RIVER STORIES
A Collection of Essays About Living Out

Mark Munger
CLOQUET RIVER PRESS

First Edition
Copyright 2002 Mark Munger

ISBN 0-9720050-1-3

Published by Cloquet River Press
5353 Knudsen Road
Duluth, Minnesota
55803
(218) 721-3213

Email the publisher at: Mlitlgator@msn.com
Visit the author's website at:
www.members.tripod.com/mungerbooks.

Printed by InstantPublisher.com
Cover Art and Design by Rene' Munger

For My Sons; Matt, Dylan,
Chris, and Jack

ACKNOWLEDGMENTS

I'm indebted to Marla Ahlgren, Creative Writing Instructor at Fond du Lac Tribal and Community College, Cloquet, Minnesota, for her many hours of dedicated proofreading of the manuscript for this collection.

Most of these essays were originally printed in my column for *The Hermantown Star* newspaper during the years 1997-2001. I am grateful to the support given me by the owners and editors at *The Star* who have guided my creative writing over the past five years. Without their interest in my work, these stories would remain unwritten.

A special thanks to Charlie Wilkins from Thunder bay, Ontario, a great writer who took the time to listen to me when things weren't going so well.

Lastly, to my wife Rene' and my four sons: thanks for putting up with this old man's dream. It hasn't been easy but I know you understand.

Mark Munger
Duluth, Minnesota
April 10th, 2002.

TABLE OF CONTENTS

MILLER CREEK DAYS

LIVING OUT

MILLER CREEK DAYS

I was born in St. Paul, Minnesota but grew up in and around Duluth, the North Star State's Inland Seaport. In the late 1950's my mom and dad built their first home in Piedmont Heights, a suburban development on the top of the high hills overlooking the blue waters of Lake Superior. Back in those days, the winters were cold and full of snow. The springs were endless days of rain and mud intermixed with the onset of new growth and games of marbles and tag.

Summers included long and languid days spent exploring the woodlands growing on top of the bluffs located above Skyline Parkway, the thread of asphalt roadway that winds its way along the hillside and offers a spectacular view of Duluth and the St. Louis River.

In many places along the Parkway small creeks and brooks intersect the road. These rivulets tumble down slope eventually uniting with St. Louis Bay. Many of these watercourses once held native brook trout in significant numbers. As young boys, we spent hours trying to convince wily fish to snap at our number ten hooks baited with worms. Some of these streams still hold native brookies; others have been denigrated to the point where they are only marginal trout habitat.

Autumn always carried a change of seasons, the turning of the leaves. In my family, fall also meant the chance to hunt grouse, deer, and ducks with adult relatives. Autumn was also the season when I first realized that I was mortal, that someday, I would pass on. Somehow the death I witnessed while hunting triggered this maturation of thought.

The first few essays in this collection are from that time in my life, from my youth and early adulthood. They are a brief taste of what life was like growing up in a white middle class neighborhood in the last half of the twentieth century.

Mark Munger

DEAD LETTER

Davey Crockett stood tall in the midst of the Mexican horde. His musket was useless: there was no more powder, no more shot. He held the heavy weapon above his shoulder like a broad, terrible ax. Gunfire rang out. Travis was already dead. Bowie would not live more than another minute or two. Santa Anna was poised to enter the demolished grounds of the old mission at the head of his triumphant army.

A boy sat on a round braided rug in his basement. The child's knees curled beneath him with the flexibility of youth. He was absorbed in reliving the grand heroism of the Alamo. Pale blue figurines of molded plastic, historically accurate and detailed in their perfection, surrounded the pressed metal walls of the fortress. There were few Texans remaining on their feet. The child, a small boy of nine, talked softly to himself as he carefully advanced the Mexican soldiers towards destiny.

His mother stood behind him at an ironing board. She watched *The Edge of Night* on an old black and white cabinet-style Admiral television. The woman concentrated her gaze on the soap opera, ignoring the flickering picture and the scratches in the walnut box surrounding the screen. Her small hands pushed and pulled the hot iron in no particular pattern as she tried to follow the parade of simulated domestic problems being portrayed in front of her.

The boy should not have been home. It was a school day. But it was November. He always got strep in November. That year was no exception. So he stayed home, nursing his sore throat and a bruise on his butt from where his mom gave him a shot of penicillin.

"Mark, what're you doing?" the woman asked, knowing full well that her son was comfortably lost within the depths of his imagination.

"Playin' Alamo," the boy responded without looking up.

"Who's winning?" the woman queried, knowing little about the Mexican-American War.

"Mexicans. Rotten old Santa Anna wins every time."

"Can't you change it so the other side wins?"

"Mom, that's not what happened. That'd be cheating," her son replied as mounted Dragoons of the Mexican Army continued to gallop towards the beleaguered mission.

"We interrupt our regular programming to bring you a special report", a male voice said on television. The seriousness of the announcer's tone forced the woman's eyes from her work.

"This morning in downtown Dallas President Kennedy and Governor Connolly of Texas were shot. Eyewitnesses say that both the President and the Governor were rushed to a Dallas hospital.

8

The conditions of both men are unknown. Stay tuned to this station for further details."

"Oh my God," the boy's mother murmured, dropping the iron to the floor.

"Is the President hurt bad, mom?" her son asked. As he spoke, he carefully placed the figure of Santa Anna next to Davie Crockett. The tip of the Mexican General's saber nudged the frontiersman's chest, foreshadowing the Texan's demise.

"We don't know yet, Mark. Just pray it's not bad. He's such a good man. Remember seeing him give that speech at UMD?"

The boy remembered. President Kennedy had been in town a month or two before at a local university. Being only nine, the boy could not remember the President's words. Because the man was the President, there wasn't any need to. Whatever the President of the United States said had to be important.

As the afternoon lingered on, the news grew worse. The woman and her son sat on the warm fabric of the rug. They listened raptly as reporters talked about bullets to the head, brains bursting apart, blood staining Mrs. Kennedy's dress. The mother held her son, embracing his sickly body, taking solace in the life that she brought into the world. They watched Walter Cronkite; his velvet voice checked by emotion and pain, announce to the world that the President of the United States was dead.

Distraught by the finality of the news, the woman rocked the boy in her arms. She did not speculate why the President had been shot. She did not contemplate whether the assassins would be found. Her thoughts were singular and were devoted to the brutal fact that the First Lady had been widowed and was left alone to care for two small children.

"What a horrible thing for those children," she whispered. Tears slid slowly down her young cheeks as she spoke.

"Do you think I should write Mrs. Kennedy a letter 'bout not being too sad?" the boy asked, pulling away from his mother's arms as he looked intently at her troubled face.

"That would be wonderful," she encouraged, her voice soft and tender.

Leaving the remaining Texans to their fate, the little boy climbed the bare wooden stairs to the kitchen. His mother remained behind, enraptured by the pain of the most horrific event she'd witnessed in her lifetime.

Studiously, he wrote his letter to the First Lady. After finishing the message, he lost the nerve to send it. His mother tucked the letter away, intending to save the document for when the boy was older, for when he would understand.

In the intervening decades, through the tumult of the Vietnam War, the deception of Watergate, and the greed of the "Me Generation", the letter remained safely stored in a scrapbook. While leafing through the memories one day, he came upon the writing and considered sending the letter to Mrs. Onassis. He thought it might serve some purpose for her to know that the children who witnessed that terrible event had not forgotten. Instead, he did nothing.

Then Jackie died. After reading about her funeral, the boy, now a man, searched his scrapbooks for the letter. The missive to the First Lady was gone. The letter had disappeared, leaving him to ponder whether it is ever possible to retrieve what has been lost.

SPEED DEMONS

"Wanna build a go-cart?" Eddy asked, sipping on a glass of cherry Kool-Aid.

"Sure," I answered. "Got any wheels?"

We sat on the weathered redwood bench of a picnic table, gazing intently across the bright green grass of Eddy's backyard. A mechanical push mower leaned against the baby blue siding of Eddy's house. The smell of freshly cut grass whirled around us on the warm summer breeze. Eddy nodded.

"You bet. My dad's got an old cart in the garage with two good wheels an' we can take two off of my sister's doll buggy."

I didn't ask whether my friend's father would object to us dismantling his garden cart. I knew he wouldn't approve. And it wouldn't make any sense at all to ask whether Diane cared that we were about to destroy her buggy. After all, she was a year younger, a brat, and a girl.

A bumblebee avoided my attempts to swat it away from my glass. I didn't want to make the mistake that Eddy's little brother Ron had and drink a glass of nectar with a bee in it. Ronny's tongue swelled up ten times' its normal size after that. The kid talked like Elmer Fudd for a week after being stung. No way was I gonna swallow a bee.

We lived on a new street in a new suburb. My house was the only one on the block not built by the guy who owned the land on our street before there were houses. It didn't make my house any better than Eddy's or anyone else's. It was just something my parents told me.

All the houses, even ours, were typical suburban tract homes. Two or three bedrooms. Wide hardboard siding painted mute colors. A single car garage with siding to match the house. Most had fireplaces, though they were generally used only around Christmas. In the summer, everyone had flowers. Only a few had vegetable gardens in the back. Eddy's dad loved his vegetable garden.

The street in front of our houses, Chambersburg, was paved with blacktop and steep. Most of the houses on our block, indeed on all the blocks in our neighborhood, had at least two or three kids. A few childless older couples made the mistake of buying houses in our neighborhood with an unreasonable expectation of quiet. They tended to get cranky when we ran through their lawns on the way to visit friends or when we darted into their flower gardens to retrieve a ball. We generally ignored them because they were old. Some of them were probably as old as forty.

"Those are some pretty nice wheels, eh Mark?" Eddy asked as he pried the cap off of one end of an axle holding the wheels on his Dad's garden buggy.

"Yep. Should really go if we put them on the back of the cart," I responded as I looked up from pounding 2x4's together to form a chassis of our vehicle.

Eddy let a wheel drop onto the cool cement of the garage floor and pulled the remaining wheel and its steel axle free of the garden buggy. We'd learned the craft of cart building from older boys in our neighborhood: boys who no longer built pretend cars but drove real Fords and Chevrolets; boys who listened to Gary Puckett, went out on dates, and generally ignored us; boys who'd very shortly go off to college or find work at the Steel Plant in Gary-New Duluth or join the Army and wind up dying in Vietnam.

The carts we learned to build were not sleek, sophisticated vehicles. Of the hundreds of go-carts that were built on our block during the 1960's and early 1970's, only one was built to compete in the local Soapbox Derby. That contraption was a heavy, foolish thing that ended up coming in dead last in the race, which pretty much ended anyone else thinking about setting his sights so high.

Most of the time, our go-carts used 16-penny spikes placed through the center of small tires as axles. The frames were constructed in the shape of a triangle, with the narrow part facing to the front. Using a hand drill (no father in their right mind allowed a kid back then to use power tools) we'd drill a hole through the two side rails and the front cross member upon which the two front wheels were mounted. A single bolt, secured with a nut and washer, passed through the three 2x4's and served as the pivot point for the vehicle's steering. Shorter 2x4's, covered with a piece of plywood or hardboard nailed to the framing, formed a crude seat.

Eddy grunted as he pulled the rubber wheels off of his sister's doll stroller.

"Ouch, that hurts," I cried.

I'd hit my thumb with a hammer. A blood blister formed. The pain throbbed into the end of the digit. Eddy smiled.

"Ssshhh. If you make too much noise, Diane'll hear us. She'll go runnin' to my Mom. Then we'll get in trouble."

"Easy for you to say. You didn't smack your thumb."

Ed passed a shiny bolt through wood. The bolt allowed the cart's front cross member to pivot. By nailing the ends of a rope to the far ends of the crosspiece, the cart could be steered. To turn left, you pulled the rope left. To turn right, you pulled to the right.

The advantage to our using purloined wheels and a steel axle was that we avoided the most common mechanical defect in go-cart design: nail-axle failure. Using spikes as axles for the wheels allowed a maximum of two or three trips down the hill before the nails would bend.

I banged away with the hammer and secured two 16-penny spikes and the stroller wheels to the front cross member. Four 10-

penny nails bent in half held the spikes to the wood. I spun the tires, checking to make sure they would spin freely. The stroller wheels turned faster with each pass of my hand.

"It's sure low to the ground," my pal observed, sitting in the driver's seat, tugging on the steering rope. He pulled on the chord. The cross member pivoted cleanly. Eddy's legs were crowded because he was appreciably taller than I was.

"It'll turn on a dime," I professed. "Let's try it out."

The August sun fell slowly in the west. It was just before nightfall. Fresh tar and rocks loomed beneath the chassis as we pushed the cart to the edge of Eddy's driveway. The City, for no logical reason, had resurfaced Chambersburg Avenue with a mixture of tar and shards of gravel leaving the once smooth roadway bumpy and brutal. My freshly scabbed knees bore witness to the viciousness of the new surface. One false move on my red Columbia bike and the flesh covering my kneecaps had been shredded.

"You go first," I told Eddy. "They're your wheels."

The big Norwegian kid looked at me with a broad grin, his dimpled cheeks and fair skin framed by clean blond bangs.

"Actually, they're Ed and Diane's wheels," he mused.

My buddy braced his black Keds against the wood. I positioned myself behind him.

"Ready?" I asked.

"Yep...let her go."

I bent at the waist and began to run. Pushing the rickety wood frame with all my weight, I felt gravity take over. In front of my house, two lots downhill from Eddy's place, I gave the contraption a final shove.

The cart bounced imperviously over the new tar and rocks. Eddy's hair flew free of his face as he zoomed down the hill. Other kids stopped playing to watch his journey. Panting and wheezing, I caught up with my pal at the bottom of the hill. He coasted into Bjorlin's driveway before coming to a stop.

"You gotta try it, Mark. These wheels are super fast."

My Dad met us at the top of the hill. We were winded by our climb. I expected a lecture about riding carts in the middle of the street.

"That racer of yours really sails," my old man said, his crewcut standing straight above his eyebrows. "Mind if I try her?"

"You bet Mr. Munger. Give her a whirl," the blond kid responded.

"You sure you want to do this, Dad?" I asked skeptically. My old man was fun loving in an adult sort of way. He wasn't usually one to join kids at play.

"Looks pretty safe to me," he said, taking a cramped position on the cart's wooden seat. His thick fingers grabbed the clothesline. The frame creaked under his weight.

"Give me a push."

We took our positions behind my dad and began to shove him towards the crest of the roadway. Our breathing became labored as we sought to make speed. Our tennis shoes pounded against the tar as the cart caught the slope and plunged downhill. At the edge of Eddy's yard, we gave the cart one last push and watched the go-cart disappear. Then I heard my father's voice. There was a note of urgency to his question:

"Where's the brake?"

I looked nervously at my pal before shouting my response:

"We use our shoes to stop."

I couldn't see my Dad's face as the contraption roared down Chambersburg Avenue. I can only guess what his thoughts were as he considered the fresh tar and jagged rocks passing beneath his stocking feet.

A QUIET EVENING AT HOME

"What is this stuff, anyway?"

Though I was only twelve years old at the time, I sensed that my father's critique of my mother's cooking was going to cause trouble.

My brother Dave, six years old and terrified of loud noises, my dad, and I sat on steel and plastic chairs snuggled against the clean Formica top of our 1960's kitchen table contemplating the hot-dish mom had placed in front of us.

"What's in this anyway?"

My question was foolish. I knew better than to chime in with my old man. But something pushed me to live dangerously that summer evening back in 1966.

I remember the smells of the old house. The place wasn't really old in terms of style or the building's longevity. It was a small three-bedroom rambler, my parent's first new home, built along with hundreds of other nearly identical ramblers in the new neighborhoods that grew out of the loose soil and rock on top of the hills overlooking Duluth. A big picture window faced the back of our lot, towards what had once been an open hay field until the neighborhood's Catholics built St. Lawrence Church and School on the empty ground. When the Papists first began to build we thought they'd ruined our unsanctioned playground. Then we discovered that a softball diamond fit neatly inside the church parking lot. We also learned that the old priest was slow to anger and generally tolerant of our attempts at sport.

Our front yard was all neatly trimmed bluegrass and newly-planted shade trees: trees intended to replace the maple forest that was cut down to make way for the homes. The only significant water for a half a mile, a small pond and rivulet that harbored tadpoles and shiner minnows, disappeared under the excavator when our neighborhood expanded.

Anyway, that's where I lived, perched high above the city in pristine, sanitary artifice. It was the place where I contemplated both puberty and the experimental meals that my mom foisted upon me. Not that my mother meant us any harm. To be fair, she was at a disadvantage. She had a hard time competing with the women in my dad's family when it came to culinary art. Grandma Munger and her daughter, Aunt Elsie, two very robust German women, made everything, from caramel rolls to pumpkin pie, the old fashioned way: from scratch. They used real whipped cream stirred to fluffy perfection by their thick Teutonic wrists and real butter, creamy and rich, in and on everything.

For whatever reason, my mom's response to such competition was hollow. When Dream Whip came out as the first non-dairy artificial whipped topping, she latched onto it like the Holy Grail. When Cool Whip emerged from the nuclear test site where it was concocted, Cool Whip became the new craze in our home. Cool Whip pies. Cool Whip and Jell-O. Cool Whip and beets.

With each issue of "Good Housekeeping Magazine", my mom's efforts to surprise and amaze us with her cooking skills reared up like an ugly neighborhood rumor.

Hot-dishes. My mom insisted on trying every possible rendition of this most Scandinavian of meals even though the closest her ancestors had ever been to Norway was England. Her relatives were not the purveyors of fine casseroles. Her kin were weak-kneed Tudors who gave up their virgin daughters to the Vikings rather than lose their sheep.

"It's something I thought you'd like."

We stared at the bowl of steaming vegetables, suspect meat, and pulpy noodles sitting in front of us on the table. My sister Annie, little more than a year old, sat next to my dad in her wooden high chair, cooing contentedly while pressing strained Gerber's vegetables into her curly blond hair. Dave viewed the baby food on Annie's plate with envy.

"I can't eat this," my dad mumbled.

My father's words were discharged matter-of-factly, as if reporting a scientific reality. In our family, he was the loud one, the one who could raise and lower his voice at will. My mom, frail, quiet, and demure rarely yelled back, though in her own, steadfast way, she seldom yielded ground. I knew that I should keep my mouth shut and just eat the stuff. There was a big bottle of skim milk (dad preferred whole milk but had lost that trial of wills as well) to wash the mixture down. Or I could stuff the casserole in my napkin when mom wasn't looking and toss it to the dog. I didn't need to speak my mind to escape eating my mom's latest experiment. And David, despite his age, should have known better as well.

"I'm not gonna eat it," my little brother chimed in.

"It smells gross," I added.

I watched my dad push his upper body away from the edge of the table. It was a hot, uncomfortable July night. A thunderstorm was blowing in from the west, ready to open up any second. Humidity clung to my dad's ribbed T-shirt in anticipation of the storm. Mom stood over the table; her serving spoon gripped firmly in her dominant left hand.

"Fine."

There it was. Mother appeared to accept the unanimous verdict of the men of the house. I chanced a sidelong glance at my dad. He wasn't smiling.

Our every-day dishware was made of Melmac, a virtually indestructible synthetic material that no scientist could explain the origins of. Mom set the wooden spoon down on Dave's plate and picked up the bowl of hot-dish. I figured that our black Labrador would be eating fine tonight and that, if we were lucky, dad would drive us down to Mr. Nick's Drive-In for a Charburger basket.

The serving dish shattered into a million shards of pottery when it hit the floor. Dave's eyes opened in horror as he watched mom's hands fire Melmac projectiles across the room at high speed. Mandarin Jell-O spattered across the wall behind my dad, covering him in a shower of orange gelatin. There was nothing we could do to stop the onslaught.

Melmac was advertised as unbreakable. I believe it was created with the intent of surviving a Soviet missile strike. It didn't stand a chance in the hands of a Slovenian mother on a rampage.

When it was over, when she had emptied the table of every dish, of every utensil, my mom snatched Annie out of the high chair and walked out the door. My dad was speechless. The two of us looked at each other and then at David. My little brother was so awestruck, he couldn't move.

Most of the hot-dish ended up on the floor though small stalactites of noodle clung to the ceiling. Fractured dishware and bent silverware littered the place. Milk and orange Jell-O stained the painted plaster walls. The three of us sat in stunned silence as we listened to the family station wagon peel out of the driveway and roar up the street.

The kitchen was spick and span when mom and my baby sister came home later that evening.

PHEASANT HUNT

Across a frozen field, a fresh wind whipped corn stalks. Stark, gray-black clouds hung low over the flat prairie. Wide oaks stood across the yellowed corn. Hundred year-old willow trees marked the end of the plowed earth and the beginning of a creek bottom.

A Jeep Wagoneer, its shine dimmed by a thin covering of mud, stopped by the side of the road. A cloud of greasy dust swirled behind the car as the vehicle halted. The dust passed the station wagon on the tongue of an approaching storm. The doors of the vehicle opened slowly against the wind. Three men placed the worn soles of their leather hunting boots on gravel and exited the Jeep. A boy and two dogs remained inside the car.

"Come on, kid. This is where we get out," the boy's father said.

The man slid his Browning 12 gauge out of its case as he spoke. Uncle Paul and Grandpa Jack stood at the rear of the Jeep. The vehicle's tailgate was down. In the car, the boy's eyes were heavy with sleep. His arms and legs felt sluggish as he struggled to exit the warmth of the car. Outside, a hostile breeze reminded him that it was near the end of pheasant season. He zipped up his canvas hunting jacket, a hand-me-down from his father, and pulled the drawstring at the bottom of the garment to keep the wind at bay. The sleeves of the oversized jacket hung below the tips of his gloved fingers.

"Harry, is it OK if I give it to him now?" Paul asked.

Paul was a favorite uncle, a relative by marriage. To the boy, Paul was a man's man; a hunter; an adventurer; an aviator who flew Corsairs for the Marines during World War II.

The boy knew the question was being asked about him. He did not know what gift was in the offing.

"Just make sure he understands his limits," the boy's father replied.

The uncle was a dark skinned Norwegian, the only son of a Lutheran minister. Prior to his marriage to the boy's Aunt, Paul had been a legendary bachelor in and around the little farming community he called home. He wore his hair slicked back and sported a delicate Clark Gable mustache. His voice was coarse and rough, the product of too many cigarettes. The boy watched his uncle unzip a gun case and remove a rifle.

"This is for you," Paul said quietly as he handed the youth a Stevens' .22 rifle.

"Thanks."

"Your dad says you've had firearm safety. I thought it was time you had your own gun."

The boy admired the weight of the weapon. The stock was light oak. The barrel was steel blue.

"Just carry the gun. You can't use it for birds: it's a rifle. I thought you'd enjoy carrying it while we hunt."

Grandpa Jack walked and examined the rifle in the boy's hands.

"That's a nice .22, Paul. Where'd you find it?"

"It's left over from the fire. It was just sitting in the garage, taking up space. Might as well put it to use."

The boy knew that, long before his uncle married his Aunt Susanne, Paul owned a variety store along the main street in his hometown. A fire ruined the store but not everything inside. The fire was the first of many streaks of bad luck that would befall his uncle during the time the boy knew him.

Deuce, the boy's black Labrador, and Flaps, his uncle's Springer Spaniel, barked inside the Wagoneer. The boy reached into the station wagon and unlatched the doors to the dogs' travel cages. The animals dove out of the car. The Springer danced across the ditch bank in unbridled enthusiasm. The Labrador trotted with an air of aloof maturity.

Morning cold slowed the men and made their fingers clumsy as they loaded their shotguns. The boy walked beside his father as they entered the corn. Terrified that he might make a mistake, the boy constantly fingered the safety of the unloaded .22. His father's admonitions, repeated hundreds of times before that day, ran over and over in his head:

"How do you know a gun is loaded?"

"It's always loaded, Dad."

"When do you point a gun at something?"

"Only if you're gonna shoot it."

Ahead, the dogs worked the dry crop. The Labrador used his physical strength to force his way through the vegetation. The Springer dodged around the standing corn, his tail beating like a dragonfly's wings.

"Hen," someone shouted.

A female pheasant escaped the stalks, its monochromatic wings beating furiously against the wind. Some distance out, the bird turned, set a course for the creek bottom, and landed in thick underbrush on the far side of the stream. All three shotguns followed the hen's path. No one shot. The dogs dove back into the field in search of roosters.

The boy's arms began to tire carrying the unloaded rifle over uneven ground. A thin mist blew out of the sky, turning the hard packed dirt to slime. It was hard for the boy to keep up with the men. Ahead of the hunters, the Spaniel turned in full, urgent circles. The dog's nose dipped to the ground. The Springer's muscles froze.

19

"Flaps is awful birdy. Watch him, Harry."

Grandpa Jack's voice was edged with excitement. The old man crouched low, near the dog, waiting for the bird to flush. The boy's father accelerated his walk and cradled his shotgun just off the dirty canvas of his field jacket.

"Get him, Flaps."

Paul's voice fueled the dog's natural inclination to roust the bird. The Springer poked his nose into a tangle of standing corn.

"Caack ... Caack... "

A rooster burst from nowhere. The bird narrowly missed knocking the Stetson off Grandpa Jack's head. In contrast to the lazy flight of the hen, the rooster immediately found the speed of the wind.

Crack.

The bird crumpled in mid-flight slightly ahead of the gun's retort. The rooster folded into itself and plummeted. The boy lost sight of the pheasant in the shifting corn.

"Good shot Harry!" Paul yelled.

The Labrador raced along a row of dead corn in search of the pheasant. Paul's Springer followed the Labrador clearly intent on stealing the rooster away from the larger dog.

"Come, Flaps," the uncle called.

The Spaniel obediently retreated. Deuce's head disappeared in the yellow of the maize. When the dog's nose emerged from the corn, the rooster hung loosely from the Labrador's mouth.

"Good dog," the boy's father praised.

Head held high, the retriever returned to its master's side with the prey.

The men gathered around the dog. A quarter-mile away, another nervous rooster rose from the field and flew off before settling in the thicket bordering the creek close to the hen that the hunters had passed on earlier.

"Beautiful bird," Paul observed as Harry removed the male pheasant from the dog's mouth.

Grandpa Jack leaned on his Winchester pump and nodded in agreement. The boy's father held the pheasant so that his son could admire the bird. The youth removed a glove and stroked the warm feathers of the rooster's breast.

In the distance, blackbirds gathered in mid-air and swung south in flight. The boy studied the dead gamebird. He looked deeply into the faces of the three men who'd brought him hunting. He felt as if the hunt, their love of him, would last forever.

What did he know? He was only a boy. That day, there seemed to be so much time. The sky was endless; the cornfields rolled on forever. To a boy of twelve, the future was far, far away.

THE BIG ONE THAT GOT AWAY

My dad rigged a dead smelt onto a large single hook and gave the small fish a substantial toss.

Splash.

"We'll let it sit on the bottom and hope a big Laker or Northern comes swimming by."

Bundled against an early May chill, I nodded and accepted the bait cast outfit, the kind with an open face reel, from my father. I placed the well-worn fiberglass rod into the crotch of a pine branch secured to the shoreline of the lake and walked back to our rented cottage seeking warmth.

My family was at the end of the Gunflint Trail for the Minnesota Fishing Opener in early May. The small two-room cabin my mom, dad, brother Dave and I occupied overlooked the ice-jammed shores of Seagull Lake. It was early morning on Saturday, the first day of the season. The sun was not yet up. As dad and I walked back to our shelter, I felt the cold grip of retreating winter emanate from the sheets of dissipating ice floating a few hundred yards off shore.

Inside the building, I fell asleep watching my old man wind spools of new monofilament fishing line onto our reels. I was supposed to be helping. He complained once or twice about my inability to concentrate when I allowed the line to slide off the spool and congregate on the floor. My old man muttered something unprintable under his breath and took over the entire job himself. I don't remember if I dreamed as I slept on the couch in the cabin, waiting for the sun to warm the water.

"Get up Mark, time to fish," my dad said, nudging me into consciousness.

"Gotta sleep," I mumbled.

"It's time to go," he repeated, a hard-edged urgency in his tone.

I rose and followed him out the door, all the while wishing I were six years old like my brother Dave, or female like my mom. They were allowed to sleep longer because of age and gender respectively.

"Something took the smelt," my dad said as we approached the casting rod.

The tip of the device surged as the restrained fish on the line struggled to break free. My dad set his tackle box and aluminum rod case on the ground and picked up the bait casting outfit.

"Holy moley," he exclaimed. "Must be a big Northern Pike."

I watched my dad struggle against his opponent. I knew there was little chance he'd hand me the rod. This fish was one for the record books and not one to experiment with. Mr. Lee and his son, our fishing partners, left their boat at the dock next to us, and came over to investigate the commotion.

"What's up Harry?" Mr. Lee asked.

"Got a big one here, Dick. It's taken nearly all of the line out. I can't budge him."

I peered into the open bail of the reel. There were only one or two revolutions of line left on the cylinder. The fish was out deep, a great distance from us, reluctant to come into shallow water.

"Let's get in my boat and see if we can chase it down," Mr. Lee offered.

"Sounds good. I'll hold onto the rod, you drive. Mark, we're going to need you to help land this monster. Let's go."

My dad kept steady pressure on the fish as he entered Dick's run-about. The boat's hundred-horse power Johnson outboard was idling smoothly, ready to respond. I loosened the ropes securing the boat to the pier as a sliver of dawn ascended in the east. Dick gently nudged the boat's shift lever into reverse. The run-about backed up in a harsh breeze as Dick eased the vessel through decaying ice.

"It's trying to get under those logs," my dad shouted over the din of the engine. My old man reeled furiously as the boat continued to chug towards the lunker's hiding place.

"Mark, get the net ready," Mr. Lee commanded.

I found an aluminum-handled landing net under my seat and stood near my dad, watching his face as he strained to defeat his prey.

"He's surfacing."

"Keep up the pressure, Harry, we don't want to lose this one," Mr. Lee instructed.

"I think I know what I'm doing, Dick."

"I know you know what you're doing," my dad's companion said apologetically.

The boat cut a swath through chunks of melting ice. My dad struggled to keep the fishing line from being severed by the sharp edges of the flotsam.

"I think I've got him," my dad yelled.

Just off the bow, a black and white torpedo exploded from the ebony water.

"It's a loon!" Mr. Lee exclaimed. "You caught a loon!"

"Crap," was my dad's only response.

The bird's flight came to a sudden halt when it reached the end of the monofilament line. Too tired to take wing again, the loon paddled furiously as it tried to outrun its pursuers.

"I'll get alongside it and Mark'll scoop it up with the net," Mr. Lee instructed.

I clambered over the windshield and onto the bow where my father was playing his "prize".

"Be careful."

"Don't worry, dad. I'm not about to go swimming over a duck."

The Queen Mary swept in alongside the stricken bird. With an awkward motion, I dipped the net under the loon and captured it. Because of the bird's weight and the angle of my arms, I was unable to hoist my catch into the boat. As I fought to lift the prize over the gunwale, the waterfowl shook its head with a vengeance.

Snap.

I watched helplessly as my father's tenuous connection to the loon was eliminated. Free of the fishing line, the awkward bird pushed itself out of the net with tired wings.

Splash.

Mr. Lee shifted the engine into neutral. The bird floated safely away from the motor's propeller. We watched the loon thrash wildly against a length of fishing line trailing behind it before the bird disappeared beneath the ice.

BROTHERS

Water gurgles. My brother and I set up camp. An attenuated stream cascades across the mossy rocks below us. The creek marks time in a way that humans only marginally understand. Quick, agile brook trout dart beneath the boiling surface of the water. We don't have a fishing rod with us. The trout are not in danger of ending up in a frying pan.

Stone towers above our tenting site. Here and there, grass has secured a foothold in the gabro and clings tightly to the rock. The ledge we've chosen to camp on is no more than eight feet wide. We call it a cliff. Really, it's just a shelf in the rock. We're only ten feet above the water. To a seven-year-old boy and his thirteen-year-old Boy Scout brother (that's me), the ledge is a cliff.

When I was a little kid, this creek was foul. Someone got the bold idea to run a sewer line up to the airport so that human waste was no longer dumped directly into the stream. Funny how now, after decades of environmental activism, the suggestion of preventing sewage from being dumped directly into a creek seems like such an obvious proposal.

By the time of our camp out, the stream is pristine. The trout are back. Being kids, we take the existence of native brook trout and clear water as a given. It doesn't dawn upon us that the creek could ever go back to the way it was.

I set our two-person canvas pup tent up on the ledge while my sibling scours the urban forest for deadfall. The green fabric of our tent is faded from use. The mosquito netting is ripped in spots but, because it's late August, bugs don't pose a threat. The thin soil covering the rock restricts my ability to anchor the tent pegs. I don't worry. There's little wind and the overhang of the rock rising above us affords protection from the weather.

My brother returns. He piles dead aspen and birch near the stone circle I've constructed to serve as our fire pit.

"Let's go for a swim."

"Sure," my little brother says.

We strip down to our underwear and gingerly thread our way down the ledge to the stream. Rock defines the shoreline of the creek. There is no beach. The water is only twelve or thirteen feet across. Earlier this summer, my friends and I placed boulders across a narrowing in the watercourse, creating a crude dam. A tentative pool has formed behind our artificial wall causing the water to rise a foot or so. Still, the creek is only chest deep; the pool is only twenty feet long. In reality, we're going wading, not swimming.

I take my time entering the stream. Once the water is over my groin, I dive in, carefully putting my hands in front of my face to make sure I don't hit my face on a rock. My brother is just learning to swim. He's more cautious about putting his head under.

"Come on you baby," I jeer. "The water's not that cold."

"I'm coming," Dave nervously responds.

The sky is overcast and threatening rain as we wade across the gravel bottom of the pond, splashing each other, yelling like fools. Our voices careen off the prominence shrouding our secluded paradise. We are less than a quarter mile from our neighborhood, a neighborhood brimming with suburban homes and noisy traffic. Despite our proximity to civilization, we hear nothing but our own cries of delight.

"Time to get out," I urge, feeling the need to make a fire and cook the hotdogs we've brought for supper.

Crystal-like water pours off our skin as we emerge from the stream and climb the slippery rocks in our white jockey shorts.

"Here's something to dry off with."

My kid brother, the minimalist in our family, accepts my offer of a towel in silence. I watch as he pats the water off of his smooth skin.

I stand in the chilling air, the day fading to dusk, and remove my briefs. Fully exposed to the cold, I note that my body is not yet going through the changes that my friends are experiencing. I feel anxious, though I know that worrying won't speed up the process. I slip on a clean pair of underwear. My Wrangler's are less cooperative. The trouser legs want to bunch up at my knees where traces of moisture remain.

I wonder why I am so at peace here, in the shadow of the trees, with my brother and so angry with him when we are at home. I don't mean to say cruel things or pick on him. But whenever my parents are gone, leaving me in charge, I go after him. He's a good kid. He doesn't squeal. Maybe he should.

I don't understand why I act this way. Maybe it's because my parents don't get along. Maybe it's because I'm small for my age and always getting picked on at school. Maybe I feel the need to retaliate and he's just the unlucky target of my rage. Or maybe I'm just a jerk. Thankfully, no trace of this part of me intrudes as I sit by the singing waters of Miller Creek.

The fire crackles pleasantly. Small sparks spiral upward, drawn towards the night sky by a draft emanating from somewhere up the valley. We eat Elliot's wieners, the thick skins of the sausages blackened by flame, on soft white buns. We have to cut the buns. Mom, always the economist when it comes to food, insists on buying uncut buns. We dab catsup and mustard across the crispy skin of the meat, drink grape Kool-Aid out of tin camping cups, and talk sparingly as the salt from Old Dutch Onion and Garlic potato chips clings to our lips.

A pair of resident mallards flies rapidly through the forest, following the downhill plunge of the water. Diminutive tree frogs sing off in the distance.

"This is neat," I observe.

"I'm going to sleep," David announces, his words slow and tired.

"Make sure you leave enough room for me."

I watch my brother unzip the fly of the tent and climb into our shelter. The soft yellow glow of his flashlight illuminates the shelter's interior, framing my brother's body in silhouette as he struggles to enter his sleeping bag. I stir the embers of the fire and add another log. The light in the tent goes off. My brother is soon asleep.

There is no moon. Second growth forest blocks out much of the sky. Faint stirrings of fear descend upon me as I look around our modest camp and realize that I'm alone. I douse the fire and climb into the tent beside my brother, wondering how he'll measure this day against all of the other days we've shared.

DUCKS ON A POND

"Those look like bluebills," my father whispered.

"Where?" I asked talking in a low voice between hard breaths.

"Over there, right in the middle of the pond."

We shortened our strides as we approached the brackish shore of the pothole. I narrowed my eyes. A high knoll rose behind us, sheltering the pond from the worst of the weather. There was no wind, no weather to speak of on that day. My eyes, far younger than my father's, took far longer to locate the prey.

"I see 'em," I replied mutely. There were a half-dozen or so dark objects bobbing out in open water, away from the cattails and wild rice.

"Keep low. Take the dog with you and circle around. The wind is coming from behind them," dad related. "They'll either take off into the wind or head towards me. One way or another, we'll get a shot at them."

I nodded. Cradling a single shot twenty gauge in my fourteen-year-old arms, I began to negotiate the thick brush surrounding the edge of the marsh. Deuce the Second, our black lab, pranced eagerly in front of me, his heavy tail beating in eager anticipation.

Approaching the edge of the water, I lowered my profile. The ground became infiltrated as I followed the shoreline. Black, putrid liquid oozed up between my boots. I sank deeper and deeper into the floating surface of the bog. The dog's weight was evenly distributed over four wide paws, allowing him to walk on top of the marsh. I was not so lucky. Muck and water climbed my hip waders until I was waist deep in mire.

The scaup could not follow my slow, pathetic progress. High reeds and marsh grass blocked their view. Breathing hard I stopped and looked back towards my father. He was standing in a thicket of sapling aspen, his shotgun resting across his chest, waiting for the birds to take wing. Deuce panted, his slick black fur shining in the clean sun, his bright brown eyes staring curiously at me, as if to ask: "Why are you so slow?"

"Let's go, boy," I urged quietly, prompting the dog to crawl on his belly across the undulating surface of the bog.

"Other," I heard my father cry out.

I looked towards the far shore of the pothole. Sweat trickled from beneath the brim of my baseball cap. Moisture built up under my armpits. I stopped and removed the Twins cap from my head. Tenuously balancing in the soft soil, I wiped the perspiration off of my forehead with the sleeve of my jacket, replacing the sweat with mud. My black rimmed athletic glasses, preposterously ugly but functional, clouded up with steam.

"Other," I heard my father yell again.

My eyes strained. I didn't see anything unusual, anything noteworthy, on the far shore. I saw nothing of substance, nothing but row upon row of defiant trees cloaked in brilliant white. The luminous birch stood in stark contrast to the dark, colorless mood of the rest of the autumnal forest.

"Other," dad yelled once more.

Deuce's ear's sat square, on full alert. Mud dripped from the bottom of my jacket sleeves as I advanced. A small patch of black alder afforded respite from the bird's scrutiny and allowed me to close the distance to my prey. I raised the barrel of my shotgun in anticipation of the ducks' hurried flight but remained crouched, nearly touching the stinking muskeg with my face as I moved forward.

Behind me, my father's voice continued to boom. The retriever quickened his pace. My heart began to pound as we broke free of the thicket. Just out of the range of my twenty-gauge shotgun, my quarry paddled lazily in frigid water. It was obvious that my prey had been watching my labored progress from the moment I left my father's side.

Lowering my weapon, I patted my dog's slick fur and watched the mammals play in the middle of the pond. A smile crept across my lips as I wondered how many times my dad would retell the story about his oldest son being hoodwinked by a family of otters.

THE LAST GAME

He was a senior in high school. Standing on an aluminum stepladder, the rungs spattered with decades of maroon and gold paint, the kid held one end of a strand of crepe paper in his right hand. With his left hand, he taped the paper to the ceiling of the first floor hallway, the hallway leading to the school auditorium. At the other end of the roll of paper another senior, a girl, stood on another ladder.

The teenager studied the girl through his wire-rimmed glasses. His classmate was short, athletic, and cute. She was also a cheerleader. She was one of the reasons that he decided, as a skinny puke of a sophomore, to forget debate and try his hand at football. He knew he'd never amount to much of a player. He knew he'd likely ride the bench for three years. It didn't matter. He'd gain the satisfaction of being a football player, of being part of the team. He'd be one of the players who, the day before a big game, got his locker all fancied up by the cheerleaders, by Betty and the others. He knew going in that was about the best he could expect. It was a bargain he was willing to make.

Perched on the ladder, he watched Betty, her feminine form agonizingly wondrous and mysterious at the same time. It was Thursday, the day before the big homecoming game against Central.

Back in the 40's, 50's, and even into the late 60's, the Central game was labeled the biggest game of the year. It wasn't really true. East had actually taken on the role, at least in the kid's mind, of the enemy. He believed that all East students were born into wealth. This perception made the "Cake Eaters" a far better foil than the rough and tumble boys from Central. Central was too much like his own school: the kids were largely from blue-collar homes, with an occasional poor kid thrown in for good measure. The kids from Central were more like kindred spirits than rivals.

His team had clobbered East the Friday before. Miracle of miracles, he'd actually been called upon to play when the contest was still very much in doubt.

"You're starting on the suicide squad," his coach and favorite teacher at the time had said. "Don't let me down."

The boy lined up on the 40-yard line as the last defender on the kickoff squad on the right side. Standing under the gloriously bright lights of old Public Schools Stadium, the only field used by the four public high schools in Duluth, Minnesota, a wave of unrelenting panic came over him.

A whistle blew. The ball was launched and the kid's feet churned furiously against the damp grass as he ran down field, towards the waiting East return man. Marko was his name. He was the Coach's kid. The East player stood motionless under the

29

moonless October night as the pigskin descended. The running back stepped to his right and took off with the ball. A wave of defenders closed the lane, forcing him back against the grain, right into the waiting arms of the kid. The boy wrapped his skinny arms around the muscular torso of the East player and held on long enough for his teammates to topple the running back onto the turf. Late in the game, he repeated his success by trapping Marko in the backfield. He dove at the halfback's feet from his defensive end position, knocking the East player to the ground for a second tackle.

Heady from his first gridiron success, the undersized defensive end looked forward to the Central game when he and the other seniors would be introduced under the lights. It was his last home game. He knew that, even though he'd grown some, at 5'8" and 140 pounds, his days as a player would end with the season.

"I'm gonna start all of the seniors against Central," Coach Marv told the team at the end of a light practice. "We'll see what you can do."

The kid knew this meant he'd get another chance to start on the suicide squad. His coach wasn't crazy enough to put him in as a starter on defense or offense. The boy was too slow to be much good on offense. Too small and, worse yet, too full of fear, to be effective on defense.

As the teenager hung the last of the decorations, he cast a long, wistful glance in Betty's direction. He knew he'd have to make the most of the few seconds of time that each kickoff occupied. Those moments would be his, his to try his best in front of his parents, his siblings, and the cheerleaders.

Late autumn's cold lingered within the hard vinyl seat of his old Jeep Wagoneer as the vehicle labored to climb the steep hill towards home. It was after 11:00 p.m. He needed sleep. He had a big day ahead of him.

It was a fitful night. A slight catch in his throat, the result of a cold, intensified. When he awoke in the morning, his mind was disoriented. Chills wracked his body. The cold had exploded into a full-blown case of strep throat.

This was his annual autumn course: catching a minor cold and ending up so sick that he missed homecoming. Illness barred his participation in two of the three "Red and Black" celebrations during junior high. He missed Maroon and Gold Day his sophomore year with the same malady.

By chance, he was healthy for homecoming his junior year. At the game, he stood in freezing rain and sullenly watched as the contest deteriorated into a fistfight after one of his teammates called a black player on the Central team a "nigger."

Now it was his senior year, his last year. He was shivering and in the throes of delirium. He forced himself out of bed and into the shower. Wet and shaking with fever, he tried to get dressed. His alarm clock told him he had twenty minutes to make the last bus down the hill to school. He pulled on his jeans and his home jersey. Number 86. He really wanted 88 but his buddy Paul, a two-way starter, had priority when it came to jersey numbers. Exhausted by the effort of dressing, the kid fell heavily onto his rumpled bedspread, wearing a number he didn't want, struck down by an illness he couldn't beat.

All day long he fantasized about getting out of bed, boarding a city bus and making it to at least one class so he could suit up for the game. The furthest he made it was to the bathroom; one door down the hall, where he rinsed his sweat soaked face with a damp cloth.

His mom checked in on him before she left for her tennis game. His dad was long gone and working downtown. His parents would be at the stadium that night. They hadn't missed many home games since their graduation from the same high school three decades earlier.

That evening, the kid listened to the game at home in his bed on a portable radio as a professional announcer ran down the starting lineups for the teams. The ailing teen could make out the voice of the Assistant Principal in the background of the broadcast calling the game for the fans at the stadium. The stricken player listened intently as the seniors were introduced. His name wasn't mentioned. Within the gloomy dankness of his basement bedroom, the kid sipped water and contemplated the roar of the crowd, cheering silently when his teammates took the game from the Trojans.

A week later, he walked hesitantly across the auditorium stage as the senior football players were introduced one last time during a pep assembly. The Coach said nice things about all of them, mentioning something about the kid being undersized in stature but oversized in heart.

That night the boy watched his teammates flail desperately against a bigger, faster, more finely tuned Cloquet team. He stood on the sidelines, wrapped in a raincoat against a hard driving snowstorm and a cruel wind. His jersey remained unstained, his meager talents unused. He never got the call, never got into the game, as the Lumberjacks rolled over the Hunters with ease.

PRAYER OF THE CREEK

You first walked with me when you were only a child. Part of a Kindergarten excursion, I think. I remember your smallish feet dangling within my pools, scampering over my mossy banks, sliding uncontrollably across the smoothness of my rocks. You were only six, though I had been since the retreat of the last ice age.

I was dirty then, my water fouled with human waste. There were few fish, fewer frogs. I was near death. But I remember how enthralled you were with my swiftly churning rapids, my noisy falls. You loved me then, I could feel it. But I was too tired, too damaged to return your love properly.

After that first visit, I knew I was in your mind. I felt you thinking about me, felt your young heart searching for me whenever the four walls of the classroom closed in around you.

From a distance, I saw your gangly limbs begin to form muscle. I saw acne creep across your brow. As you grew and came more frequently to visit, you cast your worms in my waters; you sat upon my grassy banks under the shade of balsams. You dreamed of the day you would return and live beside me.

Then, miracle of miracles, someone finally stopped the sewage from seeping into my waters, someone finally determined that the health of the children, who fished my ponds and waded my rapids, meant something. Within a few short years, I was clean; my waters flowed sweet and pure. The fish came back. By chance, you came to live within a stone's throw of my dancing path.

Through adolescence, my quiet drew you and others to play ball hockey upon my tortured ice during winter. Your passion for trout saw you draw fish with your bare hands from beneath my stones. But, like the men who built the great cities of America, like the pioneers who carved their farms from the prairie, you were not satisfied with my nature, with my graceful, shallow basins.

In front of your house, you loosened boulders and rocks from my ancient bed. You piled them in an orderly fashion across my path and dammed my current until the water rose to touch your waist. By shovel and bucket, you scooped soft sand from my shoals and filled in the cracks and crevasses of the dam until my power was confined. You caught luminescent trout by the hundreds under the rocks and released them into your private pond. Naively, you intended that they remain there, to be your private stock and pleasure.

It was then that I became not only your friend, but also your teacher. In short order, you learned that, though you are man, you cannot own me, you cannot possess my bounty, you couldn't control me. Late summer rains doubled my lazy, idyllic pace. A crest of storm water crushed your dam, bursting it asunder without mercy.

When the torrent subsided, only a few large boulders, stones too large for the water to dislodge remained. A hundred years ago, your dam may have held. Because of progress, it did not.

For you see, men continued to harm me. Upstream, where my pace was less rapid and my course less straight, men had covered my floodplains with asphalt. Greed destroyed my marshlands. Man built upon the soggy earth, built stores to feed commerce. It was man's dogged overbuilding of my floodplain, not God's rain, which caused the flood to come with such sudden fury. You knew this. You heard others cry out about it. Still, you stayed silent and the building continued.

Through high school and college, you continued to love me, to visit me, to ski and walk the narrow trails that meander through the thick underbrush of my valley. But I could not love you as I had. Your ears did not hear my pleas. Your eyes did not see my loss. Slowly, ever so slowly, you stopped hearing and seeing me at all. Your walks became infrequent. You did not introduce me to your children with the same affection and reverence you and I had been introduced. You lost your wide-eyed innocence and left me to defend myself.

I am virtually alone now. My old friends, like you, have grown up and left my side. My waters no longer run clean and cold. Salt-riddled rain washes into my course from ten thousand blacktopped parking spaces. I am too warm. In the heat of the summer, my rocks sprout green slime and mold. The frogs and salamanders have left.

You try, on odd-occasions when you come home to visit, to grasp the delicately decorated flanks of brook trout hiding amongst my stones. But there are no fish left to touch. They are gone.

I hear the politicians and the moneymen talk about more buildings, more asphalt. I try to cry out to them, to explain my worth, but they do not hear me. For they have never been my friend as you have.

As spring approaches and another construction season looms, I long for you to look at me with the awe and wonder of a six-year-old boy on his first visit to Miller Creek. For in that wondrous gaze, in that youthful passion, was my salvation. I pray that you see me that way again. Before it is too late. Before I am no more.

MEMORIAL DAY

The "Boys" made it back to the Boundary Waters Canoe Area and were camped on the shores of Omega Lake. My pal Larry and I were working a bit of shallow water between the island we were camping on and a tiny speck of rock and cedar fifty yards off the island's shore. It was early morning; the sun was just beginning to rise over the trees to the east. Above us, a pale blue sky stretched, uninterrupted by clouds, into Canada. Larry and I sat at either end of a dented aluminum canoe. The other guys in our party were still asleep.

"Coffee sure tastes good this morning," I said reverently, trying not to scare the fish as I savored a gulp of hot liquid from a tin cup.

"Ssshhh," my companion murmured. "I've got one nibbling."

"Ya, right," I retorted.

"Just a little bit more..." he said quietly, as if he hadn't heard me. "Got 'em," Larry remarked, his fiberglass rod bending in earnest.

He played the fish gingerly. The line immediately dove under the vessel, a sure sign the fish was a pickerel.

"Northern," I noted.

"No kidding."

After a few minutes, my pal tossed a thrashing, flipping, angry two-pound fish into the bottom of the Grumman. Larry searched his tackle box and found a well-used nylon stringer. In short order, the pike was back in the water, safely tethered to our canoe.

"Now that's how you catch fish, Mark," Larry said, his words carrying just a hint of superiority, as he handed me a cigar from the depths of his tackle box. He pulled a second stogie out for himself.

I sucked on the cigar and struck a farmer match against the coarse metal zipper of my trousers. I pulled hard on the tobacco and inhaled pungent smoke while I tossed a Daredevil lure towards a shoal.

The water was perfectly still. A loon paddled effortlessly across the main channel of the lake and began to fish.

"Loon," Larry whispered.

"I see him," I noted, trying to concentrate on the primeval force striking at the lure some ten feet beneath us.

"Got one," I cried out. Again, the hooked fish sought refuge under the boat. "Another Northern."

"Don't let him break your line," Larry instructed. "We need him for fish soup."

The pike fought hard against the six-pound test monofilament but the steel leader held firm. I began to reel the fish in, carefully stopping at intervals to allow the pike to play itself out.

When the prey was near the surface, I leaned over the gunwale and reached for the Northern.

My glasses started to slide down the bridge of my nose. Before I could react, the frames plummeted through the air and landed in the muskeg-stained water. I sat helplessly as the spectacles waltzed slowly towards the rocky bottom of the lake.

"Crap," I mumbled, still fighting the fish.

"What?"

"I just lost my glasses."

"How'd you manage to do that?"

"They just fell off."

"Can you see them? Maybe you can snag them with that Daredevil."

"Ya right."

I landed the fish. We resumed sitting quietly. Larry knew I wasn't happy. He kept his thoughts to himself. The loon seemed to enjoy my anguish. It drifted in close and let out an outlandish laugh before diving under the surface of the water.

We paddled towards the rocks and tossed our plugs into shore. The wind picked up and worked the water into a gentle chop. Without my glasses, I was nearly blind. I had to squint to make out the largest, most obvious details of the landscape.

Behind us, the Canadian Shield rose directly out of the water to form our rocky campsite. A few haggard cedar trees capped the summit of the primitive stone. Smoke curled upward from our camp's firepit. The breeze brought the smell of sizzling bacon across the water. We heard the voices of our companions talking in reverent early-morning tones.

Crack.

A loud noise startled me. I turned towards the small island.

"Did you hear that?" I whispered.

"Nope."

"Something's on that rock pile," I said.

"Sure, Mark," Larry replied casually between puffs on his cigar.

"There's something on that island," I implored.

I pursed my cheek muscles in an attempt to get my eyes to focus. The wind turned the stern of the canoe towards the shore of the diminutive isle. I stared hard at a small stand of cedar trees in the center of the rocks.

Slowly, as if being filmed by a severely intoxicated wildlife photographer, a blurry form emerged from the trees and waded out into the dark water. I pressed harder to see. The canoe drifted closer. Another object, larger still and black, vacated the tree line and entered the lake.

"Larry. What the hell are those?"

"Holy Moses," my buddy whispered. "It's a cow moose and her calf. We're in their way."

Larry put down his rod, picked up his paddle, and with a few gentle strokes, eased the canoe towards our campsite.

I wish I could tell you how magnificent the mother moose and her baby looked negotiating the deep water only a few yards away from our canoe. I wish I could tell you about the fine mist that formed on their dusky, elegant fur as they crossed the bay, or how their large brown eyes reinforced the link between God and all his Earthly creatures. But I can't. All I really saw were two enormous blobs of color swimming in the tannin-stained waters of Omega Lake.

WOODEN SHIPS

Tim was one of my partners in my law firm. He thought it was a great idea: we'd do the work for our client Carl and take a 1948 Chris Craft Sedan Cruiser in trade. Carl needed to file bankruptcy. Being that he was about to go bankrupt, he didn't have any money to pay us.

"Let's look at the boat and see if it's worth taking," Tim suggested.

"Sounds like a plan."

We jumped in my Chrysler Laser, fired up the turbo, and rode out to Drill's Marina to view the boat. It was early September. The leaves were just beginning to change along Grand Avenue. Thin rain settled over the valley as we made the left hand turn into Riverside. Carl was waiting for us at the Marina office when we pulled in.

"Here she is," our diminutive client advised, pointing to a 33-foot cruiser painted sharp white and bobbing gingerly on the gasoline stained water of St. Louis Bay. Tim and I walked along the suspect pier, studying the boat, trying to discern whether the vessel was worth what I'd spend in time representing Carl. "Kittiwake" was painted in delicate gold across the glossy mahogany of the boat's stern.

"She runs like a top."

I stepped aboard and listened intently to the purr of the engine.

"Single screw, 130 horse Gray Marine flathead six. Not a lot of speed but plenty of muscle."

Carl's rendition of the attributes of the vessel's power plant carried the same salesman's pitch he used to endear himself to his customers. I didn't challenge the lack of authenticity behind his words because I was enthralled by the possibilities attached to yacht ownership.

The next spring, as I dipped a paintbrush into copper-bottom paint, a preservative needed to prevent the mahogany hull of the boat from rotting, Rene' and Matthew, our oldest son, only six years old at the time, pulled waterlogged indoor-outdoor carpeting off of the rear deck of the Kittiwake. The carpeting was a colossal mistake committed by the previous owner. The covering impeded the flow of excess water into stainless steel drains located in the aft of the boat. This defect caused water to remain trapped in the fibers of the carpet, which lead to the disintegration of the wooden deck.

Stained from head to toe with rust-colored paint, I climbed a stepladder to study my wife's progress. It was evident, even to my untrained eye that the entire rear floor of the boat needed to be replaced. This was not something I'd bargained for when Tim and I cut the deal to accept the boat as a fee.

"We can both work on her," Tim had energetically offered. "Just think of it...our own cabin cruiser."

Tim showed up for one repair session. He lasted two hours and then vanished, sending his more talented brother, Charles, an electrician, in his place. Charlie spent dozens of hours crawling in and out of the bilge, rewiring the boat. He wasn't paid. He did it because, as a craftsman, the challenge interested him.

Larry, my carpenter buddy, orchestrated the reconstruction of the aft deck. It was too expensive to use mahogany. Treated timbers and plywood had to suffice. I hired a mechanic to tune and prep the engine for the season. I caulked the hull, filling in large gaps in the dry planking with marine caulk. I also recovered the cabin's roof with new canvas. Fresh paint and elbow grease eliminated some of the dry rot and decay readily apparent throughout the interior of the once elegant cabin. By the end of August, the Kittiwake was nearly ready for the water.

Wooden boats. Who'd have thought that the hull planks needed to soak up water, to expand, before a vessel can be used? I watched with interest as the boatlift, essentially a small crane with an impressive sling, carried the vulnerable boat from its wooden cradle to the launching area. After being lowered into the water, the Kittiwake rested in the gentle current of the St. Louis River, suspended in the sling, for the better part of a day as its hull planking swelled.

Charlie's wiring worked like a charm. New bilge pumps, activated by floats, pulsed busily under the decking as Rene', my sons Matt and Dylan (an infant), and Rene's mom climbed on board for the Kittiwake's first voyage. It was mid-September. The best of the boating season was behind us. My simple little project had taken up most of the summer.

"I hope you have plenty of gas," Rene' commented.

"Two tanks. The main and reserve."

I stood imperiously behind a smoothly varnished helmsman's wheel and activated fans to expel accumulated gasoline fumes from the bilge. The freshly burned remains of another wooden cruiser were mired solidly in the mud of the river bottom next to an adjacent dock. The craft had been torn apart at the waterline when a spark from the boat's starter ignited migrating gas vapors. The cabin had been blown to wee bits. All that remained of the once opulent boat was a badly charred mahogany hull. Confident that the Kittiwake's hold was free of explosive fumes, I started the engine.

There is a trick to negotiating a narrow docking slip in a 33-foot vessel boasting a single screw, a trick I'd not yet learned. The boat weighed 8 tons dry, was narrow of beam, and labored when forced to turn. After several precarious attempts to leave its berth, the Kittiwake lumbered past other stately motor yachts and expensive sailboats lining the marina narrowly missing them as it headed out into the River.

We headed up the channel past Spirit Lake, past Whiteside Island, where banks of red clay slid slowly into the dirty brown water of St. Louis Bay. Ducks and geese paddled out of our way, lazily reserving their energy for migration. A thick yellow sun hung low over Barton's Peak. It was late afternoon. The leaves had changed to scarlet, crimson, and gold. With the old Gray Marine purring softly beneath the floorboards, I felt like Bogart in the *African Queen*.

On the aft deck, Matt played with his toys. Grandma reclined in a lawn chair, sipped a cold beer, and enjoyed the passing scenery. Rene' was in the galley, a level below the main cabin, feeding Dylan a bottle. I imagined I was a rich man piloting a brand-new Chris Craft on the Ohio or the Illinois River in the late 1940's, back when the boat was freshly built and uninhabited by the aftertaste of mildew and decline.

The day waned. I turned the vessel around at the Fond du Lac Bridge and headed back towards the marina.

"I think you need to speed it up," Rene' observed, poking her head up from the galley. "It's going to get dark pretty soon."

I switched on the running lights and opened the throttle. The pitch of the engine heightened. My oldest son sat in the captain's chair helping me steer. The sound of water dancing against wood accelerated as we surged under the rusted iron trestles of the Oliver Bridge.

Then it happened. As we rounded Spirit Island with the lights of Riverside twinkling in the near distance, the antiquated engine stopped. I knew in an instant that I'd drained one of the fuel tanks. Charlie had instructed me how to switch tanks. Opening a hatch in the rear deck, I studied the simple controls for the fuel supply.

"What's the matter?" my wife asked.

"I drained the main tank. The reserve is full but I don't know how to switch it over."

Rene' looked at me with a less-than-charitable gaze.

"Dad, I'm thirsty."

"In a minute, Matt."

My mother-in-law remained calm. She devoted her time to surveying the landscape, perhaps recalling a simpler day from the 1930's when the Whiteside family farmed the island bearing its name. Try as I might, I couldn't solve the riddle of the tank. There we were, less than a half mile from the marina, with twenty gallons of fuel waiting to be withdrawn from the tank, and I couldn't get us moving.

Grandpa Don, my father-n-law, intercepted our distress call on his scanner. The Coast Guard contacted the Marina. Two scruffy looking characters, their mouths grinning from ear to ear as they pulled alongside the old sedan cruiser in a dinged up runabout, came to our aid under the rapid approach of darkness.

"Here's the problem," the taller of the men related in a voice tinged with mirth. "You need to turn this here main switch and the switch at the top of the tank. Otherwise, she's just sucking air."

My father-in-law was waiting for us at the dock. There was a curious smile on his face. Donald's smirk conveyed a desire to engage in conversation but at that point, I didn't feel much like talking.

HOW NOT TO RUN A MARATHON

I knew it was the place I wanted to live. One trip from town on a rainy Sunday afternoon convinced me that we should move to the country and live on the banks of the Cloquet River.

Actually, the dream for me began when I was still in law school. Sitting on the 25th floor of the First Bank Building in Minneapolis, working for the largest law firm in Minnesota, I knew that I could not be a lawyer in the Twin Cities. And because one of my best friends had found a nice spot on Bowman Lake, an oxbow in the Cloquet River system, I got it in my head that I had to live on the River.

Times were tight when I got out of law school. Home mortgage rates were somewhere around 16%. The most Rene' and I could afford when we came back to Duluth was a two bedroom house in town. For three years, we owned a tiny, well kept home in Duluth on St. Marie Street right by the University of Minnesota-Duluth. After watching Matt, our oldest son, nearly get killed by a car speeding down St. Marie before his fifth birthday, and after watching our beagle Corky get hit by another vehicle on the same thoroughfare, I convinced Rene' it was time to look for a safer place to live.

That spring, I came across a newspaper ad offering a hobby farm in the country for sale by owner. Two things about the description of the place caught my eye. One, it was on the Cloquet River. Two, it was a Sears and Roebuck Home from the early 1920's. I was raised by a mother who collected and restored antiques so I was intrigued by the possibility of living in a home with history.

"This house sounds like it's just what we're looking for," I told Rene', pushing the Want Ads towards her.

"Where in the blazes is Fredenberg Township?" she asked, betraying little enthusiasm for my discovery.

"I dunno. Somewhere out by Bowman Lake I guess. It's on the River."

"Well, if you want to go look, fine," she responded, "But I've got to go to a baby shower. You'll have to take Matt."

"All right. He might as well give me his opinion on his new house," I added.

To make a long story short, I fell in love with the property. A few weeks later, I dragged my pregnant spouse out to look at the place.

"How far is this place from town?" my wife bemoaned as we bounced along LaVaque Road. With each passing pothole, the low-slung frame of my Laser sports coupe slammed against crumbling blacktop.

"Just a few more miles," I fibbed, knowing that it was at least another eight miles to the homestead.

Once my spouse saw the property (not the house, mind you, which became a 16 year long renovation project), there was no turning back. In short order, we put every spare dime (and some borrowed ones) into buying the old Drew place. After exhausting our savings, there was no way we could afford to rent a U-Haul, much less pay a professional mover, to tote our stuff from town. That's how it was that we ended up with a van from a casket company (no bodies inside, thankfully), a Gurley's Cookie Truck (borrowed from my Godfather), and an assortment of friend's vehicles in front of our little house in town one Friday afternoon in June.

On moving day, as my back ached from lifting yet another box of books (writers must be readers), the foolishness of my timing finally dawned upon me. No, I wasn't having second thoughts about fulfilling my law school dream of living out, living on the banks of the Cloquet River. No, Rene' wasn't going back on her commitment despite the house's badly stained yellow shag carpeting and 70-year-old shingles and windows looming at us.

My revelation hit that evening, as a group of us sat in the front room of the old farmhouse. It was nearly 10:00pm. We were all exhausted. The cookie truck and the hearse were empty. A pile of boxes was stacked high against one wall of the living room waiting to be unpacked.

"How are you going to run a marathon tomorrow morning?" my friend Vicki asked between bites of Kentucky Fried Chicken.

"Dunno," I responded, my mouth stuffed with coleslaw.

"Mark's been training pretty hard," Rene' interjected. "But I don't know about getting up at 6:00am to drive him up to Two Harbors."

"I'll be fine," I said. "I ran eighteen miles last Sunday. Twenty six miles won't be that bad."

"On greasy chicken and seven hours of sleep?" my oldest pal Eddy quizzed. "Must be the John Belushi training method."

"You guys worry too much," I responded as I shoved my hand deeper into the bucket of grease and poultry.

The alarm went off the next morning at 5:00 am. I reclined in bed, deciding whether to tarnish my reputation as a "never quit" kind of guy by ignoring the buzzer. Something deep within my psyche made me get out of bed.

"Wake up, 'Nay," I whispered in as nice a voice as a husband is capable of.

My wife's brown eyes batted twice before easing open.

"You're not really going to run, are you?" she asked in a pleading tone of voice.

"Got to. I'll get Matty ready."

It was a cool, misty morning when we arrived in Two Harbors, Minnesota, on the North Shore of Lake Superior. I figured that there was no sense in eating breakfast. The chicken was lurking down low, waiting to be utilized as fuel.

"Good luck," Rene' said wearily, kissing my cheek. Matt slept soundly in the car. I waved goodbye and joined the throng of milling runners.

The first five miles I was blazing. I hit each mile marker at six minutes per mile, which for me was a terrific pace. After ten miles, I was spent. My left knee and hip ached, the result of going out too quickly, the "rabbit syndrome" that I'd read about, been warned about; the syndrome I told everyone would never happen to me, did me in. By thirteen miles, less than halfway through the race, I was walking. All those tortoises that I'd passed in the first ten miles were reaping their revenge, passing me in silent triumph, their slow, steady pace carrying them closer and closer to the finish line while I struggled to remain upright.

The pain got worse. My limp became more pronounced. The chicken was crying to get out. I was wet from sweat and drenched from rain. I poured water into my mouth at every aid stand. The slowest runners began to pass me by. Only the walkers remained behind me on my slow journey towards Duluth.

At mile sixteen, I began to jog. I told myself that I wouldn't be like the guy I knew from law school who trained for two years, lost 40 pounds, only to quit at milepost 20 of his first and only marathon. No way would I let that happen.

Agony engaged my left hip and knee. My back stiffened. I managed to pass the sick, the tired, the vanquished on sheer determination and lack of common sense. The chicken played along and remained quietly engaged in the process of digestion.

On London Road, inside the Duluth City Limit, my pace increased. I passed more runners, the really slow ones, on Lemon Drop Hill. I was able to shuffle my feet in something approximating a jog while other exhausted entrants walked up the incline holding their sides in pain. By the time I passed the Old Norshor Theater in downtown Duluth, I felt good. My feet were moving, my legs were working. I knew I'd complete the race.

Once I cleared the finish line, medics wrapped me in a silver foil blanket. As I sat on the cool pavement eating orange flavored yogurt, I watched other runners stagger into Canal Park, happy that I'd survived the twenty six-mile race. Rene' and Matt approached me. They hadn't seen me cross the finish line. Rene' figured that I'd quit.

"How do you feel?" my spouse asked as we drove towards our new home on the Cloquet River.

"My hip is killing me. My knee is sore. Why didn't you talk me out of doing this?"

"Like you would have listened to me."

"Well, I'll tell you this," I murmured. "I'm never doing that again."

The next year, I did do it all over again, minus the house moving and the Kentucky Fried Chicken.

LIVING OUT

In 1997, I began writing a column for a local weekly newspaper, *The Hermantown Star*. My intent in writing for the Star was to brush up on my composition skills, skills that had languished since I left high school in the early 1970's. As originally envisioned, my column, entitled "Living Out" was to focus on my family's experiences living along the banks of the wild and scenic Cloquet River in rural Fredenberg Township just north of Duluth, Minnesota.

Over the years, the column has allowed me to tinker with narrative, dialogue, and other attributes of writing, as well as recount events from my past (**Miller Creek Days**, for example) and present. Sometimes the stories engender a giggle from the members of my family featured in the tales. Other times, they're none too happy to have their failings and foibles revealed to the public. But you'll notice that, in the majority of these essays, it's the author who is the brunt of the joke.

Mark Munger

A HOUSE FOR MINNIE WILLIAMS

It was getting on towards autumn when she finally settled on the house she wanted. Model 7016 in the 1921 Sears Modern Homes catalog. The price was $1200.00 for a four bedroom, one bath, pre-cut home that Sears labeled the "Glendale." For her money, she was to get: framing; interior walls, yellow pine trim and floors, a chimney, shingles, exterior siding, exterior doors, windows, two porches, all paint, nails, varnish and hardware.

Minnie Williams tilted her head and viewed a calendar on the wall. September 1, 1921. Her eyes glanced around the dirty interior of the place. Thick smoke curled up from a kerosene lamp on the table. The lamp's dim light allowed her to see only a portion of the room she occupied.

Richard had promised when he brought her from Des Moines, Iowa to Fredenberg Township, Minnesota that she would not have to raise her children in the filthy smallness of a cabin. That promise had been made five years and two babies ago. She sighed. Richard always kept his word, eventually. The door opened behind her.

"Good evening, Richard."

She smiled at her husband as he walked into the light. He was short, no more than five foot five. He was slight of build. His eyes caught the lamp light, reflecting blue. His black hair was shoulder length, greasy from a day's work. His face was rough and bore a full beard.

"Evening, Minnie. What's for supper?"

She rose slowly and pushed herself away from the table. She stopped, pausing to rub her swollen belly. She massaged the fabric of her dress, working a cramp deep within her womb. She was pregnant again.

"Anything wrong?" Her husband reached around her engorged waist, holding her steady.

"No, just a spell. It'll pass. There's chicken and dumplings on the stove and milk in the ice box."

He eased her into the only other room on the main floor. The room held their rough-sawn bed, a leather chair, a chest of drawers and a small end table. "Sit yourself down in the good chair. I'll fix myself a plate."

Richard sat down at the table. He studied the open catalog as he ate.

"This the one? The Glendale?" He turned his head to her as he spoke.

"That's it. We need the four bedrooms. Can't cram another child into this cabin." Minnie tilted her head back in the chair, hoping the pain would subside.

46

"We got $500.00 from Great Northern Dam and Improvement Company for the flowage rights a' front of this place. That plus the money I'll get from the white pine I cut should be enough for your Sears house." Richard took a huge piece of boiled chicken off his plate with his knife and forced it into his mouth. White grease and gravy dripped onto the worn surface of the pine floor.

Minnie smiled. She leaned further back in the warmth of the chair. Long blond hair fell out from under her scarf. At thirty, she was two years older than Richard was. Plain featured and of modest figure, she stood a full four or five inches taller than her husband did.

The two boys were hidden deep in the darkness of the loft above her. They slept together on a thick homemade mattress stuffed with straw. The heat of the cook stove raced past the sleeping boys. The stove's warmth was drawn from the cabin through countless gaps in the log walls.

"Maybe we ought to ride over to Taft and catch the train to Duluth. You can go in and see Doc Smith. We'll order the house by mail from town."

"I'd like that."

It was easier than she had expected.

"Imagine", she thought to herself as she mailed off a cashier's check and order form to Sears, "imagine a world where you can look in a magazine and order your home lock, stock, and barrel."

On October 30, 1921, two months after they ordered the home from Sears, four large bundles of building materials were shipped from Homan Avenue, Chicago, on the Chicago, Northwestern Railroad, bound for Taft Station. In Duluth, the flatcar carrying the Williams home was switched to the Duluth, Winnipeg, and Pacific line. The same day, Richard Williams and five men from the Township met the train at Taft. It took a come-along and the strength of all six men to load the bundles on separate wagons for the final eight miles of the journey.

Minnie Williams and the other wives stood outside the cabin. The intensity of the sun made it unusually warm. There was no snow on the ground. The route towards them sliced through an empty land. Great white pine stumps bore mute witness to a vanquished forest.

Off in the distance, the draft team pulling Richard Williams' wagon came into view. The horses walked with steady power on uneven ground. At the edge of the west bank of the River, the farmer motioned for the other wagons to halt. The cantilever bridge that would eventually connect the two ends of the Taft Road had not yet been built. The main road over the Island Lake Dam was closed for reconstruction. There was only one way to get Minnie's new house to the other side of the Cloquet River.

Williams urged his two Percherons down the loose gravel of the hillside. The horses snorted and stomped. Their great black flanks shivered in excitement. For a brief moment, Minnie feared that the animals would turn away from the swift current. But her husband knew his horses. He coaxed them to pull the wagon out into the quickness of the River. The other drivers watched quietly as Williams advanced to the far shore. They entered the stream only when the lead wagon was safely across.

The aroma of hot food and coffee greeted the farmer as his wagon crested the eastern slope. Once on the level, his eyes fell upon a white cross singularly positioned in short brown grass. He slid out of the wagon seat. The tails of the horses twitched though there were no flies.

Richard's first wife, Cora, was buried in the cold earth before him. She had died at twenty. Minnie was her older sister. A gentle hand touched his shoulder. He turned and met Minnie face to face.

"Cora loved this place."

Minnie's voice was subdued as she handed him a cup of coffee. Her eyes floated over his face like clouds blown by the wind.

"This is no time for cuddlin'," another voice declared. "We better get this house together before the snow flies."

Emmett Johnson walked towards the couple as he spoke. Johnson was a carpenter. Short and rotund for a Norwegian, his brown hair and beard were speckled with gray.

"Got the plans right here, Emmett. Let's take a look."

Williams pulled the blueprints out of his coveralls and handed them to his neighbor. Johnson stared at the documents. Each piece of lumber was pre-cut and each bore a label corresponding to the numerical scheme of the blueprints.

Johnson whistled.

"That's the way to build a house. What are we waitin' for?"

Richard nodded in agreement. It was time to build Minnie Williams a new home.

I can't tell you what happened to the Williams family. I don't know whether their third child survived the winter or whether the couple lived a long and happy life. What I can tell you is that, on this January night, as a bitter Northwest wind assaults our seventy-five-year-old Sears home, the love of Minnie and Richard Williams can still be felt here.

BENEATH THE CANOPY

There is not much primeval forest left on the 132 acres of land in Northeastern Minnesota that I call home. Progress has disturbed nearly every inch of my farm along the banks of the Cloquet River. If you came for a visit, you wouldn't think this to be the case. Sentinel white and red pines tower over second growth forest. Deer, wolves, bear, eagles, osprey and assorted lesser creatures remain abundant despite the intrusion of humans. Notwithstanding the plethora of animal life, these woods are not the same as they were a century ago, before Europeans arrived to log the forest and till the soil. The one exception to this is a tiny, delicate labyrinth of swamp occupying a small corner of our property. Beneath the rare cedars of that refuge, little has changed.

Marsh grass grows thick between the black alders. A thin ribbon of fresh, cold water ebbs slowly through the bog, sliding gently towards the stream's juncture with the River. Two islands of red cedar rise from the tremulous ground, providing a stable platform from which to view the swamp. A scent of cedar, carried by a brisk wind, finds my nostrils, and reminds me of the age when Ojibwa hunted this ground and walked its fragile paths. An unnamed creek meanders between the trunks of the trees exposing gnarled roots to cool air. Minnows dart in the shadows seeking protection.

This bog exists in the twilight of wilderness; between the manicured pasture of our old farm and an open gash left by my neighbor's clear-cutting of the mature aspen on adjoining land. A line of maples climbs a hogsback to the south. Though the steep spine of the ridge provides a marginal barricade against progress, it does not take much imagination to conjure up the specter of skidders crawling through wet peat, crushing the vegetation, dehabilitating this rarefied garden.

Every day, thousands of vehicles pass by this spot. I can hear them now, roaring along the roadway, as I sit within the embrace of the trees. I suspect that the folks driving past on the highway aren't interested in this swamp. Their lives are too hurried, too rushed, to contemplate the secret beauty of this marsh. Perhaps that's for the best.

STRAWBERRIES

Jerry Drew warned us. I mean, it's not like he didn't give us plenty of advance notice that they were there. We just didn't understand. How could we? We were from the city.

They were in the pasture, concealed, silent, growing larger and larger, swelling from the heat and the spring rain. There was no sign, no fence, to mark their territory, to alert us to their presence. It was left for us to discover them.

I remember Jerry's cryptic words as he and his family packed themselves into their station wagon and headed out the driveway for the last time. Just before he hit the blacktop, he stopped the car and backed up slowly so that he was right alongside Rene' and I.

"Oh yeah-one more thing."

He smiled and waved his arm toward the pasture.

"You may want to keep an eye on the strawberries. We put in a few plants last year."

We had nodded, still shell-shocked from the move. My wife and I watched mutely as the Drew's departed. The strawberries were forgotten. We were eager to get to the business of making the old Sears house our home. The berries would have to wait.

It took my family a few weeks to get settled in, to become accustomed to the bats and field mice that also called the farmhouse their home. It took quite a bit longer to figure out how to connect the mower deck to the Ford garden tractor that came with the place as part of the deal. In the end, I managed to attach the deck using fewer parts than the manual called for. I saved the extra pieces. Just in case. Again, I was far too busy to look for strawberries.

Next on the priority list was the barn. The building was filled waist-deep with sheep manure and needed attention of the most deliberate sort. It took two weeks of shoveling and wheeling dung before I reached the concrete floor of the old dairy barn. Throughout my labor, the strawberries remained undiscovered.

Towards the end of June, I took two weeks of vacation. I planned to spend my time off reading, tinkering, and finding the best fishing spots in the River. I was home, reading an Ursula LeGuin novella, when Rene' finally found them:

"Mark, there must be a ton of strawberries out there."

I wasn't interested. The term "ton" reminded me of sheep manure. The acrid dust of that experience still clung to the inside of my nostrils. My shoulders and back ached at the prospect of moving a "ton" of anything.

"Uh-huh," I replied, without looking up, my nose buried in the book.

Rene' would not go away.

"You have to see them for yourself. Come on."

My wife stood there, very pregnant, very sweaty, and very determined. I yielded. I put down the book and followed her out into the field.

"See?"

Outlined in the tall grass, I could make out what looked to be about a quarter acre of green, leafy plants. The plants formed tight, perfect rows, their leaves glistening in the bright summer sunlight.

"What are they?"

"Strawberries. They're loaded with fruit."

"You're kidding. Who'd be crazy enough to plant so many?"

I didn't expect her to respond.

"The Drew's," she said.

"I knew that."

She lifted the leaves of one of the plants and forced me to bend down. I studied the fruit. The size of the berries made me rethink my feigned disinterest.

"Wow. They're huge. How many of the plants have berries like this?"

"All of them. Four to five per plant. Every last one of them."

Rene' stood up triumphantly. I continued to examine the ripe berries. The heavy fruit hung precariously in the still air. I began to dream: strawberry pie, strawberries on ice cream, strawberry jam; the possibilities seemed endless. Rene's voice called me back to reality.

"They need to be weeded."

"How's that?"

"You heard me. The weeds are choking out the plants."

My wife's arms raised. Her gesture encompassed a vast expanse, which up to that moment had seemed to be a quarter acre of heaven. Until she mentioned the weeds, a quarter acre hardly seemed sufficient for all the plans I was making for the little fruit.

"Really?"

"Really."

I began to perspire. Great beads of sweat formed on my forehead and dripped onto the plants. I thought I detected one of the strawberry plants dance in perverse delight as my body's moisture landed on its leaf. I sensed I was becoming delirious.

That evening, Rene' and I began to hack away at the weeds beneath a cloud of obnoxious mosquitoes. We pulled. We tugged. We strained at the thick-rooted parasites that were rapidly overtaking the garden. In addition, we found that there were so many ripe berries we couldn't harvest them all. Hundreds ripened and fell to the dirt before we could salvage them. Every relative, friend or neighbor we could round up was enlisted to pick. Their efforts hardly dented the crop.

Finally, we placed a sign out on the road:

"Pick Your Own Strawberries. 50 Cents a Pound."

Strangers got their fill. More berries ripened. Like out-of-control chocolates on an assembly line in an old *I Love Lucy* episode, our strawberries continued to ripen faster than we could pick them. And the weeds, despite our best efforts, continued to sprout.

By the end of my vacation, 450 pounds of berries had been harvested. Another hundred pounds or so remained in the field. My dreams of strawberry pie and jam had been replaced by the reality of aching knees, a body covered with bug bites, and a realization that, without a gasoline tiller, the weeds would always win.

The following season, the patch produced half as many berries and twice as many weeds. Conceding defeat, I fenced in the pasture and let Nicholas, our horse, eat strawberries, weeds, and grass to his heart's content. I thought I'd seen the last of strawberries on the Munger Farm.

But there's something magical about strawberries. Something compels Rene' and I to try to grow them. Maybe we share some sort of primeval hunter-gatherer need that can only be satisfied by growing strawberries. Or maybe we're both just plain stubborn. Whatever the reason, year in and year out, we add new strawberry plants to our vegetable garden. We water them, mulch them, nurture them, and try to weed them, but the weeds always win out.

You'd think we'd learn our lesson. You'd think that we could admit defeat. It would certainly be cheaper and less frustrating to simply drive to town and buy berries at the market. But I'm here to tell you: dreams of homegrown strawberries die awfully hard.

WINTER GEESE

They came to live with us on my thirtieth birthday, a gift from three of my high school friends. I'm now fast approaching fifty so that my memory of things that happened on my thirtieth birthday may or may not be accurate. That disclosure having been made, I think my mind has retained most of the details about the geese.

My pals Larry, John, and Steve gave them to me. Two white farm geese, one male, one female. Being that Larry and John were carpenters at the time and Steve was an engineer, the boys saw to it that the geese came packaged in a well-constructed cage. But the geese were large and the cage was small. It soon became apparent that the birds needed more room.

I don't remember their names. I do remember their voices. Their loud, obnoxious calls still reverberate in my mind. I built them an enclosed pen out next to the barn. The first few weeks we had them, I did my best to keep our golden retriever named Pelly, away from the birds. I tried to keep the geese fed and watered. I wasn't a farmer. I'd never owned poultry. I think the birds took advantage of my ignorance.

That November, the Cloquet River plummeted to the lowest level that it has ever been at since we moved to Fredenberg Township. Normally, because our farm is located only a mile or so below the dam on the Cloquet River that forms Island Lake, the flowage in front of our place stays open all winter. But that year, the Cloquet River froze over. Only a small oval of water, surrounded by thin, fragile ice, remained open in front of our place.

Somehow, I left the door to the goose pen unlatched. When I went out to feed the birds, they were gone. Fresh snow told the tale. I followed their tracks through the pasture, down to the river. There, out in the middle of open water, two geese swam. Even to this City Boy, it was obvious that the domesticated waterfowl had no intention of returning to their cage on their own.

After a period of contemplation, I envisioned a plan. Pelly was a golden retriever, a bird dog. It would only be natural for me to call upon him to help me retrieve the geese. I yelled to my wife Rene' and asked her to bring the dog down to the water. I didn't really intend for her to get involved in the chase. She was within days of delivering Dylan, our second son, and clearly not physically balanced for chasing angry geese over slippery ice. But she came, bringing the dog and a steady stream of suggestions as to how we might capture the birds, with her.

Pelly dove eagerly into the water after the geese. His enthusiasm concealed the fact that he was old. Ice formed on his long chest hair as he swam in circles after the panicked fowl. Honks echoed off the frozen banks of the river as the birds dodged the aged dog's lunging attempts to grab their tail feathers.

My wife and I positioned ourselves on opposite edges of the ice. The frozen surface cracked as we scurried back and forth. It seemed improbable that Pelly would catch the birds. I was convinced either the dog or the geese, if not both, would die of exhaustion before the birds were captured.

Despite my lack of faith, the old dog managed to corner the smaller goose against the rough edge of the shoreline. As the bird tried to strike the dog on the end of the nose with its bill, Pelly sank his teeth into the bird's tail feathers and picked the squawking goose up out of the water. With a leap of restored youth, the dog trotted across the ice still holding the bird.

Running to the dog's aid, I slipped on the ice, landing unceremoniously on the dog and the goose. Rene' howled in laughter. I winced in pain. To me, farming was becoming serious business. I didn't appreciate the humor.

"I'll give you a 6.5 for that dive, Mark."

I concentrated on holding the flapping bird under my arm. The bird's head twisted in defiance. It tried to break free of my grip and bite me. I held the goose tight to my body with one arm, clamping the other hand around its bill.

"Very funny, dear. Now what do you propose I do with this goose?" I asked.

The question was real. I hadn't considered what we would do with the captured bird while we stalked its liberated mate.

"You could walk him back to the pen and then come back for the other one."

It seemed like a sensible suggestion. Anyone that knows me knows that, during times of crisis, I am usually sensible. For whatever reason, I decided to take a more creative approach.

I trudged up the frozen riverbank with the goose under one arm. My Sorels slipped on fresh snow. The gander drifted in the water. Pelly dashed up the embankment behind me. As I crested the hill, the goose broke free of my grip. Her long white neck coiled. She struck at my gloved hand but she couldn't pierce the thick leather of my glove. I reestablished my grip and tucked her head back under my arm. An outbuilding blocked our path. We were not on our land. We were on a neighbor's property. Behind the shed, a small cabin sat tucked into the woods, its windows boarded up for winter. Firewood dusted with fresh snow was stacked neatly in front of the cabin.

I opened the door to the outbuilding and cast the bird into the darkness. Heavy springs automatically closed the portal.

"That should hold her for now, eh Pelly?"

The dog didn't respond. He was headed back down the hill.

Out on the river, Rene' continued to shuffle across the ice. Her movements were deliberate. She called to me.

"Where'd you put the goose?"

"Up the hill in a building by the old cabin."

"What building?"

I didn't answer. Pelly was once again in the water. The dog's pace had slowed. His panting grew labored as he paddled in aimless circles trying to corner the gander. There seemed to be no method to the retriever's approach. The dog appeared to be engaged in a mindless chase, a journey with no beginning and no end. The goose didn't tire. Snow fell. Thick wet flakes settled in the branches of low hanging trees. Muted cries of the captured bird floated down to us from atop the rise.

Suddenly, the dog broke free of the water's grip and launched himself at the gander. A bitter strike from the bird's bill missed the retriever's nose. Pelly's mouth clamped down hard on the bird's neck. Rene' grabbed the thrashing goose away from the dog. Globs of thick blood fell to the ice.

I took the bird from my wife. The gander struck out at me, narrowly missing my face. My gloved hand pressed the bird's bloodied feathers apart.

"He's O.K.," I advised. "It's just a surface wound."

Climbing the snow-covered hillock to the cabin, the bird squirmed in my grasp. Its chest pounded in fright. Behind me, my wife leaned over to pet the old dog. Her feet gave way, dropping her unceremoniously to her rump. I couldn't resist:

"I'll give you a 10."

Rene' ignored my remark and continued to stroke the hard-with-ice fur of the retriever from her new position. I climbed the slope with the second bird. When I stopped to adjust the gander under my arm, my wife asked me the following question:

"Mark, where are you putting these geese?"

I didn't answer her. My gloved fingers clumsily unlatched the door to the outbuilding. I opened the shed and stuffed the second goose inside before its mate could escape.

"I'll need a hand," I called out to my spouse. "We can each carry a bird back to the house."

Standing in the gentle vortex of falling snow, I listened to the muffled sounds of the trapped birds and observed that someone had cut the silhouette of a quarter moon through the weathered siding above the entrance to the building. I smiled and wondered what the geese thought of it all.

THE LONG RETRIEVE

The sky was blue and high. There was a chill to the air, a precursor of winter yet to come though the sun's strength retained a hint of summer. The leaves were gone: the browns and grays of late autumn having replaced the greens.

On the north bank of the River, we walked an old trail. He remained ten to twenty feet in front of me. The leaves beneath our feet were wet with dew. The ground cover made no sound as we moved. A heavy odor hung over the narrow corridor. I recognized the smell to be that of rotting aspen leaves. He kept his nose close to the forest floor despite the fetid smell of decaying vegetation.

We were hunting grouse. We hadn't encountered any partridge by the time we made Mud Lake. The dog had acted birdy a few times, pacing frantically to and fro in the dense undergrowth on either side of the trail, but didn't flush any grouse for all his effort.

Mud Lake was ominous. The pothole's water was stained black, the color of tar. Out in the middle of the pond, a flock of mallards floated contentedly out of range. The retriever lifted his nose to the birds and turned to me.

"Out of range, boy."

The words weren't important. The tone of my voice was what mattered.

"Let's keep moving. Maybe we'll kick up a partridge or two down the trail."

The dog wagged his tail and went back to working the dense balsam and aspen lining the path. I watched his thick red fur dodge in and out of the trees and sparse grass. Every now and then, I could see his white chest hair as he strained to peer over the undergrowth to look at what lay ahead of us. The fur of his ears and legs became matted and covered with burrs.

"WUMMMMMMMPPPPHHH..."

My heart stuttered when the grouse erupted. The bird took off low and behind me. My .410 side-by-side barked. Once. The bird flew on. Twice. The bird set its wings and sailed unharmed over a stand of sickly birch.

Instinctively, the dog chased the departed bird.

"Come, Pelly, come."

The dog didn't heed my calls. He was convinced I'd hit the partridge. I guess it's a retriever's prerogative to have too much faith in his Master's abilities.

In time, the dog accepted the fact that I'd missed. He came back from his quest. I sat on the cool ground and leaned against a large balsam. The dog rested quietly at my side. I stroked his soft coat, picking out burrs where I could. He licked salt from my hand.

The shade of the tree kept us cool. Pelly's ears twitched. The breeze carried the voices of the ducks towards us.

We left our place of contentment in search of prey.

As we walked south, the path disappeared into marsh. Box elders and willows formed a nearly impassable thicket. The dog dodged beneath the low branches with impunity but it was slow going for his human counterpart. My companion moved with the energy and vigor of a pup. He was twelve, a sage among Golden Retrievers. He did not hunt like an old dog that day.

Every now and then I lost sight of him in the bramble. Every so often I heard the thunderous crash of another ruffed grouse fleeing to safety. It was no use. I couldn't see the birds rise. The few shots I managed were made in complete frustration and without aim. After five or six birds escaped, I'd had enough. I was wet and tired. Due to my marksmanship, I was also birdless.

I crossed the Cloquet River downstream from my house. Pelly plunged through the cold water, swimming when he had to, walking when he could. The blue sky was gone. A seamless gray blanket covered the world. A brisk breeze rose from the east, causing whitecaps to exaggerate the current. Exiting the water, the dog bounded up the bank, his nose once more to the ground.

We found no grouse. I walked onto our hay field. The grass was short; the hay had long since been put up in the barn. The dog bounded across the yellow stubble. His ears trailed behind him in the wind. In the distance, our white house stood stark against a depressingly terse sky.

"Here Pelly."

I called the dog back. Five ducks rose behind the old cantilever bridge spanning the River. My glasses were clouded by condensation. I removed them and wiped the lenses on my shirtsleeve. The old dog and I stood behind a thin line of aspen trees on top of the riverbank horizontal to the flight of the birds. The ducks approached. I affixed my glasses to the bridge of my nose, the metal frame cold against the skin. The ducks were Whistlers.

"Down, boy."

The retriever crouched. I knelt down next to the dog. We watched the progress of the birds. The ducks came in low, with their legs extended, ready to land on the water.

I'd never fired my .410 at a duck. I had No.8 shot in both barrels. I doubted that the pellets could penetrate the chest feathers of waterfowl. Despite my misgivings, I lifted the gun to my shoulder. My right eye followed the leader. I squeezed the trigger slowly; holding my breath as the Whistlers attempted to land.

"Crack."

The leader tumbled headlong into the river. The others accelerated away before I could shoot again. Pelly dove from the bank and landed in the water on all fours. He began to swim out to retrieve the downed bird.

The combination of the river's current and the wind kept the duck away from the dog. The dog could not see the bird in the water. He paddled in circles searching for the downed bird, his head held too low to see over the waves.

Whether he did it intentionally or not, I will never know. But as I was ready to give up and call him in, the dog arched his neck and spotted the duck. With speed, Pelly closed the distance to the floating Whistler. Gripping the duck in his mouth, the dog tried to return. The current was too strong. The River began to carry the golden retriever and the duck downstream. Changing directions, the dog swam with the current, plotting a diagonal course towards a clearing along the far bank. On the opposing shore, Pelly stood contemplating my location. Water dripped from the dog's long coat. The golden retriever shook himself with a vengeance. Water flew. The bird stayed put in the soft mouth of the canine.

I unloaded my shotgun and began to walk home. On the other side of the river, the old dog broke into a trot. He kept a tight hold on the duck. Through the brush lining the riverbank, across the wooden deck of the decaying bridge, the dog carried the dead Whistler. He didn't release the bird until I took it out of his gentle mouth.

Pelly had retrieved a single, seemingly insignificant duck, a full quarter-mile. That was the last time we hunted together. During the winter of that year, a car hit my dog out on the road. His hip was fractured and he had to be put to sleep.

As I write this, my shotgun leans against a wall across the room. The wooden stock of the weapon is freshly polished and oiled, ready for another hunting season. Through the window above my desk, I can see our current dogs, Maggie and Sam, running through the yard. They are fine animals and wonderful pets. But they are not Pelly.

However, I'm consoled by the fact that, whenever the leaves turn brittle and begin to drift to the ground; whenever the geese and ducks gather to take wing, Pelly's last hunt comes back to me. It is then that I know his spirit is still here. In my mind's eye, I can see him trotting slowly through the closeness of the forest, still carrying the Whistler, still making the long retrieve.

A VERY FAMILIAR PLACE

The boy sat nervously at an old oak desk. His legs were short; they barely touched the wooden planks of the floor. He was the sort of boy prone to doodling and daydreaming. The thick lenses of his new eyeglasses gave him a studious look but his mind was wandering. His eyes were not on the Social Studies text in front of him. His eyes were focused outside, riveted on the swirling elm leaves and the retiring green of the grass. A city park stood empty across the cracked blacktop of the street.

"Hope it doesn't rain at the farm."

Jeff's voice called the boy back to the classroom. The words were whispered, in hopes that Miss Hollingsworth, their teacher, would not overhear them. Theirs was not an ordinary class. They were "special": selected from various elementary schools of the City and thrown together in one classroom. They were the geeks, the brains, the bookworms. Jeff, like the boy who listened to him, looked the part.

Jeff wore glasses as well. His glasses had black plastic frames. The frames rode high on his nose. As Jeff spoke to Wayne, another classmate, the glasses slid down Jeff's nose. Wayne was one of the few in the class who didn't wear glasses but Wayne was still a nerd.

"Can we drive the car?"

Wayne asked the question under his breath. Jeff's response was just as subdued.

"Sure. The old Ford still runs. We can drive it as long as we don't take it on the road."

The boy was curious. He had never seen the farm. He was new to the class. He had arrived late, in October. He was sent to replace a girl from his school, a girl who could not handle the pressure of being surrounded by genius. Most of the smart kids had been brought together the year before, in fifth grade. But not him. He only knew one girl in the "special" class when he arrived. The other twenty-some kids were complete strangers. He did not know them. He dared not ask about the farm.

In his mind, he saw an old white farmhouse standing alone, surrounded by uncut hay. He was certain that a lake cut through the property. Cold, October water danced in that lake. He wanted to go there, to run and play with the other boys on the shores of that unnamed pond. But he was an outsider. He was not invited. His vision of the place faded as Ms. Hollingsworth walked by.

Eventually, the others in the class came to accept him as one of their own. He and Jeff became friends. Years passed. They played football and basketball together. One day, because of their friendship, he was finally invited to the farm.

He'd never stopped thinking of the place. From the very first, his mind revised and reshaped his vision of what the farm looked like. When he finally visited the old homestead, he found that the farmhouse was indeed white. Square logs, fashioned in the old way, the Finnish way, remained hidden behind pine lap siding. The timbers were as solid and remarkable as he thought they would be.

But there was no lake. The only water on the place turned out to be a shallow creek. The lack of a lake did not diminish the beauty of the farm in the boy's eyes. He loved history. The farm's past whispered to him as he stood in the pasture contemplating mounds of stones that had been piled there. Though in his teens, he was old enough to appreciate the sweat and toil that built the place. The spirit of the immigrant men, women, and children who had farmed and died there touched him. His eyes scanned the landscape with possessive angst. He sensed that the farm could only be owned by those who had created it.

Years later, on the backside of the farm's woodlot, the boys built a ramshackle cabin of aspen. They used aspen because there were no longer any large fir trees remaining on the land with which to build.

Through the summer's heat, the incessant bites of black flies, and the buzzing of mosquitoes, the boys worked the woods. Their toil reminded the kid of the terrible price the immigrants must have paid to live there. Though the cabin was a mere shed compared to the intricate dovetailed buildings the Finns constructed nearly a century before, he felt a connection to the land once the shanty was finished.

As insignificant as it seemed, the tiny cabin was a refuge. It was a place to hunt, to ski, to play cards. It was isolated by time and distance from real life. In some small way, the cabin made the boys a part of the farm's history.

They grew older; the boys became men; they married, found jobs, and fought the battles of adult life. The cabin stood empty. After several harsh winters, the roof fell in, the logs rotted; the walls collapsed.

This night finds him back at the farm. Above him, the sky stands clear and dark. A kerosene lantern flickers in the wind. The shadows of giant spruce trees sway, dancing in time to the evening breeze.

Bang.

The screen door to the front porch of the farmhouse announces the entry or departure of each guest. The man, now in his forties, an age which seems to confuse and annoy him, sits before the warmth of a bonfire.

"Dad, have you seen Dylan? He and Evan are hiding on me."

Chris, the man's third son, casts the question out into the night where it echoes off the weathered walls of a failing shed. There is no glass left in the windows of the outbuildings. The barn has long since disintegrated. Its lumber fuels the fire. He was here when the barn fell. How long ago was it? Five years? Ten? The man can't remember.

It's October. Jeff and his wife have invited their friends and relatives to celebrate the coming of the harvest. Everyone knows that there is nothing to harvest at the farm. These fields have not known crops or cows, or the bite of a tiller, for forty years. It's not the promise of harvest but the promise of old memories, which draws them back.

Jeff sits cross-legged before the fire. He plays a timeless Crosby, Stills, Nash, and Young song on his twelve-string guitar. His fingers remember notes he has not played in two decades. Though the guitarist no longer wears the glasses of his youth, Jeff's wire-rimmed frames ride low on his nose as he concentrates on the song.

Children pull boards off of the shed. The adults don't complain. Older boys slide the seasoned pine planks into the fire. Sparks swirl up into the night and turn to ash as they climb.

The man thinks back to their old school, their old classroom, where he first heard Jeff talk about Grandpa's farm. He closes his eyes. The fire's warmth, the music, the darkness, allow him to come to a very familiar place. He sits quietly next to his wife, listening to the wind, the trees, the soft chords of a forgotten melody from an old friend's guitar and deep within himself, the man hears the lap of waves against a shoreline, a shoreline that exists only in the dreams of his youth.

LEMONADE STAND

Above the slow current of the River, the span of an old bridge stood. Rust stained the bridge's iron frame. Gaping holes in the wood timbers exposed the frailty of its deck. Noisy crows circled the tenuous arch of the cantilever, once delicate and ornate, now bowed and frail with age.

Two boys sat near the span at the end of a long gravel driveway. Workers milled around the bridge. A dry wind captured the dust caused by the construction and wrested it away from the earth's gravity. Small rocks and bits of sand pummeled the boys. The sun's heat stung their exposed necks and arms, their skin white and tender after the long winter. A young hand darted across the card table and removed the glass pitcher of lemonade in advance of the squall. The smaller boy, his dark hair hanging loose around his head in very straight, even rows, joined his blond-haired cousin under the card table with the pitcher. Despite the heat and the thirsty crew of construction workers busily dismantling the bridge, they sold no lemonade.

At nine years old, the boys' experience in commerce was limited to begging their parents for money to buy He-Man toys. But they'd watched enough television to understand the concept of selling retail: you need a product that someone wants.

"Greggy, no one's buyin' our stuff."

Matt sat cross-legged in the dirt, protecting the mouth of the pitcher from the swirling dust devils.

"Ya. Maybe ten cents a glass is too much."

"Maybe. But if we charge five cents, that's only..."

The younger cousin's brow knitted as he tried to do long division in his head.

"...Two and a half cents apiece for each glass. We'll be here all year trying to get enough to buy a Skeletor Slime Pit," Greggy blurted out.

A worker walked by the table, glancing at the crude sign:
Lemonade, 10 Scents a Glass.

"Hey mister, wanna glass?"

Matt, never at a loss for a question, poked his head out from under the card table as he spoke.

"No thanks, kid. Got a thermos full of coffee. A little too early for lemonade. Catch me after lunch."

The boys stood up and dusted off their blue jeans.

It was Greggy, his blue eyes peering at the workmen, who stated the obvious.

"You know what we need?"

"What?"

"Somethin' else."

"Like what?"

"I dunno."

Questions. More questions for Matt to ponder. Suddenly, it came to him. His round face beamed in triumph.

"Come on Greg. I got an idea."

Leaving the open pitcher to the swirling dirt, they bolted for the house.

Sometime later that day my wife Rene' searched the cupboards for macaroni and cheese. She hadn't seen the boys since early in the morning when they asked her permission to set up a lemonade stand. They would be hungry. There's nothing better than macaroni and cheese to satisfy nine-year-old boys. Having just completed the grocery shopping for the week, Rene' knew there were several family-sized boxes on the shelves. But when she opened the cupboard doors, the boxes, along with several cans of vegetables and Campbell's soup, had inexplicably vanished.

Troubled, Rene' put on her tennis shoes and went outside. The wind had died and the sun stood unusually high for late spring. Calm heat hung heavy over the valley. At the end of the driveway, she could see the boys sitting behind a table. Walking down the dirt drive, she saw that the cantilever of the old span had been removed.

"Hi, mom. We're doing really good," Matt yelled, his small voice projecting broadly.

"Yeah, Auntie Nay, we've just about sold a whole pitcher." Greggy's voice trailed after his cousin's, its pitch a bit deeper, the words slightly less excited.

Across the road, the construction crew rested in the shade of trees, used Styrofoam cups crumpled on the ground near the men.

Rene' approached the boys and caught a glimpse of their promotional sign. Freshly amended, it now read:

Lemonade, 10 Scents a glass. *Free Pryze*.

The two boys sat on folding chairs, eyes concealed by cheap sunglasses. Matt wore his Minnesota North Stars cap pulled down hard upon his head causing his ears to protrude. Greggy's Oakland A's cap sat loosely atop his yellow hair. His head was clearly too big for the cap.

"Do you boys know anything about the missing cans of soup and boxes of macaroni and cheese from the kitchen?" my wife asked.

Rene's tone was even. From the fresh marker on the boys' sign, and the three cans of peas stacked neatly on the table, she guessed what had happened to her canned goods. Looking intently at the boys, she poured herself a cup of lemonade. Waiting for a response, she took a long drink of the cold liquid.

"Ugh. Didn't you put any sugar in this?"

The tartness caught her completely off guard. She expected a slight twist of lemon, followed by the sweetness of sugar. Instead, she tasted only lemon.

"Sugar?"

Matt looked at Greggy. Smiles flowed across their sun-reddened faces.

"So that's why they spit the stuff out."

Greggy's voice was quiet as he spoke. Matt tried to contain a giggle.

"What about the soup and the mac and cheese?"

Gathering his wits about him, Matt removed his sunglasses and looked up at his mother with gentle brown eyes.

"That's what we used for prizes, Mom. See, Greggy and I figured that we'd do just like McDonald's does with a Happy Meal: give them a surprise with every glass."

"How many cans and boxes did you give away?" Rene' asked in as stern a voice as she could muster. She was having trouble keeping a straight face as she listened to the boy's marketing scheme.

"'Bout ten cans of soup and three boxes of mac and cheese."

A heavy sigh escaped from Rene as she picked up the three remaining cans of peas.

"I think the lemonade stand is closed for today. Let's go have some lunch."

"Sure, mom. Besides, we sold twenty glasses. That's..."

Again, Matt did the math in his head as they walked down the dry dirt of the drive towards the house.

"...A buck apiece," his cousin responded. "If we do this every day for a week, we'll have enough to buy a Skeletor Slime Pit."

Rene' turned her head and looked at the boys.

"I think we better have a talk about your understanding of economics. Your lemonade stand will likely cost Uncle Mark and me more than we can afford."

The two boys looked at each other, puzzled by the remark. Without much effort, and at no cost to them, they were each a dollar richer than they had been when they woke up that morning on the Munger Farm. They didn't see what the problem was.

A CHRISTMAS CAROL

Sure, you can go buy a Christmas tree from a nursery, from some Boy Scout lot, or from some dubious looking stranger lurking in the dim light of an alley. But what fun would that be?

When I was in law school, Rene' and I didn't have a lot of money. Naturally, we bought our first few Christmas Trees. Now that I'm relatively successful, we don't buy our trees. We chop them down in the woods. We don't have to pay anything for the privilege because we cut them down on our own land. But the Munger Christmas Tree, though free of charge, is never without cost.

I'm sure you've seen those cute little *Currier and Ives* etchings. You know, the ones showing the kids all bundled up in the sleigh with dad and mom gliding through the snow behind the family horse, a picture-perfect Christmas tree in tow. Sort of reminds you of *Dr. Zhivago*, now doesn't it? It's a scene that my family aspires to mimic year in and year out. We have yet, after many winters of trial, to achieve anything close to such serenity and bliss during our annual Christmas tree ordeal.

My wife and I start our annual tree trek with distinctly different values and opinions as to what we're after. Rene', being an artist, seeks to find the cosmetically perfect Christmas tree. I, on the other hand, simply want to find one that is tall, green, and absent bird droppings. I'll always head for the lowly balsams, of which our land has thousands. Rene' will always migrate to the Norway's, which are far scarcer and more difficult to find. And in separate parts of the forest, we will both locate what we believe to be the "perfect tree".

Year after year, if you're out and about in Fredenberg, you can hear the discussion from the woods. It's unchanging, as constant as the star over Bethlehem:

"Mark, that is the ugliest Christmas Tree I've ever seen."

"What's wrong with it? It's green, isn't it? It's straight, isn't it? Come on Rene', we could be out here all day and not find a better tree."

"I found one."

"What, another one of those spindly Norway's you always pick out? Get real."

You get the picture. Ultimately, as the kids disappear into the forest to avoid taking sides, the debate rages on. And always, exhausted by my wife's persistence, I yield and shuffle back to the house with her selected Norway.

Some years we used Cisco our 30-year-old mare to pull the tree back to the house on a plastic slider. Some years, when I was lazy, I'd pull the tree with our Skidoo, unless the Skidoo quit, in which case I end up pulling the snow machine and the tree with my tractor. But each slow, painful retreat from the woods finds me muttering under my breath:

"My tree was better."

But no one listens.

There was one year when Rene' was too busy to look for a tree. The kids and I picked out a dandy balsam: tall, supple and fresh, with no bird poop. You could tell by Old Cisco's jaunty gait, as she labored to pull the tree home, that even she knew we had a winner. With great care, the kids and I trimmed the tree with a minimum of arguing. To the sounds of George Bailey's angst echoing in the background we decorated the balsam in hopes of surprising Mom. The surprise was on us.

"That's the ugliest tree I've ever seen," she said as she stood in the front porch of our house.

"What? You've gotta be kidding, dear. I mean, just look at how green it is, how straight and..."

"I know, Mark, no bird poop. But look at all the bare spots. You can't hide bare spots like that."

"Sure you can. That's why God invented lights."

"You've already got too many lights in the bare spots. Look at the boughs. They're bent to the floor under the weight of the lights."

"We'll get some wire and tie the boughs to the wall."

"You're ruining Christmas, Mark. That tree is a disgrace."

Dylan, our second son defended me:

"But mom, we like it. It's a neat tree."

Rene' didn't reply. The tree spent the night fully decorated in our enclosed front porch; proudly proclaiming to all that baldness can be beautiful.

In the morning, I made sure my path to the truck took me past the tree. The balsam was, to my way of thinking, perfect in every way. I kissed my wife on the cheek as I left for work.

"Lighten up, dear. It's just a tree. Besides, it kind of grows on you."

There was only silence as I departed.

That evening coming home from work I drove my pick up truck past the front porch. Through the frost of a winter window, I saw bright bulbs, tinsel and lights adorning the firm, unyielding boughs of an upstart Norway pine. Walking up the back steps, I noted another curiosity. Where, that very morning, there'd been a lovely eight-foot high pine standing guard over a slumbering poppy bed, only a stump remained. As my eyes adjusted to the fading daylight, I discovered, nestled in the slight depth of snow hugging the rear porch, the discarded balsam that had once been our Yuletide tree.

"Merry Christmas, Mark," my wife called out from the warmth of our country home as I entered the kitchen.

ICE FISHING

"Dad, don't you think we should just park the car at the top of the hill and walk down to the lake?"

I asked that question several years ago when my father, the quintessential fisherman, invited my oldest son Matt and I to go late-season ice fishing with him.

We drove up US Highway 2 to a small, nameless lake near Brookston, Minnesota to fish for "monster" crappies and bluegills. Dad assured us that we'd catch fish. After all, the lake we were going to was one of Doctor Leppo's favorites. Everyone knew that Dr. Leppo, next to being the best pediatrician in town, was also the best ice fisherman in Northeastern Minnesota. With an endorsement like that, I figured there was no room for error.

Dad has always been the kind of guy to challenge his vehicles. Back in the 1960's, he took some pals to Canada goose hunting. Somewhere in the middle of the prairie, Grandpa decided his Jeep Wagoneer could do just about anything. He saw no reason to heed signs that read: "Road ends". It took three bulldozers and a farm tractor to pull the Wagoneer out of the swamp at the end of that road.

"Don't worry. This car has Positraction. We'll be fine."

Before I could protest further, the Cadillac rolled down the snow-covered boat landing and out onto the ice. Matt, six or seven years old at the time, looked at me. Even he realized that Grandpa was once again pushing the limits of mechanized travel.

It was a gorgeous March day. A white sun rose high above us as Dad started the power auger and drilled three perfect holes through the frozen surface of the lake. Despite the warmth of the day the ice was thick and hard.

"Matt, get me a couple of minnows, will you?"

"Sure Grandpa."

Wet up to his elbows from reaching into the minnow bucket, Matt triumphantly marched to Grandpa with two small Crappie minnows crushed between his choppers.

"Thanks."

After half an hour without a bite, I wandered away from my fishing rod in search of wood for a fire. Grandpa continued to stare intently into the cold water as if trying to will the fish into biting.

I scanned the lake as I walked. We were the only ones fishing. I pondered the reasons this could be. I kept my thoughts to myself as I gathered dry maple branches from the shoreline and trudged back make a fire.

I drew a match across my belt buckle. The sulfur caught. Gingerly, I touched the delicate flame to a dry piece of birch bark wedged under wood.

"Any luck, Dad?" I asked, keeping one eye on the rising flames.

"Just a couple of nibbles. Perch, I think," he said.

"What do we have?" the boy asked.

"Hot-dogs, chips, and candy bars," my dad responded.

"Goodie."

My son managed to drop several hot-dogs into the fire before he successfully cooked one. We sat on overturned plastic buckets, eating lunch, catching no fish and not really caring too much about it.

By four in the afternoon, Grandpa had seen enough of Dr. Leppo's secret lake. We'd pulled out two tiny perch. Both fish weighed less than the minnows used to catch them. Matt ate four hot-dogs, two candy bars, and drank two cans of Coke. He was hungry again.

The Cadillac started without incident. Dad looked at me with a confident "I told you so" smirk. Things appeared to be fine until we left the level surface of the lake and tried to make it back up the hill. Positraction could not overcome the intentions of the car's designers: a luxury automobile is meant to be driven on clear, dry pavement, not out onto an ice-covered lake. We were stuck.

I tried to help. I found pieces of discarded plywood and placed them under the rear wheels of the car. The Cadillac took offense and spat the boards at me. I pushed. I shoveled until I was blue in the face. Nothing could make that low slung, heavily armored tank move uphill in loose snow.

We left the lake without any fish and without our car. Walking down an unnamed dirt road in the middle of nowhere, my six-year-old complained about his need for another meal. When he complained that his legs were tired, I hoisted him up to my shoulders and carried him through the snow-covered silence. We stopped at each cabin or home we passed. We knocked on door after door. There was no one home on the lake.

"They're probably somewhere else, catching fish," I muttered.

Grandpa scowled.

As the sun went down, we came to a house occupied by a nice old couple. The husband gave us a ride to a tavern out on the highway.

"Hi, Rene'. It's Mark. We're gonna be a little late. The car's stuck on the lake. We're trying to find someone to pull it out."

The call to my wife was not an easy one. She was fully aware of my father's propensity to turn an ordinary day into an adventure.

"Stuck? How?"

"It's a long story. We're waiting for a kid with a truck to pull us out. Then we'll be home."

Outside the tavern, the sky was black and the wind was cold. We sat at the bar eating greasy cheeseburgers and watching "Austin City Limits". An old man behind the counter, wearing a ribbed undershirt and a two-day-old beard, scratched himself impolitely and read the paper. We were his only customers. He seemed annoyed that we were in the place.

Grandpa inhaled a cheeseburger and left with a young kid, a local farm boy, who had offered to pull the Caddie up the hill for $20.00. The closest wrecker was forty miles away and the guy wanted $150.00 to drive out to our location. Given the circumstances, the kid's offer was a bargain.

"Be back soon," my Dad promised.

I nodded and slid a couple of quarters into the pool table. Emmy Lou Harris sang softly from a Wurlitzer. Matt munched on French fries. A loud rumble shook the tavern. Bright headlights intruded into the bleak, dusty interior of the bar.

"Looks like they're back," the old man remarked, nodding in the general direction of the noise.

I pulled out my wallet and searched for money to pay the tab. Matt jumped from his stool, catsup dripping from his chin, and darted for the door.

"Thanks for the burgers," I said.

The bartender grunted. I slid my money across the lacquered surface of the bar and walked out of the place. It was ten o'clock.

We drove home nestled in quiet with my oldest son curled up in the back seat and fast asleep. Somewhere near Pike Lake, my Dad finally spoke:

"Sorry about this, Mark. But you wanna know something funny?"

"What?"

"That kid who pulled me out? He was only fourteen. Doesn't even have a farm permit to drive."

"Really?"

"Yup. Nice kid. I paid him an extra twenty bucks."

That was a few years back. Somewhere near Brookston, Minnesota there's a dairy farmer in his twenties who tells the story of two attorneys and a little kid from the City who tried to go four wheeling in a Cadillac.

THE FIREMAN'S DUCKS

"A friend of mine from the Fire Department has a problem."

Larry, one of my oldest buddies, was on the phone. His call found me at my law office during a moment of confusion. A trial loomed ahead of me. I was preoccupied.

"What's wrong?"

"Nothing's wrong. How'd you like some ducks?"

"Ducks? What kind of ducks?"

"I think they're mallards."

I paused. I already had four white farm geese given to me by Larry and two other "friends" for my 30th birthday. A cow was too expensive a gift: a goat, too destructive. So they'd given me geese. Two geese, which had, of course, turned into four geese. Four geese, which were in danger of becoming eight geese.

Did I really need more poultry wandering about the place, leaving their "packages" on our sidewalk?

"Why is he getting rid of them?"

My voice was calm and held no trace of enthusiasm. My mind was busy drafting jury instructions. I was vulnerable to suggestion because I wanted to get back to my work.

"The guy's pond is freezing up. He wants to butcher them but his wife and kid won't let him. I said you might want 'em."

There was really no thought behind my answer.

"Sure. The boys would like that. But what am I gonna keep them in? My pen is too small."

"Just put 'em in the pasture and let them use the barn at night. They can't fly."

Two days later a gunnysack full of quacking birds came home with me from work. By the light of the November moon, I untied the string securing the neck of a burlap bag and dumped a mass of feathers and bills onto frozen ground. Eleven fairly normal-looking mallards, some male and some female, and one very odd looking black and white Muscovy duck struggled free of the tangle.

As the ducks scurried around the enclosed pasture, I filled a feeder with corn. Hearing the feed fall against the metal skin of the feeder, the ducks rushed in unison towards the sound. Our geese, much larger and more aggressive than their smaller cousins, puffed out their chests and blocked the ducks' access to the food. Intimidated, the mallards and the Muscovy veered away. Darting uncontrollably across the grass, they collided headlong into the wire fencing while the geese triumphantly pecked at the grain.

Matt, our oldest child, rose with me the next morning to do chores. We dressed for dawn's chill before venturing outside to see how the ducks had fared. We found the geese nestled quietly in a corner of the barn. The pasture appeared empty. We walked through the hayfield, searching the tall grass for the ducks. They were nowhere in sight. As we approached the Cloquet River, the watercourse that flows immediately adjacent to our field, we heard the muted voices of waterfowl.

A light snow was falling. Snowflakes speckled the drab morning air with white. Standing on a gravel beach, my son and I saw our ducks, bobbing in unison, suspended in the slow current of the flowage, partially hidden by the fragile yellow marsh grass of the far shore. The Muscovy sat in the middle of the raft, looking distinctly foreign and obvious. We stared at the birds, at a loss as to how they'd escaped. The pasture gate was secured. There were no gaps in the fence. The ducks could not fly. And yet, they were free.

I placed a tray of corn on the ground near the River's edge. We stepped back, giving the birds space but the bait didn't work. All winter long, our ducks floated in front of the farm, laughing in their duck voices at the City Boy. As spring ascended, as their wing feathers grew, the mallards attempted short, experimental flights up and down the river but the Muscovy never left the surface of the water.

By Easter, the mallards were extending their flights. Each day at dawn, the flock would rise and fly off. The Muscovy tried to follow by paddling frantically up and down the River in search of his companions. Each night at dusk, the mallards came back, settling gently around their flightless friend, surrounding him with their numbers.

One day, the mallards didn't return. The Muscovy drifted up and down the Cloquet River; his plaintive quack a lonely, singular voice against the barren autumn landscape. Wild ducks reclaimed the river as their own. The migrants didn't tolerate the Muscovy's attempts at kinship. Whenever he approached, the Whistlers would dash in unison after him, driving him off.

Summer came and went. Wild mallards gathering for their great migration were more kind to the Muscovy. They allowed the domestic duck to float amongst them on the river. In October of that second year, just hours ahead of the first snow, the wild birds took wing. After their departure, I didn't see the Muscovy.

Whenever I heard a "quack" from the hollow of the River, I thought of the odd duck. I strained to see if, by some miracle, the Muscovy had returned. I knew that he'd likely met his end on the riverbank, in the smothering grasp of a weasel or a mink. I knew there was little likelihood a flightless domesticated duck could survive in the wild.

Several years later, I was walking towards our barn, intent on removing accumulated horse manure. Entering the dark confines of the old log building, the smell of horse hung heavy in the air. Inside the barn, I was greeted by a loud and obvious ruckus. Once my eyes became accustomed to the muted atmosphere of the place, I discovered the source of the commotion.

Our cat was frantically chasing a duck between the well-muscled legs of our two horses. Feathers flew as the feline pounced after the bird, clawing frantically at the duck's tail. Short, desperate "quacks" resounded from the timbered walls as the bird scurried beneath the bellies of the livestock. Our horses ignored the perturbation and remained content to chew fresh hay, unmoved by the tragic dance swirling around them.

I kicked blindly at the cat with one of my leather boots, sending the animal racing up the wooden ladder into the hayloft. The duck appeared exhausted as it adjusted its plumage and sat on soiled oat straw. I could hear its pathetic breathing as it cowered under the edge of the manger. With delicacy, I deposited my fatigue jacket on top of the shivering bird, pinning it to the ground. I reached under the green fabric and retrieved the struggling animal.

The Muscovy struggled against my embrace. I looked into the creature's milky eyes and wondered about nature, about chance. I tried to determine whether the bird I was holding was the same duck that had been released on our farm. Whether it was or wasn't, I knew there was no point in trying to reclaim something that had never been mine; at least, that's what I told myself as I knelt on the soft gravel of the riverbank and watched the duck paddle off in search of its companions.

DEER HUNTERS

For most of my forty plus years on this earth, I've been a hunter, and a deer hunter at that. But despite my personal connection with hunting, there's something different about living in the middle of the battle, about living at ground zero each November when the deer hunters take to the woods.

When my wife and I moved to Fredenberg Township just north of Duluth, it was the fulfillment of our dream come true. Well, at least my dream. I'd always, and I mean always, wanted a hobby farm in the country. Not that I knew anything about farming. It was the concept of land, of space, that captured my attention. A place out in the woods and field, one that I could call my own, was what I craved. My love of the land had little to do with an interest in hunting or fishing, though I did plenty of both growing up.

We started to look at houses. Hundreds of houses. Many of them were the same bungalows from Hades that we'd looked at before we bought our house in town. Two years passed until we found our farm. We moved to the country in 1984, on the eve of my first Grandma's Marathon. But that, as they say, is another story.

Our first summer living out, we learned a great many things about country life. Things like: what do you do when you discover you now own a quarter acre of ripe strawberries? Or what do you do with a barn full of sheep manure?

That first year living out, when the green grass of summer gave way to the yellow hay of autumn, it dawned on us that hunting season was just around the corner. Soon there'd be legions of deer hunters, fellows we didn't know, marching across the countryside with high-powered rifles. They'd surround us. Engulf us. Hold us prisoner and confine us to our land while war raged 'round us in the forest and across the fields. How could we cope? How could we protect our son Matthew?

Our first October on the place, Rene' and I bought every item of orange clothing that the Fredenberg Minno-ette, our local bait, tackle and convenience store had in stock. Gloves, hats, pants, sweatshirts: we bought it all. Then we hit Target and K-Mart in town for backup. During the weeks before Halloween, we began indoctrinating Matt to put on his war gear before he ventured out the door. We were ready. Ready for the onslaught.

My first deer season in the country, I joined the hunters. I wanted to hunt the thousands of acres of Minnesota Power land abutting our place. Uncharacteristically diligent, I went out in early September to build new deer stands for the season. By the beginning of November, I had several new hunting platforms ready for my exclusive use. On opening day, other guys found them first. One guy was brazen enough to drive his pickup truck across my pasture so he could park right underneath one of my stands. I discovered the man's boldness after I marched across the cold, snow-covered hayfield before the break of day, and found his brand new Ford pickup resting directly beneath my hunting stand. The next year I remedied the situation. I bought the adjacent 40 acres from Minnesota Power and posted all of the land "No Trespassing".

Even with our best precautions, the hunters still came. They read our signs and stopped at the house to ask if they could hunt our land. Mostly I let them. As the years passed, my own interest in hunting faded. Too many hunters; too many folks I didn't know. Hunting, at least hunting around others, requires a certain degree of trust. The other guy is ambulating through the forest with adrenaline rushing through his veins. You best know who the other guy is before you hunt in the woods with him. That was one reason my urge to hunt declined.

Then there was the fact that my boys, at least the three older ones, were involved in sports, flying kites, playing fort, or just plain goofing off on our land. I began to tell the people knocking on my door: "Sorry, our place is closed to hunting."

I found you can't say "no" to your neighbors quite that easily. I cross country ski and horseback ride on my neighbor's property. They want to be able to hunt on mine. My neighbors Al and Earl still deer hunt. They walk my ski trails each November hoping to find a big buck. More often than not, they shoot something less. Sometimes, to fill out their licenses, they shoot a spike buck or a doe. I understand that this is part of the equation, part of deer hunting.

One Sunday the kids and I were climbing into our mini-van, getting ready to leave for church. It was an unusually warm morning for November. Deer season was open but I hadn't heard any gunfire.

I knew something was up when I saw Earl, he's the father, and Al, he's the son, climbing over my electric fence. They were wearing the orange of deer season. Their rifles were carried loosely in their hands.

"Hit a doe, Mark. She ran through the pasture by the horses," Al advised.

"No way Al."

"Yep. She's down the bank, next to the river, in front of your house."

The three of us, the father and son smelling of artificial doe urine, and me smelling of Old Spice, walked over to the River. The stricken doe had severed both strands of wire to our electric fence as it dove into the Cloquet River.

"There she is, down in the water," Earl said.

The deer was neck deep in the current, hugging the shore, totally still, and partially hidden by a thicket. Standing above the animal, I watched the doe's nostrils flare as she labored to breathe. The pupils of her eyes were dilated, whether from shock or fear, I couldn't say. She remained motionless in an attempt to become invisible to her pursuers.

Crack.

Al's .30-30 barked. I heard Rene' cry out in alarm from inside our house. The doe's head jerked. Then she was still, her brown body floating lifeless in the dark water of the River.

My third son Chris and his buddy Spencer came running up to watch as we pulled the deer up the steep incline. Dylan, the second of my four boys, arrived at the edge of the bank just as the animal came to rest upon our lawn.

"Cool," Dylan whispered, poking the dead deer with a stick.

Matt, our oldest, a child who has long expressed doubts as to the wisdom of hunting, remained in the background. He was curious enough about the events to leave the protection of the van but not inquisitive enough to venture too close.

Rene' arrived. She watched in measured disgust as Al and Earl gutted the doe in our front yard.

"They shot it back on Earl's field," I said, "and she ran through our fence. She made the river but couldn't swim across. Al had to finish her off."

My wife nodded. She'd lived in the country as long as I had. She knew better than to instigate a debate about the morals of deer hunting with neighbors. In the country, hunting just is; it's ingrained in the fabric of rural life.

"Time for church," I announced, turning my back to the other men.

Rene' and I sat in the front seats of the Pontiac and closed the doors. I felt sadness and understanding in equal measure as I put the vehicle in gear.

UNDER A CATFISH MOON

I was raised like every other Minnesotan. In Minnesota, you are either a walleye fisherman, a trout fisherman, or a little of both. I grew up convinced that folks who fish, at least those worth talking to or talking about, do not try to catch fish bearing whiskers.

Before we moved to the country, I thought catfish and bullheads were slightly behind rock bass and marginally ahead of carp on the desirability scale. That all changed when I learned the secrets of fishing under a catfish moon.

Our hobby farm has a small creek running through it. The creek is short. It measures only a mile or so in total length. This rivulet is nameless. It lacks significance when you look for it on a map. But like so many small waters, its importance to the natural order of things cannot be measured by its size. In its tiny watershed, deer hide beneath the occasional grove of cedar; herons lurk in the yellow marsh grass defining its swampy course. Leopard frogs, bullfrogs and assorted peepers thrive in its slowly emptying pools. The frogs and toads provide an early spring chorus that tells us that the creek, for now, is healthy and running clean.

For the first few years we lived in the country, I watched city folk's fish from an old cantilever bridge that used to cross the Cloquet River in front of our house. These interlopers fished at night, by the light of a campfire, a gas lantern or, on rare occasion, by the light of a full moon. These tourists were after channel cats.

Sometime before the County demolished the old bridge and replaced it with an ugly concrete structure of little character and even less integrity, my wife decided to take up catfishing. I can still remember the night.

I was late coming home from a meeting. When I pulled into our driveway the summer skies were filled with the brilliance of the Milky Way. It was late. The full moon had already passed over our house. I parked my pickup truck and began to walk across the lawn towards the kitchen door dodging various toys and a kid's wading pool as I negotiated the grass. When my shadow passed over the pool, the water erupted. Startled, I bent down and looked into the pool. Despite the lack of light, I was able to make out the silhouette of the largest catfish I'd ever seen. The creature remained attached to my son Dylan's Snoopy rod by nearly invisible line. With my bare hands, I hoisted the fish out of the pool by the monofilament.

Croak.

I'd never known fish to speak. The voice of a fish protesting its capture was intriguing. "Perhaps," I thought, "I've underestimated the ranking of the catfish in God's aquatic hierarchy."

The commotion in the yard drew my wife out of the house.

77

"Who caught this monster?" I asked.

My voice was excited. The size and weight of the channel cat was impressive. Even in the darkness, I could see the extent of my wife's smile. It was one of those "I'm-a-better-fisherman-than-you-are" smiles. It's the smile you see when you're in a boat with a woman who's caught all the fish for the day.

"I did."

"Must go eight pounds or more."

I had no experience in gauging the weight of a channel catfish but my estimate seemed accurate.

"I'd say at least ten," she corrected.

I felt the need to burst her bubble. The tone in her voice was beginning to cross the line from mere pride to boastfulness.

"Maybe nine."

She didn't show any concern that I'd diminished the import of her catch.

"I think we should let him go," she offered out of the blue.

"What?"

"He's so big. He's probably the father of all the catfish around here. Put him back. We can always catch him again."

I didn't have enough energy to tell my wife that, given the creature's size; it was more likely a "mama" than a "papa".

"OK," I agreed. "I don't feel much like cleaning fish anyway."

I picked up the Zebco rod with my free hand and bit down on the monofilament line with my teeth. It took several bites to sever the eight-pound test. As I held the fish aloft by a short piece of line, I noted that the flanks of the animal were a beautiful steel blue; that the body was lean and long; that its whiskers were graceful and tipped in black. Unlike its ugly cousin, the brown bullhead, the channel cat looked like a gamefish.

The big cat swung heavily from the line as I walked across the front lawn. The heft of the fish forced the line into the exposed skin of my palm. I ignored the pain. I was convinced that Rene' was right. We should let her go. I knelt precariously on the slick earth of the riverbank as I slid the fish into the black water.

Since that first attempt at catching channel cats, my family has made catfishing a ritual. Four or five times a summer we collect down on the point, where the little creek meets the River, for catfishing and a campfire. By gathering together, we remind ourselves that we're a family. We reclaim something foreign in this rushed, panicked world. We watch clouds dance below stars; we study the night sky as evening gathers. And, incidental to all else, we fish for the big catfish that I returned to the River.

By now, she'd be approaching the twenty-pound range. If we ever latch onto her with our cheap equipment, it'll be a fight to remember. But catching her isn't what catfishing is about. It's about slowing down, about taking the time to sit and stare out at the depths of the woods or follow the path of a falling star as it speeds earthward. It's about listening to the slap of a beaver's tail against the still night waters of a pond, or understanding the poetry contained within the rustle of the pasture grass when an evening breeze kicks up.

It's about our boys, Matt, Dylan, Christian, and now Jack, sitting around the campfire, toasting s'mores, telling ghost stories. Its about their friends, Kristi, Jake, Ian, Spencer, Tim, Brian, and all the rest catching whatever the river offers up on any given night. Or about being content, on many nights, with catching nothing at all.

It's about my wife Rene', the woman who introduced me to fishing under a catfish moon, the woman who still holds the Munger Farm record for the biggest catfish we've ever caught. I keep watching her to find out her secret. If I figure it out, I'll pass it along.

BLUE BOTTOMED LADIES

There's something about the mystery of a blueberry bog that does not translate between the genders. I know of only one or two men who, with gusto, enter bogs in search of blueberries. Nine times out of ten, it's the women who do the berry picking.

I've tried it. My wife Rene' has coaxed, and begged, and pleaded with me so many times and with such determination that I've given in once or twice. The last time I followed her through the dense clouds of stinging, biting insects into a blueberry bog was just a few weeks ago. In truth, it wasn't half-bad. I got to eat a few berries while I picked. I saw the sun rise over the tamaracks and cedars. And I filled half of a gallon ice cream pail with berries, clearly establishing that I can, if motivated, pick as many berries in two hours as my wife can.

"See how many I picked? Bet you don't have as many as I do," I insisted.

I walked over to Rene', proudly holding my pail. She could see the level of berries in my bucket through the plastic because the sun was at my back.

"Almost as many as me, Mark."

I stopped next to her and looked into her pail. My view of the contents of our respective buckets didn't square with hers.

"Mine's over the halfway point. You're a little short, dear," I replied.

I smiled and stuck my hand in her pail, picked out the biggest berry I could find, and popped it into my mouth. The wild fruit's flavor was strong and sweet.

"Mark, your pail is full of green berries, sticks, bugs, and other stuff that won't taste too good in a pie. No wonder your bucket looks full."

She reached into my pail and pulled out a stem with four green berries clinging to it.

"See?"

I frowned and looked down at her bucket. My eyes searched for a hint of brown or green. There was nothing save the velvet blue of ripe berries staring back at me. Without a word, I retreated. I was determined to fill my container with splendid examples of berrydom if it took all day. Ten minutes later, my hands blue and swollen from berries and mosquitoes, I walked by Rene' on my way to the truck, a defeated man.

What is it about blueberry picking that's so inherently female? Is it patience, the same virtue that allows mothers to keep their voices low in the face of the escapades of young children? Or is it simple stubbornness, a woman's best defense in any argument with her mate?

My wife claims her need to pick berries, particularly blueberries, is simply part of the natural order. She says she has an unconscious need to enter the bog, to pick berries, no matter the conditions, no matter the berry crop. Rene' claims that only her January dreams of another blueberry season allow her to survive the depths of winter in Northeastern Minnesota. Whatever the motivation, I don't understand it. I understand bugs. I understand wet feet. I understand canned fruit.

As June fades to July in the country, cars and trucks slow as they pass by the bogs. Our women are looking for signs, signs that the berries will be thick and full. You can hear them talking in the checkout lines in grocery stores or over coffee:

"Gonna be a real good year this year. Lots of water, lots of sun."

"Where do you pick, Rene'?"

"I can't tell you. If I told you, you'd tell someone else, and soon, the whole darn countryside would be there picking."

Folks, this is not brook trout fishing, where time honored tradition between men makes it impolite, if not impertinent, to ask where someone caught their trout. Trout are hard to come by. They are a resource of limited quantity, easily over-harvested. Blueberries should not be considered in the same light. There are billions of blueberries in Minnesota. Nothing about blueberries justifies such a level of secrecy.

When the berries are ripe, you begin to notice women crouched alongside the roads, squatting in the wet grass. You can tell them by their uniform: gray sweatpants, the pant legs tucked tightly into knee-high rubber boots, the sort of boots farmers wear when they muck out the barn. They wear their hair tucked beneath a ball cap, unwashed because there is no time to shower when the blueberries are ripe:

"The shower will still be there when I get back."

They wear no perfume. The sweet delicacy of Opium or Este Lauder is replaced with the industrial pungency of "Deep Woods Off". Makeup and lipstick are forgotten. In the zeal to dive into the bog, to wade through the fetid water and pick precious treasure, there is no need for finery.

You can tell the real die-hards, the ones like my wife and her friend Ronda. The butts of their sweatpants are stained a deep, resonant blue from hours of sitting on berries, berries they should have picked instead of squashed with their behinds.

Every once and awhile, you'll find a man who has this same need, this same unquenchable desire to harvest. In fact, if you're observant, you may see a man sitting in Rene's blueberry patch picking to his heart's content. Make no mistake about it. That man isn't me. It's my friend Ron.

81

Ron sits on his hind end and picks blueberries just like Rene', Ron's wife Nancy, and all the other Blue-Bottomed Ladies. But Ronald's trousers are never stained by the task. His secret? He wears blue jeans. Rene' calls that cheating. I call it common sense.

THE PERFECT SKI

Opaque ice, the color of root beer, was suspended above the water. Ice had formed around a small pile of boulders in the River's current. Away from the protection of the rocks, the water remained open. The skier, wearing outdated cross-country skis and boots, pushed his middle-aged body through eight inches of new snow and stopped at the water's edge.

In his early adulthood, he would have glanced quickly at the River as he made the turn from swamp to riverbank. He wouldn't have slowed his pace to watch the gentle flow of water. His objective in cross-country skiing for most of his adult life had been physical exercise, not the contemplative study of nature. The change hadn't happened out of the blue. Over time, he'd been persuaded by some inner desire that the purpose of skiing was something more than mere exertion.

His stays were not long; he didn't linger idly at the places that tugged at his inner self. The stops lasted a moment or two, unless an eagle was overhead or a whitetail stood silently watching him. A brief respite was all his new philosophy demanded.

Fierce snowflakes pelted his face. He was warm from the work of pushing through the fresh snow. Thick, swirling clouds of shining flakes rose and fell. As they settled, the snowflakes lost their luster and merged with the dirty snow already on the ground. He could not see the tops of the maples and birch. The crowns of the trees were lost in the wet blanket of the storm. Wiping his nose on an old paper towel he found in the pocket of his windpants, he pushed off.

Wumph, wumph.

The skis made repetitive sounds as they broke through the heavy snow. Because of the depth of the new blanket, he trudged along. The grace and economy of a traditional Nordic glide was denied him. Other than the sound of the skier's progress, the forest was silent. The skier did not hear the legions of snowmobiles he knew must be out on Fish Lake a half mile to the south. He was enveloped in the sort of solitude that one normally finds in wilderness though he'd started his journey right out his own back door.

Despite the heavy snow, he began to develop a pattern to his stride. He was able to make near-normal progress beneath the protective canopy of balsam and spruce. The interwoven branches of the evergreens insulated the trail from the full impact of the storm.

Sweat formed beneath the wool of his stocking cap as he tried to maintain his pace. Fog clouded the lenses of his glasses, making it impossible to see. He stopped and attempted to find a dry corner of paper towel to clear the lenses. It was no use; the paper was completely wet. He folded his glasses and slid them into his pants pocket.

Moving through the woods with marginal vision, he climbed a slight rise. Five Norway Pines stood together on a hillock overlooking a swamp. Thick undergrowth forced him to surmise the perimeter of the marsh and to guess at the forest's demarcation. He examined the Pines and wondered about their ages. Though they were not Old Growth trees, they were large, 70-80 feet tall he guessed, considerably older and larger than the aspen forest around them.

"I wonder why I have ample time to contemplate the life of old trees but find so little time to hear the things my kids tell me?"

He asked the question of himself knowing he'd never really know the answer.

The River Trail joined Old Man Farley's Trail. A few feet along Old Man Farley's Trial, the Ridge Trail cut in. He skied to the intersection and studied the snow cover on the Ridge Trail. The path hadn't been skied in weeks. He felt worn out, too tired to ski through knee-deep snow. Something forced him to pick up his pace, to rise to the challenge. He plunged ahead on the Ridge Trail.

The skier found it necessary to stop every three or four hundred feet. His heartbeat was audible as he strained to climb the grade. Normally, he would have herringboned up the steep incline. But he was spent; he could not pull the tips of his skis out of the thick snow as he climbed. He turned parallel to the contour of the slope and inched his way up ridge.

He stopped again at the summit. There was nothing of significance to see at the top of the hill. His need for rest was born of exhaustion and not scenery. His breath was labored. His low back burned from the strain of lifting his skis. Leaning on his ski poles, he bent at the waist and tried to flex the overused muscles of his spine. Snowflakes, their edges sharpened like tiny shards of glass, propelled by the unceasing wind, stung his unprotected eyes. He skied on.

Fatigue caused the skier to pull himself along by his arms. His legs were merely the means by which his body remained connected to the ground and no more. He anticipated a slow downhill glide through a glade of fallen balsams. Normally, the decent was at breakneck speed. Due to thickness of the new snow, he knew the thrill would be modest. As it turned out, it was nonexistent. In fact, he had to push himself with his poles to keep moving downhill.

Climbing the last portion of the trail, he came upon the fresh tracks of a deer. There was little doubt that the animal had heard him sliding through the snow and bounded deep into the woods to escape detection. The skier thought about the whitetail, thought about the steady accumulation of snow, and acknowledged the certainty that many deer would not survive winter. They were safe from hunters but not safe from nature.

Thrupppp.

Snow exploded beneath a dying spruce. The suddenness of the event caught the skier in studied reflection. A partridge flew low, barely visible in the dim light, pelted by an infinite barrage of snow as it set its wings in retreat. Another bird burst through the thick needles of the same sickly tree. Then another. And another. In all, five ruffed grouse rose from beneath a single spruce. The skier thought he could have hit the last partridge had it been hunting season and had he been carrying a shotgun. He also had to admit to himself that he might have missed the bird.

The trail looped back. In the summer, the path forced horses and riders to revisit ground they'd previously covered. In the winter, with new snow adding depth to an already immeasurable cover, the loop allowed the skier to ski out on a trail already broken.

Over time, his arms and legs seemed to regain their strength. Gliding on snow compacted by his own toil, the skier searched within himself and located the cadence he'd learned skiing the banks of Miller Creek as a child. His skis sliced through the soft, white residue of the storm. He no longer felt forty-two. He no longer felt winded. He no longer felt a need to contemplate or gauge the world. He was a bird soaring to the sun, a dolphin diving to the depths, a stallion racing the wind. He sprinted for home.

Underneath the eves of his garage the man bent over and unsnapped the bindings of his skis. Absolute quiet embraced the farm. The wind started and stopped in an endless shifting of silent effort. The skier walked slowly along the sidewalk towards the old house. He twisted and contorted his torso in an effort to loosen tired joints. As he reached for the door handle, he stopped. Watching the wind's silent effect upon the falling snow, he realized that, while he would never live to see a perfect world, he had at least lived to experience the perfect ski.

MAGICAL CAT

Those of you that live in the country-and I'm talking about real country now, out beyond cable television, away from the lights of the city-know that you cannot live in the country without a cat.

I grew up a confirmed cat-hater. I've always had dogs. Big dogs. Labradors and golden retrievers. But since my family moved to our farm, the feline kingdom and I have reached an uneasy truce. At any given time, I allow one or two cats to reside in our garage or barn. In return for food and lodging, our cats patrol the tall grass, preventing mice, voles and shrews from invading our home.

After decades of careful study, I must admit that cats do have their place in God's scheme of things, though I'm not certain that God has a better handle on cats than you or I do. Anyway, the thing about outdoor cats is that they don't hang around too long. Since we've lived in the country, I think we've gone through a jillion or so. There have been so many; I can't remember all of their names. I do know that the first few were named after candy. That was Matt, our oldest son's doing.

We had, as I recall, and in no particular order, M&M, Snickers, Licorice, and Baby Ruth. The last one also answered to "Baby Luth" an alternative given it by our second son Dylan, a child born with perpetually swollen tonsils. Baby Ruth was a sweet white and brown fur ball who performed her mousing duties with quiet determination. She wasn't overly affectionate or particularly aloof. She accepted human attention but didn't relish it.

It was a hot summer. Dylan was four years old. In the country, it's not uncommon for a cat to go missing for several days. Country cats usually turn up alive and well after such absences, though often disheveled and marred by adventure. Baby Ruth, despite her neat appearance and well-intentioned grooming, was no exception to the general feline propensity to wander. But as a day's absence turned into several days and nights with no sign of her, even I, the reluctant cat lover, began to fear the worst. Out where we live, there's no end to the misfortune that can befall a cat. Owls, eagles, and hawks prey upon them from the sky. Dogs, fox, wolves, and coyotes snatch them on the ground.

Dylan is the sort of a child who looks at the world with a sense of wonder. He's always been that way. Thus it wasn't unusual when, in response to my wife's inquiry about Baby Ruth, the following exchange took place:

"Dylan, have you seen Baby Ruth?"

"Baby Luth 'isappeared."

"What do you mean she 'isappeared'?"

There was a lengthy pause as Dylan's blue eyes searched an overcast sky. Mother and son were walking from the garage to the house dodging rain as they conversed.

"She's a magical cat," Dylan offered.

"Magical? How is she magical?" Rene' asked.

Adjusting his Duluth Dukes baseball cap, my son turned his head so that his round face looked at his mother. His eyes were diverted. He didn't meet her gaze directly. Still, Rene' detected an element of mischief within the boy's smile. In a soft voice, Dylan offered:

"She can 'isappear."

Visions of old horror films ran through my wife's mind as she sought to understand the cat's fate. By what terrible means had our son dispatched our family pet? Her voice grew stern:

"Dylan Munger, where is the cat?"

The child left his mother's side and walked towards the garage. My wife followed. Once inside the building, Dylan stopped in front of an old barrel stove.

"She's in there."

"Oh, my God," Rene' whispered.

My spouse grasped the handle of the firebox door, offered a silent prayer for the cat, and pulled on the door. Hinges creaked eerily as wood ash trickled onto the floor.

"Meow."

Sounds of life escaped the metal chamber. Rene' bent down and peered into the rusty barrel. Despite the lack of light, she was able to determine the outline of Baby Ruth cowering against the far wall of its prison. My wife liberated the animal. Free of its sooty confinement, the cat shook its fur, releasing a cloud of wood ash into the air.

"Why did you put the cat in the stove?"

Rene' resisted an urge to smile. The sight of the dirty cat and the look on our son's face proved to be too much. She covered her face with one hand as she waited for a response.

"She was bugging me. She wouldn't listen so I made her 'isappear."

With a single bound, Baby Ruth escaped my wife's grasp and landed on top of my workbench where the famished cat immediately went to work on a dish of cat chow.

"Please don't make her 'isappear' anymore, OK?" my wife implored through a tightly restrained smile.

Dylan approached the feline and stroked its fur. The boy's face showed that he was considering the admonition.

"But she's a magical cat."

"I know. Just don't lock her in the stove."

"OK."

My wife and son walked out of the garage and into the summer night. Sometime later that autumn, Baby Ruth 'isappeared' for good. Since her departure, a succession of replacement cats has lived with us only to ultimately vanish with similar regularity. Their departures no longer concern me. I have ceased trying to determine what makes them come, what makes them go.

I've come to understand that Baby Ruth was no exception. She was the rule. Cats are made of magic. They don't abide by rules or logic. My son knew this. He also was smart enough to realize that you can't negotiate with a cat.

CHRISTMAS TOWN

White snow folds over the streets of the town like a quilt. The sky above is dark save for the blinking of distant stars. No wind touches the frozen limbs of the trees lining the Town Square. It's Christmas Eve.

Three or four children and their parents skate upon Hanson's Pond. Their movements are choreographed like the gentle motions of ballet dancers. The children don't seem to tire. They don't seem to complain. Their parents don't argue or bicker about Christmas bills, relatives or whether or not the Christmas trees that stand in their living rooms dignify the holiday that's upon them.

A boy stands atop a small rise, the white beneath him smooth as silk. He holds a sled, the old-fashioned kind with wood slats and rusted steel runners. It seems he cannot make up his mind. He gazes at the bottom of the hill, contemplating gravity. There are no other children with him, which gives his circumstance a lonely, forlorn aspect.

Here and there, passenger cars are parked upon the street. They don't move. Their engines are quiet. Looking closely, you can see the cars are empty. There are no footprints in the matted white on the ground to suggest where the owners of the vehicles have gone. The air is free of exhaust and soot. From the scene, you would expect to smell maple burning in someone's fireplace but there is no odor save for the sweet scent of spruce.

Sharp light from the Town's street lamps illuminates the sidewalks and buildings. The Town seems well watched and safe. A single police cruiser sits parked in front of the Town Hall. Like the other vehicles on the street, the squad car is from a different time. The cruiser has not moved for days. There is no crime to speak of in the Town. No one living there can remember an unkind act being perpetrated by anyone for as long as the Town has existed.

Several adult residents of the Town stand quietly on the sidewalks. If they are engaged in conversation, it's in low, imperceptible tones. They don't appear to be caught up in the infinite hurry of Christmas. They seem calm, collected, and without worry. All the Towns Folk appear well fed and without obvious need or infirmity.

Though the buildings lining the Square appear modest, they are obviously constructed to last. The paint and trim on each is immaculate. Among their number, there is a bank, the Town Hall, a hotel, a tavern, a train depot, and several homes. Bright lights shine from the windows of each, including the businesses, even though it is near midnight. No noise emanates from the structures. If work is being done, or arguments are taking place, or love is being made in any of the buildings, those things are being accomplished in relative quiet.

A lonesome whistle interrupts the silence. From behind the whitened hillside, the single light of an ancient steam locomotive casts a beam. Pulling a coal tender, two passenger cars and a caboose, the train speeds noisily into town. The "clack clack" of wheels against ties seems to be the only disturbance in the Town. No one rushes to the depot as the train passes by. No one moves to board the passenger cars, which are dark, seemingly empty. The train rolls on.

Music breaks out in the hotel. Evidently the guests are still awake and feel like ringing in Christmas with song.

"Hark the Herald Angels sing, glory to the new born king..."

The tune is clear. The organist makes no errors in timing or keystrokes. The voices of the hotel guests cannot be distinguished; perhaps due to the bellicose volume of the organ.

It's a place of utter calm, prosperity, peace and love. The perfect Christmas Town. Though it appears to be old and out of touch, its borders expand every year with new buildings, new residents, new improvements of every imaginable sort.

In truth, the Christmas Town of this story came to our house in assorted boxes. It sits upon our floor, beneath our Christmas tree, shadowed by a myriad of lights and ornaments. Year after year we've added to the display, making it grander, more perfect. Ours is but one in a dazzling collection of such Towns that are for sale, not just at Christmas time, but throughout the year.

As I sit and watch the model train chug its way around the ceramic figures and buildings, I wonder what it is that drives us to seek perfection beneath our Christmas Trees. Is it a feeling of powerlessness given the breadth of the problems that we face everyday? A feeling of having lost the simple life we knew as children? A need to create a world over which we have absolute control?

I look out our front room window as I contemplate the Christmas Town. Across our snow-covered front lawn lies the open water of the Cloquet River.

It seems to me that many of the reasons that lead us to build imaginary worlds beneath our Christmas trees also leads us to move to the country. We feel we'll have more control of our lives, of our children's safety, of our time together, if we can just escape to another place, a place far away from the City.

But in today's world, we cannot move away from each other and create another reality, just as we cannot make a wish and join the porcelain figures of Christmas Town in their seemingly perfect world.

Jesus said: "Love your neighbor as yourselves." Whether you are Christian, Jew, Moslem or claim no faith at all, these words ring true.

Watching the temperate flow of the River, I vow to myself to live by Christ's words this Christmas season. I ask that you consider doing the same.

Perhaps, if we're successful, we may even crack a few smiles on the ceramic faces of the people living under our Christmas trees.

GREAT GRANDPA'S RASPBERRIES

He stands there in my memory. His green work pants hang low on his waist. Gray hair, organized in a flat crewcut, bristles straight up from his scalp. An August sun stands behind him. The details of his face are lost in shadow. His plaid flannel shirt is rolled up to his elbows. The white and red squares remain vivid in my mind's eye.

It's been nearly forty years since he died. I knew him only briefly. He and Grandma were old when I was born. Grandma became older still, living another twenty-five years without him. I was just a little kid when he passed away. That I remember him at all says something about what kind of man he was. The word "gentle" springs to mind. Why that adjective strikes a chord, I don't know. It just seems to fit.

They lived down in Duluth, in Riverside by the railroad tracks. Their house was a modest workingman's home. Behind the house, Grandpa had his vegetable garden.

I know that Grandpa had other things growing in that garden. Potatoes, tomatoes, carrots. None of those interested a six-year-old. They were all "good for you". They were all vegetables. But the raspberries, they were something quite different. They were worth putting on your Keds and following Grandpa out the back door; worth negotiating the maze of junk on the back porch; worth wading through the sea of purple thistle that bordered the garden.

When Rene' and I bought our place in the country, it came with raspberries. I think the memory of Grandpa's raspberries convinced me to have a vegetable garden. I know my decision to have a garden wasn't based upon visions of fresh cauliflower.

Bending at the waist, I search the canes for ripe berries. Dew hangs heavy off the fruit, glistening in the early morning sun. Each raspberry wears a thin veil of moisture and shines like a precious gem. Between the plants, intricate lace spans the stems, the handiwork of spiders living within the forest of canes.

Trapped water, suspended on the webs, shimmers to the beat of my footsteps. I pick only the ripest berries. I'm not picking for jam or for the freezer. I'm picking for myself. I want just enough fruit to fill a bowl to eat with milk and sugar for breakfast.

Insects catch currents in the moist air and fly between plants. Here and there, honeybees glide from fruit to fruit. I see many bumblebees each summer at our place. I rarely see honeybees. This summer there are more of the small bees around. I watch them closely. I've heard they are on the decline; that some sort of mite is killing off their hives. Even commercial honey farms in Iowa, which rely upon domestic honeybees, are losing hives. I say a prayer, a small prayer for a small creature.

Our riding horses snort and blow in the tall weeds of the fenced pasture. I watch them swish their tails, heads bent to the ground, grazing. It's still cool. A heavy fog is just beginning to lift off the valley. The black flies are not out, though a new hatch of tiny mosquitoes finds me as I pick the last of my berries.

I stand upright, stretching my low back, loosening a kink. The rows of canes remain heavy with ripe berries. We have already picked fifteen quarts of fruit for jam and freezing. We have no more room for them.

Maggie, our female black Labrador, snuffles along next to me. Her nose drags through the sandy loam. Stopping at ripe berries, she inhales the fruit and moves slowly on. Sam, our yellow Labrador who has forgotten how to swim, sits deeply in the loose soil. At nine, he is lazy. I select a purple berry and toss it towards him. The raspberry disappears in the pink and black of his mouth. The dog's tail beats steadily against the ground.

At the end of a row, I stare at the remnants of our unkempt strawberry bed. I spent hours last year building the elevated bed for the spoiled little plants. I added new shoots. I tore out every weed I could find. I lost the battle. Most of the plants didn't survive the winter. The few plants that did survive cannot be seen. Weeds the height of a small cow stand silent guard over my now-abandoned effort.

My eyes deceive me. I think I see Grandpa smiling at me from across the garden. Does he know that I'm no longer a little boy, that I'm a man with three kids and another on the way? His thick jowls wiggle up and down as he walks towards me. I perceive he is a ghost, an illusion from childhood. But I listen to him anyway. He speaks in the same ragged voice I last heard forty years ago.

"You didn't see me plant any strawberries in my garden, did you, Mark?" he asks.

"No, Grandpa, I didn't."

"Too much work, unpredictable, those strawberries. Stick with raspberries and you'll be fine."

I want to ask him more. You know, big questions like where he is, about whether he and Grandma found each other again, those sorts of things. But he isn't here to answer the mysteries of the ages. He's here, however briefly, to help me with my garden.

EULOGY

We were at dinner, my oldest son Matt and I. We were sitting with my dad and a group of his cronies. Our table overlooked the ice sheet of the Duluth Curling Club. As we waited for our sandwiches, curlers practiced sliding their rocks across smooth ice in the rink below the dining room windows. As the stones moved effortlessly towards the house, the target, our attention was called back to our table. The waitress stood over us with a tray of beverages.

"Who had the tap beer?" she asked politely.

"Over here," one of my companions said.

The woman placed the beer in front of the man. Effortlessly, he reached into his pocket and removed a money clip. Deftly, the customer pulled out three crisp one-dollar bills. The waitress accepted the money and gestured as if to make change.

"Keep the extra," he said.

"Thanks."

The rest of us were served our drinks. Matt, nine-or-ten-years-old, watched the guy draw the beer to his lips and drink. My son continued to stare as the beverage disappeared from the glass.

Our food came. The adults began to eat. We talked sports and watched the curlers. Matt was slow attending to his cheeseburger. He continued to watch the man in the gray beard and glasses. Matt scrutinized the manner by which our companion brought spoons of hot soup to his lips. When the soup bowl was empty, the man contemplated the burger in front of him.

"Mark, would you open the catsup bottle?"

"Sure."

I twisted the cap off the bottle and handed it to the guy. He poured red sauce over his fries. With deliberate ease, he took the top of the bun off of his burger and sprinkled catsup on the sandwich as well.

"Matt, do you play any sports?" the man asked.

"Hockey," my son replied.

"Great sport. What position?"

"Center."

"We call him the 'Junk Yard Dog'," I confided. "He likes to stand in front of the net and wait for easy goals.

"Just like Phil Esposito," the man commented.

"Who?" Matt queried.

"One of the greatest goal scorers of all time," our companion replied.

Matt smiled when he understood the compliment.

After dinner, my son and I walked back to our car through the deserted skyway. Our conversation echoed off the bare concrete of the viaduct.

"Did you see that man drink beer?" Matt asked.

"What man?" I responded.

"The man with no hands."

"Oh. You mean Bruce," I offered.

"Yeah. It was neat how he could drink beer without hands."

I studied Matt's face as we walked. I felt my mouth turn upwards into a smile.

"He does a lot more than that, Matt. He golfs. In fact, he beats Grandpa regularly. He also curls. And he's a writer."

"A writer?"

"One of the best sportswriters around."

"How can he write without any fingers?" my son asked in a quiet voice.

"I'm not sure. But he's been doing it for a long time."

Over the years, our paths would occasionally cross. When I'd see Bruce, I'd often remind him of Matt's incredulity. The sportswriter would smile. I think he got a chuckle out of the story even though he'd heard it so many times.

Years later, my GMC Jimmy was being pummeled by a summer storm. As the car rounded a curve, I noticed a man with a dog on a leash making slow progress through the heavy weather.

"That looks like Bruce Bennett," I said, slowing the vehicle.

"The sportswriter?" Matt asked from his position in the front passenger seat.

"Yeah. He lives somewhere around here."

I pulled my utility vehicle onto the gravel shoulder, stopped, and rolled down the driver's side window.

"Hi Bruce," I shouted over the noise of the storm.

Bruce blinked as rain found its way around the protective hood of his poncho and into his eyes.

"That you, Mark?" he asked with a hint of recognition.

"Yep," I said, pulling my left arm away from the open window, the fabric of my flannel shirt already damp.

The man stopped next to the car and instructed his dog to "sit". The canine tentatively placed its rump on the road's wet pavement.

"You remember my son?"

"Sure do. How are you Matt?"

My son grinned and gave a slight wave of acknowledgement.

I found it remarkable that a man with so many friends, so many admirers, would remember the name of a boy he'd met only once.

"We're headed up to Highway 2 to do some brook trout fishing," I explained.

"You've got the weather for it," he replied.

"You're getting wet. You better get home," I suggested.

"Good luck guys," Bruce said.

Tugging gently on the leash, the writer drew his dog close to his side and began to walk away. In my rear-view-mirror, I watched the man's form merge with the thick rain. Inadvertently, my attention focused on his uneven gait. It was then that I remembered that Bruce's unusual stride was caused by impairment to one of his legs.

As the sportswriter retreated through the mud, it dawned on me that although Bruce Bennett was a man who made his living selecting adjectives to describe the world, he never used the adjective "disabled" to describe himself.

RUNAWAY CHILD

"Where's Christian?" I asked my sons Matt, Dylan, and their friend Tim, the Ninja Turtle Boy.

"I dunno."

"He was right here, right next to me," I said, leaving a "Magnum Force" video game for someone else to play. Panic had set in.

"He was over there, by the pinball machines, last I saw him," Dylan, my second son advised.

I glanced around the room, a small game room on the main floor of our hotel in Orlando, Florida. Chris was nowhere to be found. It was the morning of Easter Sunday. We'd just come back from sunrise services at Sea World with our friends, the McVean's. Rene' was resting. I was in charge of the boys. I'd blown my assignment.

"Matt, you guys go look around the pool."

"OK dad."

I watched the three older boys move out quickly, as if despite their ages, they recognized the seriousness of a three- year-old being left on his own in a strange place, full of strange people. On a hunch that my third son might be missing his mother, I went into the hotel and checked the lobby. Nothing. I began to climb the stairways, checking the hallways of each floor. Again, nothing. I knew I had to get Rene' involved. I knew she'd panic, become distraught that her baby was now missing in the middle of a mammoth hotel complex. The place was huge with two separate towers of 500 rooms each, several swimming pools, a private pond, and numerous alcoves containing concealed hot tubs behind native vegetation.

"Rene', open up, it's Mark."

The door opened slowly. My wife was dressed to go to one of the local theme parks.

"Where are the boys?"

"There's a little problem."

I watched a frown descend across Rene's face.

"What sort of problem?"

"I lost Chris."

Anxiety blossomed across my wife's face.

"You what?"

"He walked away from me at the video arcade. I've checked the building. He's not here. The boys and the McVean's are looking outside."

We scurried down to the front desk. Soon the entire place was crawling with concerned folks looking for our youngest son.

"Did you find him, Matt?" I asked as I approached my oldest son by the pool.

"Nope. No one's seen him."

My eyes wildly scanned the lush greenery of the grounds.

"Help me, God," I prayed silently.

Our friends arrived. Rene' joined us. Still no Chris. We split up, vowing to redouble our efforts. Walking a path leading to an outdoor spa, the dazzling white exterior of another hotel, a companion tower to the place we were staying in, caught my eye.

"Is it possible?" I asked myself.

Ignoring a "Stay on the Path" admonition, I forged a short cut through vegetation. Moisture rolled off of my nose as I pushed myself to move faster, to make it in time, before some unknown person or persons took my child, for whatever reason, away from me. My feet slipped in the moist interior of my tennis shoes as I opened the front door and rushed into the lobby of the adjoining hotel tower.

"Have you seen a little boy, about this high?" I asked the desk clerk, gesturing. "Big brown eyes, red shirt, and blue shorts, sandy brown hair?"

"You the father?" the man asked.

I nodded affirmatively.

"Security is looking for him right now."

"Good," I thought. "The word made it over here as well."

"Thanks," I replied weakly.

Ding.

The doors of the lobby elevator began to open.

"Come on," I murmured, impatient for the occupants of the car to be revealed.

"You looking for this little guy?" a muscular security guard in full uniform asked, his left arm protected by a plaster cast.

Standing in front of the officer was a three-year-old boy, the object of my commotion and distress. I threw my arms around my son's neck as the guard escorted the child out of the elevator.

"What were you doing?" I asked my son through a steady parade of tears.

"I wanted to see momma," Chris responded in an unconcerned, matter-of-fact voice.

"You trained him well," the guard interjected. "I asked him if he was Chris Munger. He told me 'I can't talk to strangers'. I thought he was the kid but he refused to tell me anything. He seemed put off by this thing," the man continued, raising his cast.

I examined the earnest face of my son and offered an amendment to our standard parental instruction:

"Chris, it's OK to talk to strangers in uniform."

SPRING DANCE

Winter's grip on the land was released early. Last year, spring was punctuated by panicked warmth after an early May snow, a rapid awakening before the fresh rains of June. This year is different.

I stand silently in our front yard, where the neatly clipped grass of last autumn falls gently towards the steep, brambled bank of the River. The rake in my gloved hand supports me as I gaze across yellowed fields, past decaying mounds of horse leavings that retreating snow has exposed behind a fence. This day is the reason I live here. It's a day offering a glimpse of the summer to come, a day of delight and possibility.

I drop the rake and walk slowly towards the water's edge. At twenty-five, I would never have left my chores unfinished to sit and study the world. At thirty-five, I would have pawed and scraped at the sand and filth collected about the lawn until, exhausted, I'd completed the task. At forty-two, the River pulls me to it, away from the never-ending jobs of our hobby farm. I yield to the water's power.

Sundays are made for such journeys. Fresh from the spiritual fulfillment of Church, steadied in Faith and Grace and instilled with belief, it's without remorse or regret that I allow myself a few minutes to act on impulse, to observe the world around me. My leather boots, the uppers unpolished and aged beyond their years from my lack of concern for them, walk the steps down to the Point, where, in a week or so, our canoes will sit upon their wooden racks.

On the Point, the slow turning silver flow of an unnamed creek intersects the ebony water of the Cloquet River. I take a seat on the horizontal remains of an old willow. My eyes follow the banks of the River. Here and there along the shore, beaver are pursuing their engineering. A beaver lodge sits only a few yards from my perch. The River's current swirls around the projecting mass of the crude home, stops for an instant, and then regains its motion as it laps against a second lodge.

A stick bobs up and down to the pulse of the water. The River beats a steady rhythm, keeping time to a song that has no words. A pair of mallards making for the far shore of the stream accents the open sky. Sunlight warms my face. The glare catches the emerald green of the drake's head as he pulls up to land. His mate drops next to him. The hen's drab color blends in with the grays and browns of the maples occupying the riverbank behind her.

I strain to focus on the distant edge of our pasture. Sharp stubble covers the sandy soil of the field in a uniform carpet of gold. Soon, bumble bees and butterflies will dance above the greening meadow. The grass and clover will become lush and then turn brittle as the seasons change again. I search for white-tailed deer at the far edge of the hayfield. None show themselves in the openness of the late afternoon.

Loud, obnoxious voices echo from down river. Two Giant Canada Geese glide in. The birds settle noisily on the water. The geese remain suspended in the swiftness of the current, churning their legs to remain in place against the weight of the River. Their cries reverberate off the sloped enclave of the stream as if they are disappointed that there are no others of their kind to share the day with.

The log I sit on remains warm despite the receding day. Dusk is near, though there will be light enough to finish my chores. Somewhere in the woods, a drummer adds another beat to the symphony. Percussive tones boom out from the aspen forest adjoining our land. The urgency of procreation requires a male ruffed grouse to hasten his song in hopes of securing a mate. The cacophony gains speed, ending in an exhausting crescendo. The woods fall silent.

As I stand up to return to my work, a final, amazing waltz originates between the thick froth of the clouds. Two Ospreys circle each other, dodging and weaving in vast, intricate patterns. Though I am not expert enough to know which of the birds is the male, which the female, I recognize the promenade. It is as primitive, as emotive, as the first awkward steps young humans take toward romance during the beginning days of spring. I close my eyes and recall the smells, the sounds, the wonder that the dance has always held for me.

In a frenzy, the birds come together. Their frail bodies interlock. Lost in the ritual of life, they begin a free fall towards the ground. Then, in no more than an instant, the fish eagles tear themselves apart, soaring upwards in the indigo. Nothing I've ever witnessed in the wild readies me for the perfection of their cotillion. I watch as the Ospreys catch wind. Their forms fade, becoming mere dots against the distant horizon.

"That was really something," my wife whispers.

I turn to find Rene' standing next to me, shielding her eyes from the low sun. I was so enthralled with the birds that I never heard her arrive.

"Listen," she says.

I tilt my head. In the failing light, frogs have begun to sing.

"Peepers," she opines.

I nod in agreement.

"Supper's ready," she offers, her voice soft and respectful.

I take her hand. We walk up the hill towards the house. As we get closer, the sound of our boys playing eclipses the chorus of the frogs. As we pass the piles of dead grass and debris, I have the urge to stop. I want to tell her:

"I'll be in as soon as I get these cleaned up."

This day, I say nothing. I walk on past, ignoring the work. The chores will be waiting for me tomorrow. For now, I choose to listen to the melody of the season.

CRAWDAD BOYS

"I need to go to town and pick up some groceries," the woman tells the two boys.

Ian, his blond hair tossed to one side by a light summer breeze, smiles. Dylan, the woman's second son, his hair darker than his friend's, grins as his hand grasps to the wooden handle of a landing net. The boys stand unsteadily on hot blacktop. Rubber boots two or three sizes too large for the boys cover their feet and end just shy of their thighs. A galvanized metal minnow bucket, the lid secured by a spring latch, sits on the pavement in front of them.

"OK, mom. Ian and me are just gonna count our crayfish and have something to eat," Dylan replies, casting an eye at his buddy.

"Ian and I," the mother says quietly "Ian and I."

"Ian and I," Dylan responds, coloring the phrase with a somewhat perturbed inflection.

"If you make lunch, clean up the kitchen," she implores the would-be naturalists.

Dylan's smile broadens.

"No problem. We're gonna eat outside anyway, right Ian?"

The mother notices Dylan's impish grin leap from her son's face onto that of the other child. She discounts the observation and studies the blonde boy as he responds:

"Sure, anything you say, Dill-pickle."

"Make sure you put all of the dishes in the dishwasher and all the food back in the fridge," she warns. "And don't leave those crayfish out in the sun. They'll die and stink like crazy."

She starts the family van and turns on the air conditioning. She doesn't hear Dylan's final words as the vehicle lumbers down the driveway:

"Don't worry about the crayfish, mom. We'll take care of 'em."

It takes two hours to complete her errands. On the way home storm clouds begin to roll in from the west. An urgent, new wind lifts the stagnant humidity of the summer afternoon.

As the van turns into the driveway, the woman's eyes are drawn to the River. In the near distance, white smoke rises against approaching weather. Small flames leap and dance within the fire pit on the Point. Ian and Dylan sit next to the fire, preoccupied with an unknown task.

She walks towards the boys. A thick carpet of unmown clover cushions her feet. The clouds pass by, hanging low and fat with rain.

"Hi, mom," Dylan shouts from his seat on a log. Ian crouches by the fire, stirring ashes with a willow switch, urging the flames to climb higher. A steel pot rests on a rusted grate above the heat.

Bubbles form and burst within the metal container. Steam escapes, colliding with smoke, captive of the energy of the advancing storm.

"Hi, Mrs. Munger," Ian says, the words chirping out in a raspy voice.

"What are you boys up to?" Rene' asks, peering into the depths of the boiling water.

"We're having lunch," Dylan explains between gulps of Coca-Cola. Beads of sweat gather on the exterior of the Coke can as he chooses his words. "They're really good," he adds.

My wife stands over the boys. Her eyes are drawn to the minnow bucket, which is lying on its side, lid open. Small bits of cracked crustacean shell rest in the grass around the boys' feet.

"You've got to be kidding. Tell me you didn't eat them," she whispers.

"Yep. We each ate ten of 'em," Ian quips as he spits bits of crawdad skeleton into the fire.

Swallowing the last bit of meat, the blond child spreads his thumb and forefinger three inches apart:

"Some of 'em were big, bigger than this," he boasts.

"You're going to get sick," the mother opines.

Dylan grabs a set of metal tongs and reaches into the swirling water.

"Want one?" he asks, displaying a very red and very dead crayfish.

"They're great with a little butter and salt," Dylan offers, his voice genuine.

"No thanks. I think it's time to put out the fire and head on up to the house. It's gonna pour any second."

The boys dump the pot of water into the fire, sending ash and steam skyward. Scattered drops of rain splatter against them as the mother and the two boys walk towards the house.

"What possessed you to do this?" she asks, quickening her pace.

"My dad told us they were good to eat," Ian replies.

"And you told us not to make a mess in the kitchen," Dylan quickly reminds her.

The mother smiles, remembering the frogs, turtles, and crayfish caught and examined in her youth.

"I hadn't figured on seafood. I was thinking more along the lines of peanut butter and jelly," she remarks under her breath.

"What, mom?" she hears her son ask.

"Never mind, Dyl," she replies.

My wife escapes the steady pulse of the rain. From inside the farmhouse she watches the boys scurry towards her and observes:

"I'll have to caution Ian's dad to be more selective about the recipes he shares with his son."

ARAPAHO

Above us, the mountain rises. Stark rock pierces a thick quilt of Colorado snow under the steady glare of the sun. The chair lift pulls us resolutely upward.

As a child, I was fortunate enough to accompany my parents on ski vacations to the Rockies. In those days, you had to drive through Loveland Pass, near the base of Arapaho Basin ski resort, in order to reach Aspen. On this trip, my first to Colorado since my youth, I'm astonished. The mountain has been hollowed out. A freeway tunnel threads through the stone heart of Loveland Pass. It isn't necessary to climb the Pass to cross over. We simply drive under the mountain.

Arapaho does not climb leisurely towards the sky. Impatient, arrogant, and with immediate urgency, Arapaho thrusts its bold crags and precarious steeples towards heaven. The mountain's disdain for the gradual is the secret of its seduction.

Two of my sons ride the chair lift with me. Below us, nutrient starved spruce and battered pines shelter the base of the peak. As we climb, we leave the trees behind and follow the exposed face of the mountain towards the sky. Skiers and snowboarders dance beneath the chair lift. They carve vast patterns on a canvas of fresh snow. A sharp wind greets us in the open country. The breeze battles the high altitude sun for supremacy.

At the top, we slide off the chair and come to a stop.

"Take a look at the back of this run," Matt exclaims.

A yellow nylon cord ropes off the precipice. A sign indicates that the area is closed to skiers, as if any rational human would attempt to negotiate the stone, ice, and pitch displayed below. It seems like a million miles to the bottom of the valley. In reality, it's a little over 12,000 feet.

"Don't get too close," I caution, pulling Dylan away from the edge.

My second son smiles. The dark lenses of his goggles conceal his eyes. Matt stands next to us. His face is pale. The difference between the two boys' expressions has nothing to do with courage and everything to do with age. Matt is thirteen. Dylan is eight. Eight-year-old boys know nothing about mortality.

"What are those guys doing over there," Matt asks in a timid voice.

His gloved finger points to two single file lines of skiers climbing parallel trails hewn into the face of the mountain.

"They're going to ski the bowl," I respond.

We watch as skiers drop from the trails and leave personal legacies in the virgin snow. As each makes his or her decent, a rooster tail of powder rises from behind the skier. Here and there, intrepid explorers fall and careen uncontrollably downward, propelled by the steepness of the run.

"Why don't you try it, dad?" Dylan asks, his words filled with challenge.

"That's an unpatrolled area. I'm too old to be skiing with those kids."

"Come on dad, you can do it," Matt joins in, his tone of voice less convincing than his words.

I look across the slope. I look at my kids. For a brief moment, I'm a twelve-year-old boy in an old Jeep Wagoneer driving through Loveland Pass. I remember the awe of seeing this mountain for the first time. It doesn't belong in the Rockies. The Rockies don't have ski hills like this, steep insolent chutes of gleaming powder that cry out to challenge all who pass by.

"All right. You guys find an easy way down. I'll give it a try," I say with as much confidence as I can muster.

"Good luck."

My sons pole away in search of a path down the hill.

"I'll need it," I mutter to myself.

I release my bindings, shoulder my skis, and begin to walk up the mountain. It does not take long for me to realize how out of shape I am. In the sparse air of high altitude, each breath becomes a gulp, an attempt to suck in every possible molecule of oxygen carried by the wind. I fall in line behind twenty or so young skiers. Their faces show no fear; their voices are filled with the strength and confidence of youth. I envy them.

At the entrance to the bowl, I encounter a large yellow and black sign. It reads:

Caution: Unpatrolled area. Expert Skiers only. Ski at your own risk!

Intoxicated by delirium, I ignore the warning and continue on. My thighs burn and my heart pounds. Absent-mindedly, I miss the turn for the easier of the two trails and continue to climb towards the highest point of departure. One by one, those in front of me stop and lean against the ice wall rising behind us to put on their skis. Silently, each contemplates the landscape falling away from the trail. In an instant, each embraces the powder, carving magnificent paths through untouched beauty.

I find a ledge to my liking and stop. Others pass me by, wishing me good luck. There's that word again: luck. It's not luck I need but strength and skill. Then it's my turn. There's only one-way to the bottom of Arapaho. My K2s balance on the razor's edge. My mind tells me to stop, to take off my skis, and retreat down the path. My heart tells me I cannot. I've waited twenty-five years to ski this moment.

My first turn in the waist-deep snow is a disaster. I haven't skied mountain powder for over two decades. I forget to lean back to keep the tips my skis free of the snow. I catch a tip and tumble headlong down the slope, thrashing and spinning out of control. I come to rest fifty feet from where I started. Urgently, I touch my face with my wet glove. I'm lucky. My glasses didn't come off.

Because the incline is so steep, I have to press my body against the mountain to prevent from sliding down the run. Both bindings have released. I reach into the depths of the snow searching for my K2s. They have not gone far. Gingerly, my body prone to the grade, I pull my right ski towards my right boot and snap the binding in place. I repeat the exercise with the left.

There is no one near as I rise. I dig my edges into the icy base. I gain a moment of respite before gravity begins to draw me downward. Leaning back as if I'm sitting in a rocking chair, I put all my weight to the rear. As I begin to carve the snow, I claim a rhythm. I weave a tapestry into the softness of the slope. The fabric of this run is mine and mine alone.

"Did you do it dad?" Matt asks as I glide to a stop at the bottom of the hill.

"Didn't you watch me?"

"Nope. Dyl and I got bored. We took a run."

"Well, you missed one hell of an exhibition of mountain skiing," I brag.

"Did you fall?" Dylan asks, staring at the snow packed inside the collar of my parka.

"Of course not. I'm an expert skier," I fib.

"Are you sure, dad?" my oldest son inquires with skepticism.

"OK, maybe the take-off was a little rough," I admit. "But once I got going, it was wonderful."

"Gonna do it again?" Matt prods.

I shake the snow away from my exposed neck.

"Not this trip," I reply.

My eyes focus on the mountain. Though I can't follow the tenuous climb of those seeking to create art in solitude, I know that they are there. And for a brief moment, I shared their muse.

KEYSTONE

At 10,000 feet, the air is sparse and rarefied. Dylan, my eight-year-old son; Matt, his thirteen-year-old brother, and I have arrived at the top of Outback, the last of three contiguous slopes comprising Keystone Ski Area in Colorado. Outback is not only the furthest peak from our rented condo at the base of the hill; it's also the most difficult and serious mountain at the resort.

Above the chairlift's reach, we glide on well-packed snow. This is the first time my boys have skied the West. I want them to feel challenged, to experience the things that I experienced when I came to Colorado as a boy on family ski vacations.

"You want to try some powder skiing on North Bowl?"

I study a large trail map painted on plywood. North Bowl is off to our right, above the tree line. There is no lift in place to carry us to the summit.

Matt ponders the map through the thick plastic lenses of his goggles and leans forward on his ski poles as he thinks about my proposal.

"Are you sure it's OK? It's marked "Expert-a Black Diamond.""

Dylan sways slowly from side to side to fend off the impact of the thin air and the stiff wind as we talk. The few trees at this altitude provide little protection from the cold.

"There's nothing in front of you on a bowl. If you take a header, you just fall until you stop. You'll be fine."

"How do we get there?"

My oldest son's eyes are riveted on the trail map. I detect a hint of understanding and a slight reluctance to his voice.

"We walk."

Groans escape from the two boys in unison. Despite the grumbling, I persuade them to follow me. Our breathing is labored and our steps difficult as we leave behind the last vestiges of forest.

"It's a long ways down" Matt says quietly, staring at the bowl falling beneath us.

We're poised on the lip of the slope. The sky extends above us in an uninterrupted pallet of bluebird hue. Carbon dioxide forms small clouds of moisture around each of us as we exhale. I ponder what course we should take down the mountainside. The snow beneath us appears to be soft and delicate. I envision three perfectly sculpted tracks left behind as we float through the powder, exit the bowl, and reclaim the trail through the trees. It doesn't concern me that there are no tracks left by previous skiers marking the hill. That detail eludes me as I silently praise God and ready my spirit for the plunge.

"Here goes."

My skis drop over the cornice. Instead of the soft, lacey embrace of powder, I experience the jolt of hard-packed snow. Before I can warn my sons that the scene before us is a hoax, I'm rushing downhill, my skis trapped inside the icy crust of the snowfield. I'm unable to turn or slow my descent. Being a skier of experience, I'm able to ride out the bowl and coast to a stop on a level plateau several thousand feet below the summit. I watch as Dylan, then Matt, become victims of the ice. I'm reduced to being a mere observer as I watch them tumble down the pitched surface of the Outback. When the snow finally settles, I realize that my sons are stranded hundreds of feet above me.

"Are you OK?"

Dylan's sobs resound from the cliffs surrounding us.

"I can't find my left ski," Matt responds.

"I'll come up there to help you. Stay put," I urge.

The snow is thigh deep. The slope of the mountain precludes me from herringboneing up the snowfield to my sons. I remove my skis. My ski boots sink into the deceptive snow. I reach Matt. Dylan is further up the bowl, a mere speck of blue and gray clothing covered in snow. His sobs diminish but it's clear he can't move without assistance.

"Nice powder."

I don't respond to my oldest son's sarcasm. I search the snow around him for his missing ski. I find the appliance and hand it to Matt. Using my shoulders to steady his body, the boy locks the wayward ski in place, picks up his poles, and readies himself for another attempt.

"Ski straight down to the flats. Don't try to turn-the snow grabs you so you can't."

"Good thing mom and Chris aren't here."

He's right. It's a darn good thing my wife and my five-year-old son are contentedly plying the intermediate runs far below.

"There's no need to tell mom about this," I urge.

"Sure," Matt responds, a promise of mischief coloring his words.

Dylan's tears are nearly dry by the time I reach him. Both of his skis are lost in the depths of the snow. I dig into the crusted surface surrounding my son until I locate the concealed skis and retrieve them.

"Walk down to Matt."

Dylan doesn't answer me. He simply works his way through the deep snow towards his brother in angry silence. After an exhausting walk down the hill, I arrive at the plateau. I hand Dylan his skis. He doesn't acknowledge my presence as he snatches them from my grasp. I slip my gloves through the loops of my ski poles. My attention is drawn to the magnificent height of the mountain behind us. In the shadow of that great peak, I contemplate the magic that might have been.

ALL DONE IN

Soft light forms a golden blanket over gently rolling fields. A spring sun hangs just above the poplar and birch trees delineating the far edge of our pasture. Peepers begin a melodic chorus, announcing their presence to others of their kind. I begin the day, a Saturday, by raking up piles of gravel. The gravel is misplaced.

Pushing snow with my International 606 in November, I inadvertently removed a few yards of crushed bluestone from our driveway with the bucket of the old tractor. Putting the rocks back where they belong requires hours of hard, physical work. It's not easy to wrestle the gravel free from the stubborn grasp of our lawn. I haul wheelbarrow after wheelbarrow of the stuff. As I strain under each load, I constantly remind myself that a second of foresight in November would've saved hours of work in May.

I finish raking and begin to sweep the porches of our farmhouse. Winter's dust and debris flies though the cool air with each stoke of the broom. Dylan and Chris, my middle sons, help carry outdoor furniture from the garage. It's the only assistance I receive from the boys. Matt, my oldest boy, is nowhere to be found. He's eighteen years old and capable of disappearing in an instant whenever he hears the word "work".

Late in the day, I realize I have to drive to town. Our two dogs, possessing the collective wisdom of a hamster, chased Bob the cat under our deck. With little effort, the pursuers forced their way through the lattice enclosing the underside of the porch. The dogs managed to demolish one panel on the way in and one panel on the way out.

My wife Rene' rides with me to the lumberyard. It's a good thing she's along. In my hurry to get back to work, I misjudge the size of the lattice panels. Lumber occupies nearly all of the interior space of our van. With limited commentary, my wife extends her arms and keeps the wood away from the top of my head as we bounce towards home.

Back on task, I replace the lattice. The barricade restored, I turn my attention to the garage. Inside, I find the cat's litter box overflowing and malodorous. Someone (Christian) has not done his job. He hasn't checked the box in weeks. After replacing the litter and eliminating the overpowering fragrance of cat from the building, I begin to clean.

I empty the garage of its contents so that I can sweep the floor and clean the shelves. It's not a job for a rainy day. With the sun high and bright, I'm able to finish the task in a couple of hours.

Just before dark, I notice that the Munger's Farm sign on our front lawn needs repair. Two chains hang from a wooden frame and sway slightly in the passing breeze. High winds last week apparently tore the placard free. The sign lies on the ground nearby.

I kneel on soft grass. With a gloved hand, I brush a clod of dirt away from the face of the sign. My eyes focus on the message:

Munger's Farm Est. 1984.

The painted image of a channel catfish, our family "crest" as it were, remains smooth and shiny though applied more than ten years ago. Standing up, I hold the sign steady and reconnect its chains to eyehooks imbedded deep in the wood. A graceful wind touches the message, causing the sign to sway in slow measure.

My chores completed, I open the back door to our home and enter the kitchen. In our upstairs lavatory, I run myself a bath. Steam from the hot water rises lazily, drawn by the temptation of an open window. I disrobe, gingerly enter the antique claw-foot tub, and immerse myself. The near-scalding water turns my legs crimson.

Our downstairs bathroom has a Jacuzzi tub. Though the sophisticated pulse of a whirlpool has a certain appeal, I prefer the quiet embrace of the old tub when I'm all done in.

Despite the water's heat, the white porcelain surface of the tub is cold against my bare back. I remove my eyeglasses and place them on the windowsill. The bottom half of the window is open to the screen. It's quiet outside. The boys are inside the house watching television.

Reaching over the edge of the tub, I palpate the tile floor. My hand searches for the copy of *Cold Mountain* that I'm reading. Dry fingers curl protectively around the book as I lift the novel through ascending vapor. Opening the volume to my bookmark, I concentrate on the last few pages of a soldier's journey home.

"Time for dinner," Rene' yells from the kitchen.

"I'll be down in a minute," I respond, slightly annoyed at my wife's intrusion into my space.

"Better make it quick or the food'll be cold," my wife warns.

"All right."

I want to placate Rene' but I know I'll be more than a minute. I've still got ten pages left to read and I want to find out whether Inman marries the girl.

A VERY GRAVE STORY

It was cold outside. A cat cried in protest. In the garden, the last of the summer's corn, the stalks brown and dead, rustled. Pumpkins sat atop the hard, near-frozen earth, waiting to be harvested.

Our cat at the time was jet black with angry, yellow eyes. Her name was K-Mart. She was fidgety and unpredictable. She was also pregnant. Her belly, heavy with kittens, dragged on the ground. She gained our attention by climbing the screen of one of our windows.

"I oughta knock her off that screen with my boot, that's what I oughta do."

My wife scolded me.

"It's not her fault, poor thing. It's cold. Let her in before she rips the screen."

My response was, as I recall, unprintable. It didn't matter. The cat came in.

That evening, in the middle of our oldest son's bedroom, the cat delivered her litter. The stain on the white carpet is still there. Over the next few weeks, Mickey, Minnie, Darts, Daisy, and their mother occupied Matt's closet.

A few days before Halloween, I determined that the cats had to go. Gathering the kittens in an old blanket, dodging K-Mart's claws, I carried them out to our old chicken coop. I deposited the cats on a thick bed of fresh straw. I shut and latched the door to keep the little ones from wandering.

A day or so later, Rene' and I were out in the garden harvesting the last of our garden's squash. A low sun hung in the autumn sky. K-Mart sat warming herself on the top of a fencepost. Sam, our Yellow Lab, paced excitedly. You could almost see the miniature wheels of his miniscule dog brain spin as he eyed a slender crack at the base of the door to the chicken coop.

Without warning, the dog leaped towards the coop. A kitten squealed. Tossing my hoe to the ground, I reached the dog just as his jaws clamped down.

"Meowwwww..."

K-Mart flew from her perch. Her claws dug hard into the soft nose of the Labrador. I pulled the kitten out of the dog's mouth and booted Sam in the rump, sending both the dog and the mother cat end over end across the grass. The dog regained his balance and tore off after K-Mart, chasing her up the pitch-covered trunk of a spruce tree.

"I think it's dead, Rene'."

My wife pulled off her work gloves and touched the kitten's head. The cat's fur was wet with spit. There was no blood. Its eyes were shut.

112

"Mickey's okay, he's just sleeping."

Christian, our youngest son at the time, walked over to my side and retrieved the kitten from me.

"He'll wake up, you'll see."

"Bring him up to the house, Chris. We'll put him on a hot water bottle."

"OK, mom."

Though Mickey survived this first ordeal, his walk was unsteady; there was a hint of palsy about his movements. Two days after his near-death experience, the kitten appeared well enough to rejoin his mother. Christian, dressed in his yellow rain slicker against the weather, returned the battered kitten to the chicken coop. I walked with the boy, striving against an awful rain. A penetrating cold front had nestled over the River. It felt like it would snow. All it did was rain.

Heavy October fog greeted me when I went back out to check on the cats the following morning. Hoarfrost coated slumbering grass. A shallow pool of rainwater had formed in front of coop. I discovered Mickey submerged in the water. The little cat's fur was stiff with ice. The animal was dead.

"What's that, dad?"

Dylan walked up behind me. I showed him the body of the kitten. He'd already buried his share of animals on the farm.

"It's Mickey. Will you take care of him? Chris is too young to see this," I said as I handed the little ball of fur to my son.

"Sure dad."

I returned to the house for breakfast. Chris and Rene' sat at the kitchen table eating hot cereal. My youngest son's attention was instantly riveted to Dylan's jeans as my second son entered the room.

"What were you doing?"

"Nothin'." Dylan lied.

"Don't' tell me nothin'. You're all muddy. What were you doing?"

I couldn't bear keeping the truth from Chris.

"Mickey died in the storm, son. He must have been scared by the thunder. He went out in the cold and rain."

The little boy's eyes widened as if to cry.

"Where is he?"

"Dylan buried him by the barn."

"I made a nice cross for him. Wanna see?"

Chris' reply was barely a whisper:

"Ya."

The boys came back a few minutes later. Chris held the tiny, muddy corpse of the kitten in his hands.

"He dug up the stupid cat. I told him not to. He wouldn't listen," Dylan whined.

Chris stood silently in the hallway. Water dripped from his eyes, the tears exposing patches of clean skin.

"Why did you dig the kitten up?" my wife asked.

Rene' placed her hand on Chris' shoulder. The boy trembled.

"I saw him breathing."

"You're kidding," I said, trying not to sound irritated.

Christian's preoccupation with an obviously dead kitten was too much to bear.

"I saw the dirt move."

I stood up, ready to approach Chris and take the cat. I was prepared to explain the meaning of death, the finality of it all. Rene' stopped me.

"My God, he's right. The kitten is alive."

"No way."

"It's still breathing."

I studied the dirty, wet stomach of the kitten. Its respiration's were shallow, almost non-existent, but Christian was right. I'd told Dylan to bury the cat while it was still alive.

"I thought it was dead. I swear."

For some reason, I felt as if no one believed me. I'd like to tell you that the kitten recovered and lived happily ever after. That's how Disney movies end but that's not real life. Mickey died on Halloween night. That particular evening, the moon was high and full, an omnipresent harvest globe of orange. Eerie shadows formed along the ground, lured into motion by the patterned march of clouds. I walked alone searching for a forgotten corner of forest as my children slept soundly in their beds at home. Hidden by darkness, I disposed of Mickey's body. I'll not relate to you the sordid details of the burial or the location of the kitten's unmarked grave.

When it comes to the offspring of black cats, I no longer leave anything to chance.

114

JOHN MUIR'S WOODS

During our vacation, we've toured San Francisco, seen the Golden Gate Bridge, and climbed aboard our share of cable cars. We've attended the local production of *Phantom of the Opera*. Someone, I can't remember who, cautioned us not to miss the redwoods. After the cultural significance of the City by the Bay, visiting old trees seems anticlimactic. But we follow the advice.

Along Highway 1 there are no guardrails. The asphalt road disappears at the corners. There is no forgiveness to the two-lane highway. Rose-frosted hills fall away to the Bay as the road climbs to the clouds. Once on top of the rise, the road spirals down the other side with equal abandon, becoming lost in the shade of grand trees. I park the car beside an old oak, a tree that would be magnificent in any other setting. In Muir Woods, the oak is but an insignificant weed.

It's cool at the base of majesty. Little of the day's heat penetrates the redwoods. Rene' and I realize we are in a sacred place, a place that contains plants that germinated before the birth of Christ. The average age of the trees that surround us, that dwarf us as we walk the valley floor, exceeds eight hundred years.

We stare upward at the straight, thickly armored trees as we enter the forest. Ancestors of these redwoods protected the eggs of dinosaurs before the dawn of mammals on the earth. We spy a tiny doe and her diminutive fawn scratching thin black soil. Elk, cougar, bear, and wolf have vanished from this place. Urban sprawl has invaded the surrounding valleys and hills, spreading out from San Francisco along the Bay. A single pair of Spotted Owls, a rallying cry against loggers, still nests here. We do not see them on our walk.

Despite the closeness of Metropolis to our sanctuary, bright clear waters course through the Woods. The main path, covered in asphalt, veers to the left. A dirt trail winds upwards on the right.

"Come on, Nay'," I urge my wife, "let's take the dirt trail."

"Where does it go?" my very pregnant and skeptical spouse asks.

"To a picnic area on the top of the hill."

"How far is it?" she inquires, familiar with my inability to assess distance.

"Looks to be about a mile and a half or so. But the trail winds uphill. It should be an easy hike."

I turn around. A shadow of doubt clouds Rene's face.

"Mark, I don't want to end up walking for half the day."

"You won't. I promise."

My wife accepts my reassurance. We begin our walk.

Leaving the other visitors, we begin our climb towards the summit.

Redwoods close in, interrupting the surface of the trail with their root systems. I walk to the edge of a small brook that borders the path. I peer into the clean water and watch Pacific Steelhead, no more than four or five inches long, dart along the stony bottom. We pass scores of trees, many nine or ten feet in diameter. The trunks of the redwoods are scarred by fire.

"Must be caused by lightening," I guess out loud.

"No, that's from a forest fire that swept through here a hundred and fifty years ago," Rene' corrects. "I overheard a Ranger explain it."

"But it looks like it was just burned," I respond.

"That's because of the strong bark and the weather conditions. The scars don't fade."

I ponder the fact that the wound on the tree in front of me is nearly the same age as the sentinel white pines remaining on our farm. My mind tries to picture what our place looked like before the forest of old growth pines were cut. I try to shrink the height of the redwoods in front of my so as to create a corresponding white pine forest. I try to imagine I am in Minnesota in the 1850's.

We cross the gurgling stream on the trunk of an unlucky redwood. Park workers have nailed rough sawn lumber to the tree creating a bridge. Shards of white sun, allowed in by openings in the trees, touch my face as we ford the stream. Across the creek, we are once again cloaked in cool shadow. The walk to the picnic area takes longer than it should. Finally, I emerge into daylight.

"Here it is, Rene'."

I pull out a trail map. I discover that the reason it took so long to reach our destination is that we missed a turn. We've added a mile to our trek. I look down the path for my spouse. I don't see her. I weigh the proper course of action:

"If I walk back to get her, she'll be mad that I'm treating her like a kid. If I don't show concern and go back, she'll think I'm a jerk," I muse aloud.

Before I'm forced to make a decision, Rene' comes into view.

"We took a wrong turn," I say quietly when she stops next to me. My wife sits down on a bench and draws cold water from a plastic bottle in urgent gulps.

"No kidding."

"It's not nearly as far back," I offer. " Plus it's downhill."

"Good."

We sit in the shade of small redwoods, infants in the great scheme of the Woods. A large hill rises across the ravine. With a little imagination, I could be standing on Eagle Mountain in Northeastern Minnesota. But this is not Minnesota. We are in Muir Woods, one of the last remaining old-growth redwood forests in the world. A man and his wife purchased this land at the turn of the century with the idea that this forest would be logged and this land would be developed. On their first walk through the Woods, the couple realized that the place was holy, that redwoods do not exist to be cut into lumber.

The man later became a United States Congressman. However, his most enduring legacy was not legislation he drafted as a lawmaker. It was his donation of this forest to the public in the name of John Muir, a California writer and naturalist.

Well-rested, we begin our descent. The crowns of the redwoods obscure our view of the sky. We are cooled by forest older than our culture. Entering the valley floor, I smile. I smile because the Congressman who saved Muir Woods from the ax, and the President who championed Muir Woods becoming a National Monument in 1908, were both Republicans. Imagine that. The ideological ancestors of Ronald Reagan, Rush Limbaugh, and Newt Gingrich were tree-huggers, just like me.

OF LITTLE BOYS... AND COMETS

Earlier tonight, I stood outside with my wife and my third son Christian watching the great astronomical event of 1997. Hale-Bopp, the comet of the moment, flew above us, seemingly stationary against vast twilight containing a blue so perfect and seamless that the depth of its color appeared contrived.

Inside our house sits a cheap telescope: a lesson learned. Never buy anything containing cheap optics, be it a camera, eyeglasses, or a telescope. Our telescope makes a lovely conversation piece and nothing more.

Sometime in the 1960's, I fell in love with space. Maybe it was growing up glued to the old black and white Philco television back in elementary school. I remember watching in awe as John Glenn and other Mercury astronauts flew solo into near-Earth orbit. As kids, as little boys and girls, everything stopped at school when another rocket took off from Cape Canaveral; everything except the pounding of our hearts as we prayed for the safe return of our astronauts.

Gemini came next, and with Gemini the buddy system arrived in space: two astronauts linked by a common fate in a cramped, claustrophobic capsule. Commander White pushed our envelope of piety and faith by leaving the protection of his capsule and walking into the inhospitable void of the universe.

Finally, Apollo with its triumphs and tragedies, lunar landings, and unnecessary deaths, brought us to the end of manned space exploration, at least for this century. NASA has not yet, as it once contemplated, sent men and women to Mars, Titan, or anywhere beyond the close confines of our own atmospheric neighborhood.

As each rocket sped away, as all of America's children grew older, the television sets came on less often: the surprise of space grew less moving. As a nation, we became complacent, even bored, with launch after uneventful launch. Until Challenger.

Challenger proved to those of us who had been children in the 1950's and 1960's that humankind's exploration of unknown space could never be safe or taken for granted. The tragedy of Challenger was not that accidents take place, but that, in today's world of instant media, horrific accidents can take place in front of tens of millions of school children.

But what of comets and little boys? There's a page in one of my picture books from my childhood that comes to mind whenever the approach of a new comet is announced. I was perhaps ten, maybe eleven. The book contained a timeline of Haley's Comet, which theorized that the comet would be back to visit earth in 1986. I figured I would be 32 years old in 1986. 32! Wow, that would be really old. As old as my parents. I recall wondering, as a little boy sitting on the smooth hardwood floor of my parent's house, whether I would be around to see Haley's spectacular return.

The book said you only get one shot in a lifetime to view Haley's unless you're lucky enough to be four years old or younger when it came around the first time. The odds of being coherent on either side of that equation didn't hold much attraction for me. All I had to do was make sure I was breathing and vertical come 1986 and Haley's would do the rest. Seemed pretty easy at the time. Of course, things always seem easy when you're ten.

After reading about the comet as a child, I spent many nights scanning the Minnesota sky with my hand-held Bausch and Lomb 10 power telescope. The instrument didn't add much in the way of discovery potential to my observations but it did make the process seem scientific. Through that weak lens, I watched falling stars, the moon, and high-flying satellites. I never saw a comet. It didn't bother me. I figured God was saving that for 1986.

Sometime after junior high my little telescope found a resting-place in a drawer at my parent's house. I went to college, chased girls, caught one (or she caught me-still an ongoing source of debate at our house), left for law school, got married, and had kids. Through it all, I never observed a comet in the night sky. Of course, I wasn't really looking. I was waiting for Haley's.

Sure, there was Comet Kohoutek back in 1973-my first year in college. I remember the excitement of the twenty or so young men and women that gathered for our Comet Kohoutek party...and the despair we felt when the comet turned out to be a total dud. I mean, twenty college kids, rock and roll, "refreshments" and pizza...and no comet. What to do?

1986 finally came. Somehow, I forgot about Haley's. I'd waited years for the celestial event of a lifetime. And I missed it. I don't know if I was working, engaged in some deep philosophical debate with my wife, or off on a lark during the appointed hour. I just plain blew it.

Once I figured out that Haley's had come and gone, I did some rough figuring. The math depressed me. I'd have to live to be 108 years old to have another chance of seeing Haley's Comet. Even if I lived that long, the probability that I would remember the year Haley's was due back did not, given my forgetfulness at age 32, seem likely.

Time slipped by. The 1980's slid into the 1990's. A third son came along. For some inexplicable reason, I began to find myself staring more often at the night sky during our long Minnesota winters. As I scanned the heavens I tried to recall why space meant so much to me as a child. Perhaps, I postulated, it was the sky's limitless possibility that attracted me. Perhaps it was the idea that looking into space is like looking back at the beginning of time. Whatever the reasons for my interest, as I aged, I became more intent on reclaiming the sense of amazement and wonder that astronomy held for me as a child.

Comet Hyakutake teased my family last winter. We watched the comet's faint light stand nearly vertical above us. We stood in the snow and watched its display during bitter below zero nights. Even though Hyakutake was only a dim pinprick of light, it was a real comet despite its failings. But it wasn't spectacular. It wasn't Haley's. It didn't completely erase my sense of loss, my sense of having missed my comet-watching destiny.

When the comet Hale-Bopp burst onto the scene, I shrugged my shoulders.

"If it comes," I thought, "it'll be another bust. There's only one real comet and I missed it in 1986," I theorized.

In the middle of typing this, I leave my notebook computer and walk out the back door. Standing in the warm spring air, looking to the Northwest, I realize that I was wrong to prejudge Hale-Bopp. This comet, this bright splash of light, which last came to visit us five thousand years ago, stands triumphant in the sky. Contemplating the history that has passed during this galactic voyager's absence, dusk's mantle fades, revealing an ebony backdrop to God's latest celestial production. Uncountable suns appear as distant points of light, framing the wanderer's path. Against this curtain, Hale-Bopp is amazingly brilliant.

I've never seen anything like it. Watching the comet's show, I realize that God has brought me to this moment. I'm infinitely happy to live in a place where stars dance and little boy's dreams come true.

CLEANING THE BARN

Let's be candid. Owning animals means dealing with crap. Owning big animals means dealing with lots of crap. I should have anticipated this truth when I went looking to buy my first horse. Something like that should be obvious.

It's Sunday afternoon and the spring sunshine is warming the metal skin of our pole barn. Christian and Dylan, ages eleven and fourteen, reluctantly load piles of horse manure into the bucket of my International tractor. Chris' buddy Spencer is behind another shovel pushing a mixture of soiled pine shavings and manure towards the other boys.

Our new pole barn may be a modern building but the labor the boys are engaged in is thousands of years old. As I watch them push the waste of three horses across the smooth concrete floor it's easy to imagine Roman stable hands doing the same task with the same tools thousands of years ago.

"Hey, make sure you get that stuff in the bucket, Dylan," I call out from deep within another stall.

"Ya, right," my teenaged son responds as he drops nearly a quarter of his load on the cement. My criticism doesn't seem to improve his aim or his ambition.

I'm working on my own, away form the boys, so that I can listen to *A Prairie Home Companion* on the radio. The AM/FM radio that I'm using is the same one that I use to catch Minnesota Twin's games when I'm weeding our vegetable garden. The radio is a reject from my mother-in-law. The black plastic case is misshapen (someone left it next to an electric heater). Today the appliance is covered with the fine dust of disintegrating horse apples. Every so often I lose the Public Radio station we're listening to, which gives me an excuse to sit down and fiddle with the channel dial.

"Come on dad," Chris whines. "We'll never finish this if you keep taking rests."

"Shut up Chris," Dylan scolds, his blue eyes flashing. "I want to hear the rest of the show."

"Don't say 'shut up', Dyl," I remind him. "Just tell him to be quiet."

I try to decipher what Dylan says to Chris under his breath but I find the station and miss the exchange between my boys. It's a good time to do a thorough spring-cleaning in the barn. The air is still cold. The stable flies haven't hatched. Our three very fat and content horses stand outside in the pasture munching the last of August's hay. I try to remember the last time one of them was ridden. I draw a blank. I know it was before the first snow. Maybe October? Maybe late September?

The bucket of the loader is full. I climb into the seat and push the starter. A comforting "pop": the engine purrs. I pull levers to raise the load. Water drips from the hydraulic cylinders on either side of the bucket as the manure is elevated. When the manure is chest high, I put the tractor into first gear and pull away. Rusted tire chains beat a rhythm against the concrete floor as the tractor advances towards an open door.

"Dyl, unhook the fence," I yell over the din of the tractor's engine.

The teenager runs ahead of the International and reaches cautiously for a plastic handle connected to an electric fence.

"Is it off?" Dylan asks.

"Yep."

"Are you sure?" my son asks again, his voice betraying skepticism.

"I'm sure."

Dylan lifts the insulated handle. The wire disengages. I drive into the pasture. Mud and horse feces become compacted beneath the tires of the utility tractor. The pasture is a quagmire of slime and pooled water. Our horses scrutinize my progress as I pull alongside the manure pile. The heap began as a small bump on the landscape. Over 13 years of owning horses, the mound has grown. One day, our manure pile may challenge Eagle Mountain as the highest point in Minnesota.

I pull a lever and raise the bucket to the limit of the loader. The scoop tilts. Waste and shavings free-fall onto the pile. The process is repeated until all of the stalls are clean. Dylan latches the electric fence after my last trip. I park the tractor outside. Mud and dirty water drip from the metal frame of the old International. My tractor will be rinsed clean by the next passing rainstorm. It's done its job since 1962 without much fanfare or fuss. A little mud won't hurt it.

"You guys can take off," I tell the boys." I'll clean up what's left."

The kids don't stand around waiting for me to change my mind. They're long gone by the time Garrison Keillor begins his weekly monologue. I listen to the humorist in the quiet of the barn as I push the remaining bits of pine and horse manure onto a shovel. When the scoop is full, I carry the mess outside and deposit it by hand on the compost pile.

My back aches from heavy lifting. Bone tired, I turn the radio off before the "News from Lake Wobegon" is over, close the big sliding door, and walk out into tenuous sunshine. I sit on a porch swing under the barn's covered porch and watch the Cloquet River, its waters impatient from the thaw, rush by our farm. Rocking gently, I wonder whether my boys will ever understand what this place means to me.

SEARCHING FOR PATRICK ROY

Western Ontario's wilderness gave way to rolling farmland. Montreal, Vermont, and Massachusetts came and went like a dream. After ten days traveling by train across Canada, we returned to our home along the banks of the Cloquet River satisfied that we'd seen and done as much as we could during our summer vacation. Only Matthew, fourteen years old at the time, seemed unsatisfied with the trip.

"I never got to see inside of the Forum," he lamented. "And I never got to meet Patrick Roy."

Roy (pronounced "wha", as in "what") played goalie at the time for the Montreal Canadians. To Matt, a first year Bantam goalie, Roy was the ideal, the best goaltender in hockey. To my son, not meeting the tender for the Habs was a grating failure. It bothered him to no end that our family had ridden Via Rail from Reditt, Ontario, 150 miles north of International Falls, to Montreal and back without ever finding Mr. Roy.

"Sorry about that, Matt. We didn't have the time," I said in as conciliatory a voice as I could muster.

"We had time to walk around and look at old churches," he retorted.

I contemplated a reply. I thought about pointing out how much it cost to take a family of five across Canada, through Vermont, to Boston, and back on a train. I thought of computing all of the expenses in neat rows and presenting the evidence, as I often do in court, to my son. But I knew it would only fuel further debate.

A few days later, I came in the house from weeding our family vegetable garden. I found Matthew studiously writing at the kitchen table. A high summer sun cast intense light on the boy's work.

"Whatcha doin'," I asked.

"Writing to Patrick Roy," he replied without looking up.

"Sortof a long letter, isn't it?" I noted.

"I want to make sure he knows how great I think he is."

"You know, maybe Mr. Roy is too busy to read such a long letter," I offered, hoping to prompt the boy to exercise restraint.

Matt ignored my assessment and continued to write. Dylan, nine years old at the time, ambled into the room, his light brown hair bleached blond by the season, his arms and legs tanned deep brown from constant exposure to the sun. The bright blue of Dylan's eyes peered over the edge of the table.

"Whatcha doin', Matt?" he asked.

"Writin' to Patrick Roy. Stop botherin' me."

"Why ya writin' to Patrick Roy, Matt?" Dylan persisted.

"I want him to autograph his rookie hockey card. I'm sending it with the letter."

I drew a cold glass of well water from our kitchen tap and feigned disinterest in the conversation.

"Maybe I'll send one to Gretzky," Dylan observed, canting his head to one side in reflection.

"You're an idiot. Wayne Gretzky doesn't have time to sign cards for every little kid that sends one. He's the greatest hockey player of all time. Get real!"

I wanted to intervene, to tell Dylan to go for it. I wanted to try and massage the hurt I saw creep into the little boy's eyes at his brother's rebuke. There was no need.

"Oh Ya?" Well I'm gonna send him a letter 'n a card. You'll see," Dylan replied with confidence.

"Go ahead, you're still an idiot."

Later that afternoon I came back into the house for a snack and found Dylan occupying the same table, surrounded by crumpled balls of paper, his face gripped by serious thought.

"How's it going," I asked, leaning over to examine his work.

"Great. I got the letter done. I'm doing the outside of the envelope."

I watched my second son cram a very messy, nearly indecipherable letter into an envelope. The complete address of the Los Angeles Kings, Gretzky's team at the time, was scrawled in purple marker across the face of the envelope. The boy tucked a trading card of the Great One into the packet and licked the flap, sealing the envelope.

Matt entered the room holding his letter to Patrick Roy in one hand.

"Mail this for Dylan, will you?" I asked, handing him the younger boy's message to his hero.

"Lot's of good it'll do'im. He's wasting a perfectly good card," Matt observed as he snatched the envelope from my hand. "Gretzky's too busy to worry about some stupid little squirt hockey player," the older boy added as he left to mail the letters.

Six weeks to the day, I handed Matt a thick, slightly distressed manila envelope bearing the return address of the Montreal Canadians. Dylan stood to one side of his big brother as the adolescent ripped open the package. The smaller boy's eyes welled with tears. No similar package from the Kings had arrived.

Inside the manila folder Matt found publicity photos of Mr. Roy in goalie poses, Montreal Canadian bumper stickers, and countless other promotional materials from the team. But there was no letter from Mr. Roy. In addition, the rookie trading card had not been returned.

Matt's eyes scanned the form letter from the Canadians. It related how busy Mr. Roy was, how impossible it would be for such a great star to read every fan letter and personally autograph each trading card submitted to him by his legions of admirers.

"At least I got some really cool stuff. See Dyl, I told you that you were wasting your time," the older boy advised, his voice tailing off as he climbed the stairway to his bedroom. I turned to console my younger son but he was gone.

Four additional weeks passed. Labor Day loomed. The letter to Mr. Gretzky was forgotten. A thunderstorm threatened the sky above our farm. Late summer rain began to splat the sheet metal of my pickup truck as I pulled into the driveway. Dodging dollops of moisture, I covered my head with my briefcase and sprinted across the sidewalk into the back door of our farmhouse.

The house was quiet. I noticed Dylan watching me as I shook rainwater from my hair onto the finely polished oak floor of the kitchen. He stood next to the sink, a broad grin across his face, obviously waiting for his old man.

"How's it goin', Dyl," I asked as I stepped towards him.

"Great. See?" His smooth hand produced an envelope.

"Master Dylan Munger" and our address were carefully typed on the paper. There was no return address.

"Matt's stupid," the boy whispered.

"Why do you say that?" I asked, accepting the document from him.

"He doesn't know anything."

The packet was small, smaller than letter size. I carefully withdrew the contents, a single piece of cardboard undamaged by the rain.

"He signed it, dad, he really signed it."

Sure enough. Scrawled in thick permanent marker across the face of the trading card was the unmistakable autograph of the Great One.

THE LAST HUNT

It's quiet in the November forest. I'm ill prepared to be out hunting deer. I didn't plan on hunting this season. A last minute call from my father convinced me to buy a license and come up to the old shack to hunt with the guys.

I've been coming to this place, a ramshackle shanty on the edge of a vast aspen and alder forest, since I was 14 years old. I've been hunting in these woods since 1969, the year I turned 15. In all those years, I've never taken a deer here. Not that I haven't shot deer. I have. A doe up at my pal Jeff's farm. A couple of spike bucks right out my own back door in Fredenberg. But up here, in the dark confines of the valley of Coolidge Creek, I've had no luck at our deer camp.

I arrive late Friday night in my Dodge Dakota pickup. As I bounce over the logging trail towards the shack, I see stark light illuminating the battered front door of the place. A biting wind causes the propane lantern hanging above the entrance to swing from side to side. I park my truck and shoulder my gear. I don't have a rifle with me. My grandfather's 30-30 Winchester is being repaired. I'm set to borrow my dad's 20-gauge over-and-under shotgun. I've never hunted with slugs before but then my prior history with the place isn't filled with successful encounters with whitetails even when I carry a rifle.

"Hello," I call out as I step inside the crude building. Heavy air greets my face as I step over the threshold.

"How you doing, Bro?" my brother Dave asks sipping contentedly from a can of Budweiser.

"How's Mark?" Mr. Red, one of the older hunters, and a life-long friend of my father, asks.

"Fine," I respond walking through the kitchen towards the bunkroom.

A steady buzzing, the by-product of fluorescent light echoes off of the bare walls of the place. Each wall is constructed of fir doors salvaged from railroad boxcars. Plastic cords lead from the lights and weave in and out of the ceiling supports. The other ends of the cords are secured to the lighter sockets of vehicles parked alongside the shack. This electrical system works but requires a high level of diligence to remember to start the involved vehicles every so often to recharge their batteries.

"Anyone using this upper bunk," I ask, swinging my backpack and sleeping bag onto a vacant platform.

"Nope," I hear Poncho, one of the younger hunters say between chaws of tobacco.

I roll out my nylon bag. The mattress, one my father donated from my childhood bunk bed, is lumpy and smells of mice. A kerosene heater percolates. Its coils glow orange at the far end of the room. My bunk is constructed in the same primitive style as the rest of the place. The supports for the double-decker bed are roughhewn 2x4's. The sleeping area is made up of a single grain door from a boxcar placed horizontally across the supports. I toss my backpack under the bunk.

Jimmy, his father Jim, Poncho, Mr. Red and his son David, my brother Dave, and my father sit around an oval table in the kitchen. An antique LP range and an oil stove occupy one wall of the room. The oil stove gives off just enough radiant heat to keep the inside temperature bearable. A plywood counter supports a sink. The plumbing? A hole drains water into a plastic pail underneath the sink. Clean water, carried up from a spring several hundred feet from the cabin, stands ready for use in two plastic drywall buckets stored beneath the sink.

Dishes and food occupy elementary shelving. A black and white portable television plugged into my father's Suburban sits on the top shelf. A University of Minnesota-Duluth hockey game plays on the set. Mr. Red, nearing seventy and an expert on the sport of ice hockey, grimaces in disgust at the progress of the contest:

"Those Canuck kids don't know the first thing about hockey," he growls.

Jimmy once played college hockey at Harvard. He knows how easy it is to bait Mr. Red. He can't resist the temptation:

"I'm sure you could straighten 'em out, eh Red?"

"Darn right. Those boys need to learn how to take a check and how to give a check," the old coach mutters.

I settle in next to Jim Senior and open a can of Sprite, my days of over-indulging at the deer camp long behind me. I pull out a stack of quarters and join the poker game in progress. Unlike most years, the game proceeds with a minimum of arguing.

Dawn comes quickly when you go to bed late, sleep poorly, and come to the woods unprepared. My dad is in the kitchen with Mr. Red frying bacon and eggs. I stumble past them, slip on my hunting boots just far enough to cover the bottoms of my feet and walk outside to go to the bathroom. It's cold. I refuse to negotiate the twenty frigid steps to the outhouse. I find a spot behind my truck to do what needs doing.

Later on I walk the woods I wondering why I'm here. I don't like venison all that much. I forgot my rope for dragging deer. I'm carrying a borrowed shotgun loaded with slugs. I left my hunting knife at home. I don't have a deer stand to sit in that I can call my own. Nothing about this hunt seems right. I walk down the main trail. The sky is high and gray, typical for the Opener. There's a trace of snow on the ground, which covers the debris from the dormant aspen forest. I find one of my old stands but quickly decide that it's no longer safe. I amble on, alert for sounds of deer on the move. I hear nothing beyond the subtle bend of the trees in the light breeze.

I come across a platform located a fair distance above the ground in a triangle of birch. There's an old rope hanging from the railing of the deer stand. It's well after daylight. The stand is in an area my camp traditionally hunts. It's unoccupied. I decide to use it.

In the security of the trees, I shift my weight and settle in to wait for a passing buck. My eyes close. I snatch small bits of sleep. I've heard no shots and I've seen no deer. My head comes to rest against my shoulder and my thoughts drift off. My slumber is disturbed. I hear a noise behind me. I remain calm and control my breathing as I shift my position. My rear end slides across the triangular seat of the stand until I face the direction of the perceived intruder. I pull the edge of my orange stocking cap away from my eyes and place my gloved right index finger on the trigger of the shotgun.

A branch breaks. I stare excitedly into the mystery of an adjacent spruce swamp. Tan shoulders cautiously emerge from the browns and grays of the winter forest. I steady myself and search for antlers. I don't have a doe permit. I didn't apply for one. I've never applied for one. I shot one doe, one time, on someone else's permit because it was the only deer we saw all season. I'm uncertain if I'll ever do that again.

I count the tines on the animal's rack. He's a healthy six pointer. The buck's black eyes survey the territory between us. I study him as his head dips to smell the ground. The buck's nostrils flare as he detects something.

"Me?" I ask silently. I don't wait for an answer. I point the muzzle of the scattergun at the target's front shoulder and steady my aim.

Boom.

The 20 gauge barks.

Thwack.

The slug strikes solid muscle, tumbling the animal to the ground. Pulling a Swiss Army knife from my jacket pocket, I cut the old rope free of the stand. I'll need the rope to drag the deer. I know the rope belongs to someone else. I vow to return it after I'm done with my task. On the ground, I realize that the buck is not dead. I raise my meager blade and contemplate slicing the beast's jugular vein. The thought is fleeting. I can't do it. I raise my father's gun to my cheek.

"Boom."

The deer dies swiftly. I begin the unpleasant business of gutting a 140-pound animal with a jackknife. When I finish slitting the animal's belly and removing its entrails, the heart and liver saved in an old plastic bread bag and tossed into the game pocket of my orange coat, I loop the rope around the buck's rack. Checking my compass, I begin the laborious process of dragging the carcass back to the deer shack.

"Hey, that's the deer I shot," a voice says from somewhere behind me.

I turn and observe another hunter clad in vibrant orange emerge from the underbrush.

"How's that?" I respond, breathing heavily from my efforts.

"I'm sure that's the one I hit in the hind end," the man replies.

I study the guy's face. He's unfamiliar. Given that both of us have weapons and given that his tone is accusatory, I want to placate him if I can.

"He walked out from the trees," I explain. "He didn't seem to be hit."

The other hunter bends over the hindquarters of the animal. His hand brushes through the thick winter fur of the hide until the man seems satisfied.

"How many times did you shoot?" he asks.

"Twice. The first one hit his shoulder and knocked him down. I shot him once more in the head to kill him."

"I hit him right here," he says, pointing to a small hole through the rear portion of the left leg.

I look. There's a clean through between the tendon and the bone. It doesn't appear that the wound caused any lasting damage to the buck.

"I see it," I admit. "But he wasn't limping when he came out."

"I don't want to get into a hassle over this but I've been tracking him for a long time," the other man said.

Right then, I tell myself that I'll never deer hunt at the shack again:

"I don't need this," I think.

"If you really want the deer..." I offer half-heartedly.

"No, no. You keep him," the hunter mutters. "What camp you with, anyway?"

"Liston's," I disclose. "How about you?" I ask.

"Davidson's.'

Davidson's is the next camp down the trail from us. We've shared more than one drink with the Davidson Camp over the years.

"Never had this kind of trouble with you guys before," the hunter mutters through his teeth, the words terse and bitter. "You shoot out of that stand back there?"

"Yes," I admit.

"That rope come from that stand?"

"Yes."

"Well, that's my stand and my rope. See that you put it back when you're done."

I stare at the upset hunter through guilty eyes as I watch his orange form disappear into the tightly woven fabric of the forest. I take a deep breath, resume pulling the deer to the road, all the while wondering why I ever accepted my father's invitation.

OLD HORSES

We've nearly always had horses since we moved to the country. Our first horse, Nicholas, was a mixed breed stallion given to me as a fee by a client. We had him gelded to calm him down. The surgery did little good. Even the efforts of my neighbor Peg, a dedicated horsewoman, couldn't tame him. In the end, after he tossed me to the frozen ground on one cold November day, Nicholas left us. My wife Rene' traded him for two used saddles.

Barbara was the next horse to live with us. She was a purebred Appaloosa mare. White with black leopard spotting, Barbara was the first horse I ever mounted and rode by myself. When I bought her, she was being kept over at Earl's place with her daughter, Minnie, because her owner had moved. I paid Earl $500.00 for her. She was a bargain. She was 14 years old when I bought her. She was 18 years old when I found her dead in the pasture one hot summer day. The Vet said it was Lyme's disease.

Having never grown up with horses, I was mystified how a person could love such a stupid animal. Galloping Barbara full tilt across our pasture, wading with her through the River on cool spring days, holding out my hand and having her nuzzle it with her moist snout, I learned the secret of old horses. Obedience and a willingness to trust rewarded my patience. Barbara taught me that in our short time together.

After the Appaloosa died, a succession of ill-tempered mares came to live with us for brief periods of time. Minnie, Barbara's daughter, a beautiful red-roan mare, came to me on approval. That spring, she bucked my sister off in the middle of our hay field, prompting me to trade horses with Annie. I was determined to re-establish authority over the beast.

During my sister's spill, one of the steel clasps securing the reins broke free. I didn't know it. I found out about the defect only after Minnie took off for the trees at full gallop with me clinging to her back. With only one rein, I had no control over her. I rode the mare as long as I could, hanging on like a rodeo cowboy as she bucked her way towards the woods. Just before the trees, I rolled off the horse, landing unharmed in soft grass. The mare glanced back at Annie and I. With a flourish of her red mane and tail, the App turned and trotted home. I walked Minnie back to my neighbor's place that same day.

My sister-in-law at the time was a horse lady. She and I drove all over the county looking for a decent horse. On her recommendation, I paid $1,000.00 for a 10-year-old Registered Quarter horse mare. The horse's name was Pumpkin. She acted like a perfect lady when my sister-in-law test rode her. The mare was toying with us.

The first time a boat and trailer passed Pumpkin on the road in front of our farm, she reared up on her hind legs and dumped me unceremoniously on the gravel shoulder of the roadway. From there, things only got worse. My sister-in-law vowed that the horse would not best us. She arrived at my farm outfitted in a riding helmet and riding boots ready to square away the mare. My sister-in-law landed on her butt four times before she too finally admitted defeat.

Harry came to live with us. A young, roan-colored quarter horse gelding of no particular distinction, I traded Pumpkin and $250.00 for him. Harry, despite some stubborn traits and an affinity for biting cats and the hair of small children, was a good companion for my wife's old mare. They've been together for more than seven years.

She stands in the bright sunlight. The ground glistens white around her. Tufts of loose hay interrupt the snow. It's been a hard winter and she's getting ready to die. The old mare looks across our pasture with sad eyes. Her head stays low. A rear leg is held up in pain. We cannot tell if the leg is broken or merely sore. The Vet has come and gone, saying only that the mare is old. I don't want to put her down because there's no easy way to bury her. The snow is too deep. The earth is frozen. I pray she lasts until the thaw, when she can be put to rest with dignity and peace. I don't think she'll make it.

Last week, I found the horse lying on her side in her stall. She had soiled her tail and could not get up. She was weak. I'd run out of geriatric horse food and had been feeding her straight grain. It was not complete enough to provide all her nutritional needs. The food was too hard for her to chew. Her big eyes looked at me in sorrow. I knew I'd let her down.

With a leather strap under her hindquarters, I tried lifting her to her feet. Even in her poor condition, she still weighed over 900 pounds. I didn't want her to die in the barn. There would be no way to get her out. Snow blocks the main door. My tractor is broken. She tried to rise. Her feet slid on the concrete floor, pushing away the bedding. She was weary from the fight, tired of struggling to stand. I was convinced she would never get up. But she did.

She moves across the snow in painful steps. Harry, her companion, stays close to her. I sense that the gelding realizes that the mare is sick, that she's about to die. Normally, Harry's obnoxious in small doses. During her illness, he's constantly irritable, holding his ears flat against his skull whenever I come to lead him into the barn at night. He's stubborn. He doesn't want to leave the mare, perhaps because he senses that her time is short.

They stand together in the pasture, the old mare and Harry. I think they both know that this will be their last spring together. I feel the need to go out and talk to her, to comfort her, even as I write this story.

She has carried my children, my wife, myself, as well as our family and friends upon her sturdy back. Before she came to us, she did the same for her prior owners. She never complained, never bucked, never bit, never refused to do what was asked of her.

Her name is Cisco, a name she had been given long before she came to live with us, a name she bore long before the movie *Dances with Wolves* was ever made. I bought her for Rene'. She cost $150.00. It's the best $150.00 I ever spent. I fear there will never be another horse like her on the Munger farm.

(Postscript: Cisco died at the age of 32. As the Vet's needle carried her spirit away, Harry cried out from his stall. His voice shook the metal skin of the pole barn as Cisco drifted off to where ever it is that old horses go.)

DOWN AT THE AMAZING GRACE

It's a typical October evening in Duluth. Raw, untamed wind blows across Lake Superior. The sun has set. The night sky is thwarted by low-hanging cumulus clouds waiting to release rain. Only the yellow streetlights of Canal Park, weak and insignificant in the universe's grand scheme, provide illumination as my wife and I park our van in a nearly deserted hotel parking lot. Because the leaves have fallen, because winter is nigh, the Minneapolitans have retreated, leaving the Zenith City to the natives.

"I'm really excited to see Lucy," I tell Rene' for the third time in the past ten minutes.

"I can tell," my wife replies.

"I first heard her ..."

"I know, I know. When we were up in that little gift shop in Ely. You found one of her CD's and fell in love with her," Rene' interjects, having heard the story too many times.

There's no point in responding. We pass beneath the gentle light of the antique street lamps. As we walk, I marvel at how the collective vision and intellect of the people of Duluth has transformed Canal Park. In my youth, the waterfront was an industrial wasteland. Salvage yards, food-processing plants, machine shops, warehouses, and accompanying filth defined Lake Avenue. Someone, somewhere, had a vision to reclaim the place for the people and brought the vision to fruition.

We're going to see Lucy Kaplansky, a folk singer and songwriter. She's playing at the Amazing Grace Café, a venue that fits an urban folk singer like a well-worn pair of Levi's. The café is a small, intimate space that allows the audience to sit only a few paces from the performer. Folksongs, and folksingers by the very nature of their craft, are intimate, making the smallness of the setting a virtue.

A driving rain begins to assault us. We break into a desperate run. Our feet splash through puddles as we make the stairs and descend to the Amazing Grace. I open the door and start across the threshold before I remember my dating manners. I retreat, allowing my wife to pass by.

"Thanks," she says.

"My pleasure," I reply, using formality to conceal my guilt.

We're a half-hour early for the show. I finger the tickets in the front pocket of my corduroys in anticipation that someone will want to see evidence that we've paid for our admission. There's no one inside the café interested in stopping us.

"Do you want a cup of coffee and something to eat?" I ask. Rain drips from Rene's hair onto a well-worn oak floor. She passes a hand through the limp, disorganized mop. I know what my wife's going to say before the words are formed:

"Just coffee. I'm going to fix my hair," she notes as she walks away.

"Two coffees," I say to the young woman behind the counter. My eyes focus on the rows of cookies, muffins, and other bakery items displayed behind glass as I wait for my purchase.

"House blend?" the cashier asks, obviously noting that I'm not the flavored coffee-cappuccino type.

"That's fine," I remark. My attention is drawn to the young lady's face. Her skin is clean and youthful. Her eyes are light and quick. She's someone's daughter. She could be my daughter, age-wise. I hand her a ten. The clerk hands me the change and moves on to her next customer.

The seating for the concert is minimalist. There are hard wooden benches and hard plastic chairs lined up ten or so to a row, ten or so rows in all, facing a grand piano, an array of small speakers, a microphone, and several acoustic guitars resting in metal stands. A Lucy Kaplansky poster hangs against the yellow bricks of the wall behind the stage. Rough-sawn timbers of white pine support the weight of the building lurking above us.

Rene' returns and sits down on the unkind surface of a plastic chair. I hand her a ceramic mug filled with coffee. Steam rises from our cups in opposition to the cool climate of the basement. One of the owners of the café steps up to a microphone on the stage. He's wearing a well-traveled hat of unknown lineage. The fedora rides low across his forehead concealing the intent of his eyes.

"Ladies and gentlemen, please give a warm welcome to our friend and national recording artist, Lucy Kaplansky."

The singer appears in jeans, a bulky sweater, and black lace-up boots. Her hair is dark and wildly attractive. Her eyes are deep brown. As if unable to expend all of her intimacy on strangers, Lucy's eye contact with us is selective and fleeting throughout the show.

The singer selects a guitar and secures the shoulder strap to the neck of the instrument. Bathed in the unkind light of the stage, her fingers begin to work the frets and her voice begins to craft a sweet, sad melody. I know the song and I begin to sing along in a whisper.

"Ssssh." Rene' cautions. "You're too loud."

My wife's rebuke stings me far more than it should. I refrain from any further accompaniment. I've always loved songwriters, those fortunate poets blessed with the ability to weave compelling lyrics and creative tunes into memorable songs. Sadness, angst, and life's struggles are things that folksingers seem to rely upon for inspiration. Their songs, Lucy's songs, are filled to the brim with tragedy, unfairness, and prejudice.

Ms. Kaplansky does not disappoint. For an hour and a half she sings, she plays the guitar and, at times, sits behind the grand piano, immersing the room in tales of ordinary experiences made extraordinary. During breaks, she talks frankly, with a hint of regret, about her life on the road as a married, female musician and engages the crowd in dialogue:

"Well at least this is better than the last time I came to town," she relates with a pensive smile. "I agreed to come here in February last year and the warmest it got was twenty below."

A few more songs, an entreaty to come and see her upcoming shows with Dar Williams and Richard Shindell, one last lament, a tender, lilting song, and then she is gone.

The house lights flare. Rene' and I leave the cellar ahead of the crowd. As we exit to confront the weather, I revisit the words and music of the evening, I examine the texture of Lucy's songs, bits and pieces of which continue to dance across my mind. In an instant, I'm filled with understanding. I realize that, by temporarily wrapping myself in a stranger's art, I've come to appreciate what a tenuous and wonderful gift love really is and I reach for my wife's hand.

LOOKING FOR MOONLIGHT GRAHAM

Sometimes we are destined to be good, not great.

The Chisholm Ice Arena is loud. Fans scream, urging their respective team on. My son is in the nets for Hermantown. It's a choice he made some years ago, to be a goalie. I tried to talk him out of it. I tried to make him understand that if he wasn't the very best at the position, his chances of playing high school hockey were nil. But he loves it. He loves the mental part of the game, the pressure, the accolades when his team wins.

At one time during the season my son's team of ten skaters and a goalie was ranked as high as seventh in the State. That was before a back injury ended Michael's hockey career and before we lost another player to a misconduct disqualification. We went into District playoffs with eight skaters and a goaltender. We lost to teams we'd licked during the regular season. We lost not because the kids didn't try: we lost because the boys were exhausted, worn out by skating short.

We're in our third overtime period against Proctor. We've been able to stay with the Rails in the championship game of this invitational tournament only because we picked up extra players from other Hermantown teams.

Both goalies are playing fine games. Matt stands tall. He does not know that this will be his last game, that he'll tryout for the varsity next year as a sophomore but not make it. Right now, occupying the crease, protecting the tie score for his teammates, focusing on the game in front of him, he's playing one of the best games of his career.

Our defense is tired. A Proctor boy breaks across neutral ice and gets behind the Hermantown defensemen. A pass finds the Rail winger all alone in the Hermantown end, two steps beyond our last man.

Matt bears down. He shifts his position to cover the left pipe. The Proctor player skates in from the boards. He lets fly with a high, hard wrist shot. The puck strikes the goaltender's shoulder and lands in front of the net. A skirmish breaks out as our defense and the Rail player scramble for the puck. Matt moves across the crease, staying low, trying to see. The Proctor forward wins the battle. Another shot is launched towards the opposite side of the net. Matt scrambles across. He's too late.

The teams line up to shake hands. My son is nowhere to be found. His goalie stick, helmet, and gloves are scattered across the ice. I know better than to follow him into the locker room.

My wife Rene' and our two other sons at the time, Dylan and Chris, join me to watch the awards ceremony. We applaud lightly as the Proctor team hoists the championship trophy above the ice. The winners, their sweat-streaked hair flowing behind them, circle the rink with their prize. Loyal Proctor fans cheer as their team takes a victory lap. My family exits the ice rink to wait for Matt in the lobby of the arena.

One by one the Hawks emerge from the locker room. The Hermantown players carry their heavy equipment bags and their sticks into the concession area. Each player asks a parent for money. It's a ritual that has been repeated after every game since the boys were Ice Mites in kindergarten. All of the Hermantown players but my son are dressed and standing in line at the concession stand.

"Where's Matt?" I ask the head coach.

"He left awhile ago," Pete responds.

"He's not in the locker room?"

"Nope. He wasn't too happy. He left before anyone else came off the ice."

"We better go find him," I say to Rene'.

"I'm not pleased with the way he's acting," my wife advises.

"Me neither. But it was a tough loss."

"That doesn't give him the right to be a poor sport."

I pick up Matt's abandoned equipment and carry it out to the van. It's evening. The March night is wet with the melt of spring. I search the parking lot. Matt is nowhere to be found. We climb into our vehicle.

I begin a slow drive through downtown Chisholm, Minnesota. Street lamps cast shadows across the paved streets. Only the town's taverns and bars are open. Neon lights crackle in the cool night air. I turn around on the town's main street and head back up the hill towards the arena. My child has vanished. There is no trace of him anywhere.

"Where the hell did he go," I ask in a frustrated tone.

Dylan slides between the front bucket seats and points through the windshield.

"There he is," our second son exclaims.

Matt is walking towards us, his hands shoved deep into his pants pockets, his shoulders slumped, as if someone has placed the weight of the world on him. His eyes are focused on the sidewalk. His progress towards us is labored.

I drive up to my oldest son and stop the van. He looks at me. Moisture pools in his brown eyes but tears do not break free. Matt approaches my side of the vehicle. I push a button. The driver's window slides down. Cold air touches the bare skin of my face.

"What's going on Matt?" I ask.

My son is silent. He simply stares at me.

139

"Do you realize we've been driving all over town, looking for you?" his mother queries.

Again, there's only silence. I feel compelled to speak, to break my son's poisonous mood.

"Did you find him?" I ask in as soft a tone as I can muster.

Matt's eyes search my face.

"Find who?" he questions.

"Moonlight Graham," I respond.

I watch as the boy fights back a smile. He's unsuccessful. The darkness of the overtime loss fades from his face. He casts a backward glance at the Chisholm Arena as he enters the Pontiac from the passenger side.

It's a quiet ride home.

TOO MANY YEARS

The hills rose behind them enveloping the boy and his father. A train trestle stood silent against the night sky. Their campfire was meager. Fuel for the fire was limited to a few dry branches stolen from the top of a beaver lodge. The beaver had eaten everything else.

A transistor radio sat between them on the ground. It was not on. A battered tin coffeepot sat upon the stainless steel grate of a camp stove. They sipped coffee from cheap plastic cups, talking in low, respectful tones.

"Twenty two years ago. That's the last time I was at this place."

The man didn't look at his son. He was looking upward, into the distance as he spoke.

"I came here with my dad, my Uncle Bob, and my cousin Kevin. We sure caught fish that day."

The son stood up, walked over to the stove, and poured another cup of coffee into his cup. The heat of the liquid caused the cup to sag, to droop until it nearly released its contents. Noise from a passing taconite train interrupted their peace.

The locomotive emerged from the solidarity of the woods. Despite the fact that the engine was pulling an empty train, the diesel labored. It faced a steep and difficult climb from the shoreline of Lake Superior to Minnesota's Iron Range. They sat quietly and watched, as the single headlight of the locomotive grew larger. The racket made by the ore cars passing over the ties denied them wilderness. Light from the engine's interior allowed them to see the engineer and his crew. The man and his son waved at the strangers on the train. A lonesome whistle answered.

In the morning, they ate cold sweet rolls and drank more coffee. They had no idea of the time. The boy pulled on his hip waders and began to work the edge of a pond near their camp with a dry fly. The father rigged up his fly rod with a barbless hook and a nightcrawler.

"Got one."

The boy lifted the slender tip of his fly rod. He pulled a tiny, silver fish out of the cold waters of the beaver pond. It was not a trout but a shiner no more than three inches long.

"That won't be much good in the fry pan, son."

The father grinned as he chided the boy.

"At least I caught something."

The boy's reply was curt. He removed the fly from the minnow's mouth and gently placed the shiner back in the water. The fish skipped across the surface of the pond, disappearing to wherever it is that wounded minnows go. The humans moved downstream from the pond, testing the ripples of the tiny waterway for brook trout. On his third cast, the father felt what he had come to that place to feel. A series of sharp tugs bent the tip of his rod. He set the hook. The fishing rod arched. A trout's spirit had been harnessed.

He pulled the fish out of the water and grasped it in his hand. It was a brook trout, no more than four inches in length. The creature's flanks caught the first light of the sun. Explosions of color dotted the trout's skin. The fisherman loosened the hook from the trout's jaw and released the fish into the stream.

They fished the creek for two hours but never caught another trout. After a cup of instant oatmeal, the boy and his father loaded up the truck and left their campsite. The day was still new. The sun had just risen and they had no idea where they were headed.

"I think if we stay on this road, it'll take us to another spot Grandpa Harry and I used to fish."

"Sure dad. Just keep an eye on the gas gauge, OK?"

They drove for an hour. Descending a steep grade, they came to another creek. The truck slowed as they arrived on the valley floor.

"Want to try this one?"

"Sure. Looks kinda tight, not a lot of room to fly fish, but I'll give it a try."

"You could use worms. It's no sin to use worms."

The boy grinned. The father eased the truck off of the road.

"Dad, you're just like that drunk guy with his coffee can full of worms in *A River Runs Through It*. Didn't you learn anything from that movie?"

The father stopped the vehicle at the water's edge, turned in his seat, and smiled:

"We'll see who catches more fish."

They pulled on their waders. The father took off up stream. The water came at him in a steady current. Black alders and maples hung low over the surface of the creek making his progress difficult. The boy waded a quiet pool below the culvert. A cloudless morning warmed the day.

It was on that unnamed creek where they learned how to fish. Every set of rapids, every stretch of fast water held trout. Most were five or six inches long. Only the boy caught fish large enough to keep. At noon, they left the creek in search of larger waters and bigger trout.

"Want to try this spot?"

Dust from the gravel road wafted by them as they skidded to a stop. The truck idled on a concrete bridge. Below them, a wide expanse of clean water cut through stones and dense undergrowth.

"Isn't this the place we thought about camping at last night?"

The father surveyed their location. The boy was right. It was the same spot they'd passed up the night before. They'd made a complete circle, following unnamed roadways across unnamed streams, ending up essentially where they'd begun.

"This time you go downstream and I'll go up, Dad."

The father nodded. Baiting his hook with a fresh piece of nightcrawler, he plunged down the bank. His pace was awkward because of the hip waders. He entered the stream where it passed beneath the road. Concealed by the shadow of the bridge, he watched the boy walk upstream.

The father tossed a nightcrawler into the water. The worm landed near a pile of debris. The current caught the worm and dragged it beneath the surface. A sharp tug told the fisherman that there were brook trout hiding under the logjam. He tried to set the hook. The line went limp. He retrieved the monofilament line and tossed the worm next to the debris. On the second cast, the trout was not so lucky.

They fished in silence. The rounded peaks of the Sawtooth Range folded off to the west framing the solitude of the place. They learned that the tranquil pools of the river held no trout. The brookies were in the rapids where the water bubbled and boiled. The father was stubborn. He thought bigger fish were holding in the pools. The stream proved him wrong.

They met at twilight in the middle of the river and compared creels. Though the worms caught more fish, the boy had done what he'd set out to do. He'd fished the day in grace, using only the subtle touch of a fly to tempt trout. And the father had accomplished what he'd set out to do as well. He'd found and caught brook trout, something he had not done in a very, very long time.

They departed the serenity of the river as the sun slid behind the hills. Watching his son walk towards the truck, the older man realized that his boy was no longer a child. By the strength in the youth's shoulders, by the determination of his will, the father could see, for the first time that his son was growing up. Standing at the guardrail above flowing water, the fisherman averted his gaze and listened to the percussive song of the river.

THE MAYOR'S BIG SWING

Rain threatened to end the game before it began. Thick thunderheads broiled and rolled over the field. I looked up, hoping that the storm would hold off and allow us to play our annual Summerfest Softball contest.

What began nearly a decade ago as a friendly amateur athletic contest between the Hermantown School Board and the Hermantown City Council has, over the last four or five years, taken on the earmarks of serious physical combat. I think the change can be traced to the advent of new people in the positions of Mayor and School Superintendent.

"Mark, where do you want to play?" Dr. White, the School Superintendent, asked me.

"Left center or left," I responded, tossing a softball to my wife Rene'.

"Rene', how about right field?" the Superintendent queried.

"Sure," my spouse replied, knowing that Dr. White's competitive nature would probably only recognize catcher, right field, or pitcher as possible placements for women on the School District team.

Leading 1-0 after our first at-bats, we took the field. Our team included three women occupying the predicted positions. I glanced into the dugout at the City bench, the home team. There was one woman ready for play, the City Attorney's daughter, a high school softball player of some note. I wanted to call this gender inequality to the Mayor's attention. I didn't, despite the fact that the informal rules of the contest required that each team have a minimum of two women on the field at all times during the game.

Ms. Helmer took the mound for the School. With deliberate concentration, she mixed up her delivery. She threw inside. She threw outside. She dropped the occasional pitch right down the middle of the plate. Understand that no slow pitch hurler is ever unhittable; that would defy the intent of the game. Slow-pitch softball, unlike its fast-pitch progeny, is designed to be a hitter's game. A strike out in slow-pitch is as rare as a triple play in baseball. Ms. Helmer wasn't striking batters out; she was getting them to make poor decisions.

"Come on, Mr. Mayor," I yelled as Mayor Urshan walked up to the plate. The Mayor's dark features glared out across the diamond as he positioned himself in the batter's box. The first pitch was outside. He did not swing.

"Watchgonnado, wait all day?" I taunted from left field as the second pitch left Ms. Helmer's hand.

Crack.

With a mighty swing of his aluminum bat, Urshan lofted the ball deep into left field.

Smack.

The ball landed in the webbing of my mitt, ending the inning.

"Good catch," Dr. White said.

As I passed the superintendent on the way to the dugout, I admired his neatly pressed jersey and shorts, an obvious bow to his former days as a shortstop in the highly competitive Duluth fast-pitch leagues.

"Got lucky. Another inch up the bat and that ball was outahere," I responded.

In the fourth inning, the School Board went up by three runs. Ms. Helmer continued to confound the police officers, street workers, and city councilors with her mixture of pitches.

The Mayor came up to bat for a second time. He leaned over home plate as if to claim ownership. He took a wild and mighty swing at an inside pitch and missed. His second effort resulted in a fly ball so far to the left of third base that it threatened a group of kids playing soccer on an adjacent field. The crowd, mostly spouses of the players, turned as if one in their seats to follow the high arching trajectory of the ball. The ball landed just short of the kids.

"Hey, Mr. Mayor, the field is this way," one of the School players yelled derisively.

Serious color flushed the batter's cheeks. The wind picked up, piling clouds above us in a towering cascade of gray. The Mayor raised his hand and stepped back. He adjusted the waist of his athletic shorts and leaned in. The pitcher reached back and tossed a high, fat inside pitch towards the catcher.

Rotating his feet and body towards third base, Urshan swung the bat in a low, powerful curve and connected with the ball before it crossed the front of home plate. I began my run towards the leftfield line long after I should have. The ball was headed over the fence. Just before the ball cleared the outfield, a fierce, ornery blast caught the ball and pushed it foul.

Relieved, Ms. Helmer threw an ugly, outside offering to the Mayor. Badly misjudging the arc of the pitch, he swung under the ball and popped it up to the third baseman, ending the inning. The Mayor looked out at the bases and realized he'd left two runs stranded. He slammed the handle of his bat into the dirt and walked back to the dugout.

In the seventh inning, a cagey relief pitcher for the City mesmerized us. We went down one, two, three waving uselessly at his spinning offerings. Despite the setback, we were ready to take to the field and preserve our three run lead. I was confident we'd hold on. Ms. Helmer was doing great. In the last two innings, the City hadn't scored. She was nearly unhittable.

Then I heard our team manager, Dr. White, utter these fateful words:

"Robyn, I'm gonna make a pitching change."

A male teacher strode to the mound with confidence as our star pitcher took a seat on the pine. The reliever tossed a couple of warm-ups towards my wife who was now catching.

"I'm ready to go," he announced.

I took up my position near the left field line. The first batter was confounded by the new pitcher's delivery. A quick scoop and a toss to first by Dr. White at short and we had our first out. A pop-up to first. Two out. One more and the game would be over.

The next two batters hit sizzling grounders past our infield. With two out and runners at first and second, Dr. White called time and approached the mound for a conference. After a brief discussion, play resumed.

An outside pitch drew no interest from the batter. An inside pitch was similarly ignored. It was clear that our relief man did not have the art of deception on his side. His third pitch, an obvious toss down the middle of the plate, met the barrel of the bat and erupted towards centerfield. Our centerfielder broke into a sprint, caught the ball on one hop off the dry grass and fired the ball to third. The runner held up, the bases were loaded. The Mayor came to bat.

0 for 2. The man was 0 for 2. But I knew what he was thinking:

"Gotta be just a little more patient. A little more bat, a little less pull. Give it a ride. Grand slam. We're outta here. End of story."

I looked at Ms. Helmer sitting in the dugout. I knew she had the Big Man's number. That wasn't going to do us much good now. I backed up as far as I could. The crowd cheered. Dr. White bent into a crouch at short, ready for a game-ending grounder. An ugly, terrible feeling ebbed into my gut as I watched the pitcher go into his windup.

Silver flashed in the big man's hands like a lightening bolt coming out of the stormy sky. The offering was at belt level and slightly inside, thrown right into the power of the man. I heard the resounding "ping" of metal against leather and I knew the ball would clear the fence, clear the swamp behind the fence and likely even clear City Hall.

Helpless, I turned my back on the field and watched the ball climb to the epiphany of its orbit before it came crashing back to earth.

THE HOCKEY PLAYER

The first thing I noticed about him was his hands. They were large, thick wristed, but soft. Then his nose. His nose plunged from between his eyes towards his mouth. There was no bone remaining where the bridge of his nose had been. The remainder of his face was rose colored and kind. Age lines crossed his forehead. Sparse wisps of hair, neatly combed, rested upon his scalp.

I sat in a restaurant booth with my wife. I was talking quietly to another lawyer at our table. The old man was in the booth in front of us. His head was tilted to the side so that he could hear our conversation.

We were talking hockey, not law. We were in Thunder Bay, Ontario and had just played in the Barrister's Cup Hockey Tournament. The lawyer across from me had fared worse than I had during the games. He was the Ramsey County goal tender. His chin bore seven stitches. The old man listened to us and smiled.

"Hockey players, eh? Who you play for?"

You could see the old man's wife, a cheerfully dressed woman in her early sixties, grimace at the question.

How was I supposed to answer him? Should I admit that the two games I'd played the day before were the first two ice hockey games I'd ever played in my life? To say I "played" hockey didn't ring true. The other attorney responded, sparing me any embarrassment.

"We played in a lawyer's tournament. Minneapolis, Duluth, Thunder Bay, and St. Paul all brought teams. I played for St. Paul."

The other barrister motioned towards me.

"He played for Duluth."

The goalie stood up from the table. The old man stared at the bandage on the tender's face.

"Stick to the chin, eh? Stitches?"

"Puck. Got up under my mask when I was down. Seven stitches."

"Used to stitch those up right on the bench. Hurts worse if they poke you with a needle first. Better without anything. Took lots of sticks to the face. Nine broken noses."

The old man's nose vouched for his statement. The attorney from St. Paul grimaced as he stared at the stranger's face.

"They used Novocain. It's fine. Something to talk about at the office tomorrow."

The lawyer reached down and picked up his infant daughter.

"Nice to meet all of you. I've got an eight-hour drive home. See Ya."

The old man turned around so that he could talk to me. There was much life, much character in his face. My wife and I stood up, intent upon leaving. On reflex, I extended my hand to the old man and introduced myself. His grip was firm but polite. He didn't try to crush my fingers in his hand. He smiled. His teeth were white and shiny and didn't appear to be original equipment.

"I'm from Port Arthur. Used to play some myself."

I took in the old man's broad shoulders and bowed calves. Age had not diminished his physical presence. I guessed that he'd played more than "some". His wife feigned disgust. Her eyes betrayed a sense of appreciation measured by years of sacrifice.

"Oh, don't get him going. He'll want to show you his trading cards."

"Trading cards?"

My interest grew. Who was he? When did he play? Who did he play for?

"I'd like to see them."

The woman's smile broadened. Her hand dug into her purse. She withdrew two cards encased in plastic and handed them to me. Rene' stood next to me, looking over my shoulder.

The cards were ancient. The pictures were black and white photos re-touched with oil paint, colorized like a Ted Turner movie. The face on each portrait was that of a man-child, a hockey player no more than 18 or 19 years old. The player's nose was full and smooth, without any evidence of fracture. The young man's hair was thick and youthful.

"Played for the Red Wings and the Black Hawks."

Our companion's voice was quiet, as if he'd been called back to a different time and place by the mere presence of the cards. His wife spoke:

"The Black Hawks card was just re-issued. Still gets four or five fan letters a week because of it."

I stared at the trading cards. I wondered if Dennis Rodman, Jack Morris, or Patrick Roy would ever look back at their lives in sports with the same breadth of pride the old man seemed to. I knew, at best, he'd probably made a few thousand dollars a year playing hockey. He'd played not for money but for the sake of the game itself.

They'd lived all over the United States and Canada. For parts of three decades, they continually moved their home, following his career. Even with the moves, they were often separated by his time on the road. During those lonely winter nights, she would sit next to the radio and listen to the games, cheering whenever his name was mentioned.

Some years, he played for minor league teams. Other years, he made it to the NHL. She showed me the ring he'd won as a member of a team from the 1950's that won the Stanley Cup.

"It's not as fancy as the rings they have now. No diamonds. Just a ring."

In my mind, I disagreed with her. I thought the beauty of the ring was that it mirrored the subtle strength and dignity of her husband.

"It was a pleasure to meet you both."

I handed the cards back to the woman. We left the couple to their hot coffee and memories. Retrieving our sons Chris and Dylan from the hotel pool, I felt as if I'd left something unfinished. I convinced Rene' we needed to go back to the restaurant.

The old man was just getting out of his booth. Six decades of hockey and life made his ascent from the bench seem labored.

"Mr. Woit, I'd like you to meet my sons Dylan and Christian. Dylan's a hockey player too."

A strong hand reached out to each of the boys in turn. I asked the old man's wife to show the boys the cards. Without hesitation, she produced them from her purse. The boys held the faded cards in their hands. They read the statistics.

With more penalty minutes than points, Benny Woit had never been a goal scorer like Brett Hull or Wayne Gretzky. Until that day, I, like most hockey fans, had never even heard his name. But none of that mattered. Standing next to the old man, it seemed clear that there's more to sports, more to living a life, than mere numbers.

"Mr. Woit is from Thunder Bay. He played hockey for the Red Wings and the Black Hawks. He played back in the days when they didn't wear helmets, when goalies didn't wear masks."

The old man grinned. A long, far away look enveloped his face. Perhaps, for an instant, as he stood talking to my sons, Benny Woit was once again a young man, with young legs, skating in the Stanley Cup Finals.

THE QUEST

"Do you have any maps of Lake County?" I ask a young woman behind a counter.

"Lots of 'em."

The clerk walks over to the wall and pulls open a large drawer in a filing cabinet.

"Help yourself."

I scan maps for the place I've heard about, Cloquet Lake, the place where the Cloquet River begins.

"Why are we going to the source of the River?" my oldest son asks as we leave the Two Harbors Holiday Station behind.

"I've always wanted to see where it starts," I explain.

"Why?" Matt prods, munching on a submarine sandwich, sipping on a Coke.

"I dunno. I just like to know where things start, I guess."

"You sure there are brook trout up there?" my son inquires between bites of bread and salami.

I'm quiet. "No," I admit to myself, "I'm not sure." I'd read something about brookies being planted in the brackish headwaters of the Cloquet River back in the 1930's. Something about a "fish car", a rail car that carried tanks of brook trout fry for planting in remote areas. But who had written it? Where had I read it? I don't recall.

"I read somewhere that there are supposed to be oodles of big ones up there. No one fishes 'em," I respond, trying to sound confident.

I glance in my son's direction. His eyes are riveted on the road. Lush forest, painted the vivid green of late summer, rushes past us. Intervals of dead birch, their tops rotted by disease, stand in contrast to the healthy, supple aspen crowding the highway corridor. We leave the blacktop and follow a well-graded gravel road.

"There it is," Matt points to a thin black ribbon of water emerging from a culvert beneath the roadway. I stop the van.

"Might as well give it a try," I offer, seeking to retain my confidence. I want to convince myself that somewhere in the dark water, fat trout, a generation away from human pursuit, wait for us.

"Are you sure about this, Dad?" the boy asks.

"Sure, the book..."

Before I can finish my response, Matt pulls up his waders and heads into the stream with his rod. The sun sits brutally high as I pack my wader pocket with tackle. Grasshoppers sing in the heat as I climb down the bank. Cool water rushes past my waders. I wade into a pool. God has handcrafted the place for brook trout. Gravel bottom. Low brush overhanging the edges of the stream. Still, I find no fish.

"What was the name of that book again, Dad?" the kid asks as we turn onto a minimum maintenance forest road. Neither of us prompted trout to rise from the depths of the water. I don't answer. A glance at the map makes it plain that Cloquet Lake is not the headwaters of the River. Katherine Lake is. We drive a primitive road through absent forest. Loggers have claimed any trees of value. Scrub balsam, spruce, and adolescent aspen cover the landscape.

I'd envisioned the source of our River to be a quiet, spring-fed wilderness pond protected by steep, rocky banks and towering white pines. In my mind's eye, incredible vistas define the path of the River as it tumbles southward over glacial boulders. The reality of the place causes disappointment.

Katherine Lake sits near the center of Lake County, Minnesota, miles from nowhere, surrounded by swamp. The terrain is uninteresting. There is no shoreline to the lake. Swamp grass yields to the depths, creating an illusion that the lake is a true body of water. In reality, Katherine Lake is but a sad teardrop set amidst miles of desolation.

A cottage occupies the lake's only island. The building is inaccessible by land. A foreign-made station wagon is parked on shore. The car is unlocked, an open invitation to mischief but our location is so far from anyone else, it's obvious the car's owner is playing the odds, odds which are long in his or her favor.

A trickle of water escapes the marsh bordering the southern limit of Katherine Lake. The creek winds and twists through reeds and cattails. An ancient, rusted culvert allows the beginning of the Cloquet River to cross under the road. "Cloquet Lake," a sign reads. We follow a pathway through cedar and spruce. Sunlight breaks through the forest to reveal a small campsite. A public boat launch allows access to Cloquet Lake. We exit the van and walk to the water's edge. The water is calm; the lake's surface is black and haunting.

"Cool," Matt whispers, tossing a stone into the rot-stained water.

Soft, thick clouds float above us. We stand silent, touched by peace.

"Doubt there are any fish in here."

I watch the wind gently sway stands of wild rice. The movement of the rice breaks up the monotony of the water.

"Too shallow. Might be good for duck hunting, though," I add.

"It's still pretty neat," Matt says reverently.

We drive away from the lake. The map indicates that the road we're on ends soon. The landscape changes. Our van plunges down a hill. At the bottom of the slope, a wide, slow moving stream meanders through broad marshlands. I sense that this is the real beginning of the Cloquet River. A primitive urge compels me to stop.

Removing my fly rod from its case, I toss a dew worm between lily pads. Matt stands at the rail of a planked bridge and watches me. The result of my effort is predictable. My son smiles as I break the rod down and put it away. He doesn't say anything as we enter the van and turn around.

We leave our destination, our quest partially fulfilled. Disappointment does not deter my resolve. I know, despite hard evidence to the contrary, that somewhere on the upper Cloquet River, brook trout wait for us.

THE QUEST-A REPRISE

We're parked just off the road. Rene's van is tucked into a small clearing. I've hooked and landed several dozen minnows in the river next to our campsite. I've also landed two brook trout. The minnows are larger than the trout. Matt is having similar luck.

An earlier trip to the source of the River was marginally successful. We found the headwaters of the Cloquet River. But we had also hoped to find brook trout of mythical proportions. We found no fish at the headwaters, at Katherine Lake. We found only a sense of desolation, desolation so strong that it forced us back to the North Shore, back to familiar country.

I'll admit it. I didn't spend sufficient time planning this trip. I didn't bring a tent. Before we left home, I removed the rear and middle seats from the van so that we'd have space for our sleeping bags. Looking at the cargo area as I roll out my bag, it's clear space is at a premium.

Outside, the late summer heat won't abate. The night air makes me sweat. I watch perspiration roll off Matt's temple as we try to eat our bratwurst, beans, and chips by the light of a battery-powered lantern. Swarms of insects taunt us.

"Let's hit the rack," I urge. As I speak, I swing wildly at a cloud of mosquitoes attacking my sweat-streaked hair.

"Sounds good to me," my oldest son replies.

With military precision, I open the sliding door and motion for him to jump in. I follow as quickly as my forty-something body permits.

"There are a billion skeeters in here," my son observes, disappearing beneath the fabric of his bedroll. He buries his head deep in rayon leaving his old man to battle the bugs.

"Thanks, Matt. You could've killed a few more," I remark, crushing dozens of mosquitoes against the windows.

"Nite, dad."

I continue to kill insects until I can no longer hear them droning in the dark. The air begins to chill. Our breath collects and turns to water on the windows. Matt's respiration's are loud and deep. I climb into the warmth of my sleeping bag. I attempt to dream of brilliantly colored trout rising from silver water. My son's snoring makes such dreams impossible. Somewhere between rest and deep sleep, I realize my bladder is full. I reach over and search for the door switch.

Tnnkkk.

The lock on the driver's side pops up. The lock on the passenger's door does not move. The lock is stuck in the "open" position and is disconnected from the exterior handle. The passenger side door can only be opened from the inside. I remember that the car is scheduled for repair next week. I climb over a bucket seat and exit out the driver's door.

"Where Ya going?" Matt asks.

"Outside. I gotta pee," I reply. Absent-mindedly, I lock the driver's side door.

I stand outside in my briefs and nothing else admiring the evening. The bugs are gone. Cool air has forced the humidity of the day out of the river bottom. Ground fog cloaks the road. I stand on chilly gravel. My task complete, I turn towards the van. My eyes adjust to the darkness. I watch as Matt exits the van and shuts the passenger door.

"Matt, don't...."

It's too late.

"What, dad?" the boy asks, his eyes barely open. I point the beam of my flashlight angrily at him.

"You just locked us out of the car."

"No way."

"Yep."

We pull and pry at the doors. The passenger-side door lock remains unlatched but the door can't be coaxed open.

The sound of another vehicle approaching causes me to seek the underbrush. I mull over asking for help as I shiver in my BVD's. Pride vetoes the idea. I let the pickup truck pass.

"What are you hiding for, Dad?"

I begin to shake.

"I don't see what's so funny. How're we gonna get back home?" I answer.

I begin to formulate a plan. Picking up a large rock, I walk over to the van and search for the pane of glass that will be the least expensive to replace.

"You're not serious. Mom'll kill you."

I know he's right. I drop the rock and wedge my fingers between the glass and the window frame on the sliding cargo door. The glass moves.

"I think I can pry it open."

"Don't break it."

"I won't."

I apply force. The latch is on the verge of yielding.

Snap.

Plastic flies past my ear. The window opens, allowing me to reach the door handle.

"What'd you do, Dad?"

"It's just a plastic latch," I opine. "Bring me the light."

Wearing only my underwear, I search for the pin that held the window latch together by crawling on my bare hands and knees across the stony ground.

154

"Here it is," I exclaim, holding up a small shard of metal between quivering fingers.

My son shakes his head. I thread the pin back into place and close the latch. We climb into the van and go back to sleep confidant in the knowledge that we're secure against the outside world. The next morning we drive home over back-roads.

"What're you going to tell mom?" Matt asks.

The unsecured window rattles. I pray that the latch holds. I visualize the pane of glass falling onto the road, shattering into a million pieces as it strikes the pavement.

"Nothing," I answer. "And neither will you."

Matt smiles.

"Anything you say, Dad."

My oldest boy has been around long enough to know that God allows secrets between a father and a son, secrets that shouldn't be shared with his mother.

PASSING OF THE LION

The year was 1993. My sons Matt, Dylan, and Chris, along with my wife Rene' and I were in the Twin Cities, on our way to visit friends in Chicago when I thought that my boys needed an impromptu civics lesson.

"Let's give Uncle Willard a call and see if he can get us in to watch the House in session," I urged Rene'.

"That sounds fun," my wife responded as she packed the last of our clothes into a suitcase as we prepared to leave our hotel.

"What we gonna do, Dad?" Matt, 13 years old at the time, queried.

"We're gonna visit Uncle Willard and watch the Legislature debate."

"Cool."

"What's the debate about?" our nine year old son Dylan asked.

"Who knows," I responded. "But wouldn't it be neat to see your Great Uncle in action? " I quipped.

Both boys nodded their heads in agreement.

"Is Willard in?" I asked when I called his office in St. Paul later that morning.

"He's down on the House floor. Can I help you?" his secretary responded.

"Sure. This is his nephew Mark from Duluth. I'm in town. I'd like to have my boys see their Great Uncle at work."

"I'll call him," the woman advised. "I'm sure he'll want to see you."

Twenty minutes later, Matt, Dylan, and I were standing on the floor of the Minnesota House of Representatives with Uncle Willard. Rene' and Christian watched from a gallery perched high above the crowd of politicians. We listened as speaker after speaker rose to voice support for or opposition to a bill. After one heated exchange, Matt turned to Willard and asked:

"Why don't those people agree with you?"

"Because they're foolish," Willard answered in his customary curt tone. There needed to be, in my uncle's estimation, no further explanation.

"Why don't they want poor people to have insurance?" Matt asked me as Willard turned to discuss a point with a colleague.

"I don't know Matt," I said. "Cost, I guess. There's only so much money in the State Budget. Maybe other things seem more important than medical care."

"It's time to vote," Willard said, standing next to me, a young man's mind in an 83-year-old body.

"You two are going to cast my vote," he chortled, motioning the boys to follow him.

Matt and Dylan positioned themselves in front of Willard's voting station. I watched from a distance. A huge electronic board began to light up with the votes of the House members. Red meant a "no" vote, a vote against the bill's passage. Green meant a "yes" vote; a vote in support of the bill becoming law. I didn't need to guess what color would appear next to the name "Munger" on the board. All the same, I held my breath. I prayed that Dylan and Matt would push the right button.

My boys smiled wide as their great uncle pointed to the board. Suddenly, a green light sputtered then glowed next to the name "Munger". Thanks to the integrity and dedication of a life-long public servant, many disadvantaged people in the State of Minnesota became eligible for health care coverage that day. Thanks to Willard, my boys were an integral part of the MinnesotaCare vote, though their names do not appear in the official roll call of the House of Representatives.

Today, the Cloquet River flows by our home, its waters swollen and engorged by two weeks of torrential rain. I know I'm fortunate. There are few places on the River that one can still build a home. And I've learned, in planning to build our new house that many protections and restrictions apply to our property. Some say this shouldn't be. Some say that the banks of our lakes and rivers should be developed by who ever wants to do so, in whatever fashion the owners deem appropriate.

The dean of the Minnesota environmental movement, the lion of the wilderness, would disagree. He would say that our children and our children's children need wild places, that all of us need access to forests, prairies, streams, and lakes that have not been used to exhaustion. As I sit next to the boiling water of the River, I seek solace. I am haunted by his eyes.

It's funny. Until I stood over him in the hospital saying goodbye I didn't know the color of Uncle's Willard's eyes. Having looked into them intently for the first time in our relationship, I cannot forget them. Even at the last, Willard's eyes reflected a bright and brilliant blue, the color of Lake Superior, another body of water he fought desperately to preserve.

Staring into those eyes, I told my uncle that I loved him. I told him that he had done well. He smiled weakly and fell asleep. Two days later, he passed away.

State Representative Willard Munger will be remembered by many people for many things. My children will remember him as the Great Uncle who let them vote on the floor of the Minnesota House of Representatives. I'll remember him as the man who saved our River.

A COACH'S TALE

(In Memory of Coach Pat Andrews)

He shuffles across the hard ice of the outdoor rink. His black rubber overshoes are unzipped. The uppers of his boots flop with each step. A battered hockey stick, the old kind, the kind made of wood, fits snugly in his gloved hand. He relies upon the stick to keep his balance.

"Smurf, get up off the ice. Go after the puck," the man says in a gruff voice. The words flow out from beneath a well-trimmed mustache.

A dozen or so Squirt B hockey players, boys 9 and 10 years old, skate lazily under the glow of floodlights. Some skate with cautious, wobbly steps. Others, like his son, the one he calls "Smurf", skate with strength. The names of the boys are familiar. Allen. Jason. Patrick. Michael. Matt. Tim. Chris.

He doesn't look like a hockey player. He can't skate. He's short and can't hear well. In fact, he wears a hearing aid. But the kids listen to their coach. Their attention hangs on his every word. They work hard at every drill. He's toughest on his own son. The boys see that and don't complain because he's fair.

Because they are Squirts, nearly all of their practices are outside. I stand next to the boards in my Sorels sipping hot coffee. Steam from the Styrofoam cup circles lazily into the February night. I watch the coach stop my son and explain something to him. There's no yelling. There's no chastisement. He is the teacher and the boys are his students.

Tonight, we sit on freshly lacquered benches in the New Barn, the new Cloquet Arena. The Hermantown Hawks have been behind for most of the game. Late in the third period, they tie the score. With only minutes to go in regulation, the possibility of overtime looms large.

I look out across the ice at the young men wearing blue, yellow, and white. Not so long ago, they were Squirts learning how to play hockey in the open air of the country. Now they're high school seniors, nearly grown men, playing inside a magnificent new arena for the sectional championship.

With a man advantage, our kids fail to hold the zone. The puck squirts free and rolls. A Proctor forward races to center ice and draws the puck in. He crosses the blue line with one of our defensemen trailing him. The puck explodes towards our goal. It bounces off the goaltender's leg pad and slides harmlessly away. A battle ensues along the boards. A referee's whistle stops play. A penalty is called against the Proctor Rails. There is less than a minute to play.

I don't know if any of the others see him. I don't know if anyone in the crowd recognizes him. Down low, just outside the face-off circle, he stands, big as life, giving his players encouragement. He's wearing his overshoes and his bakery uniform. He holds the old wooden stick in one hand. Its blade rests on the face-off dot. How he got out onto the ice, how he got passed the troopers and cops, I don't know.

Thirty seconds to play in regulation. I keep my eye on the man. He doesn't move. I wonder why the officials haven't stopped the game to get him off the ice. The puck goes out to the point. A hard shot deflects off the Proctor goaltender into a corner. A pass finds its way out to the left of the goalie and onto a Hermantown stick. Caught in the middle of the play, the man in the overshoes doesn't move. The distraction caused by the apparition allows the boy to break free of the defense, to find space to set up. The puck glides true across the front of the goal.

"Shoot from the pass," the boy hears his father say. "One-time it," the man whispers.

Thousands of shots over a decade of time have prepared the son for this moment. Instinctively, the winger hoists the puck towards an opening. The red light flickers, then comes on. Time expires. The game is won.

From the bench, blue, yellow, and white uniforms cascade onto the ice in celebration. Gloves, helmets, and sticks fly through the air. Coaches smile and pat each other on the back. The Hawk Band breaks out in the school rouser. Fans cheer and clap as the players roll around on the ice in a mass of unbridled joy.

Down in the Proctor zone, defeated players kneel in agony. Their season is over. The Proctor players think victory was in their grasp. They believe they let triumph slip away. They're wrong. Victory didn't escape the Rails. The little coach in the rubber overshoes did them in.

THE MIRACLE OF THE RED SHOES

I watched his downcast, hound-dog body language as the boy walked away from the soccer field. I followed the slow, heavy-footed progress of his spikes across the muddy turf. I leaned against the hood of my pickup truck and studied my oldest son.

"How was practice?"

"I'm going to quit. Coach hates me," he responded, poison coating the words.

"What are you talking about?"

"He doesn't think I work hard enough. I'm doing the best I can but it just isn't good enough. I'm gonna quit."

My son stopped next to me and avoided direct contact with my eyes as I scrutinized him. Dirt and mud covered the blue and white of his stockings. His burly knees and thighs were bruised from the abuse of playing soccer in October in Northern Minnesota. His new shoes, highlighted with red stitching, sank into the grass as Matt nervously shifted his weight.

"That wouldn't be too smart. You're a senior. You've been on the team since 10th grade," I said, trying to instill a importance of commitment without using the word.

"So what? I don't play that much. And when I do, like against East, the next game, I'm back riding the bench."

I thought about talking to his coach. My dad would have done that for me when I was a benchwarmer back in high school on the varsity football team. In fact, he did do it. And I resented the intervention. I hated the fact that, at seventeen, I wasn't given enough credibility by my father to fight my own battles. Would Matt feel any different if I stepped into the fray on his account?

"I hate to see you quit with playoffs coming up. You've put so much time and effort into soccer. Hell, you've done a lot more in soccer than I ever did in football."

It was true. I'd started playing football as a sophomore to get a closer look at the cheerleaders. By the time I was a senior, the cheerleaders were still doing their thing and I was still riding the pine. Matt had been given an opportunity to actually play his chosen sport, albeit not as much as he felt he deserved. He had a leg up on the old man, even if he wasn't in the mood to admit it.

"There's no use in staying on the team. I'm not gonna get to play much," he lamented.

"There are probably reasons why others are playing in ahead of you. Speed, ball-handling skills, effort. I'm not the coach so I can't make those calls. But I still think it'd be a mistake for you to give up with the season nearly over, especially in your senior year."

I stared at the boy. He raised his face so that I could see his fierce brown eyes, eyes clearly steeled against my logic. I knew that a direct approach was doomed.

"Why don't you talk to Mack?" I suggested, referring to a long-time friend and assistant coach. "He'll tell it to you straight."

"I'll think about it."

The lights of Corey Veech Field blazed white against the autumn sky. Down on the field, the Hermantown Hawks, my son's team, battled the Cloquet Lumberjacks. Despite a disparity in talent, Cloquet clung tenaciously to a 1-1 tie late in the second half of the soccer match. A large crowd occupied the bleachers, urging the hometown Hawks to bear down and put the game away. Mack took the time to talk to me before the game.

"He'll be fine. I think I got him settled down. He's starting tonight," the Assistant Coach said.

"Thanks," I replied. "I didn't want to see him hang it up."

"I told him to make the most of it," Mack replied. "Those new shoes seem to have given him a fresh outlook. He can really nail the ball with those things."

As the game extended, Hermantown pressed but could not score. An upset was in the wind.

A Cloquet defender sent the ball over the end line, preventing a certain goal. The crowd stood and began to exhort the Hawks. Over the public address system, I heard my son's name:

"Number 38, Matt Munger, is lining up to take the corner kick," the announcer proclaimed.

Matt never took corner kicks. One of the regular starters, one of the more talented players, was always called upon to do the job, to set the ball down on the corner of the field and loft the orb towards the opposing goal. I was dumbfounded that my son was being given the honor of taking a corner kick in a crucial playoff game.

I dug my hands into my jacket pockets and prayed. My plea was that my son would kick the ball high, clean, and hard. I knew my prayer was selfish, the kind of petition that God rarely grants. It didn't matter. Only my wife, Mack, and I knew how important the kick was to my oldest son. Years of self-doubt would be magnified or reduced by the simple flight of a leather ball across the October sky.

Matt positioned the ball in the left corner. The sleek fabric of his gold and blue uniform caught the lights and shimmered as he moved. He raised his left hand, stepped back and took aim. Keeping his head down, bearing down hard, he stepped into the sphere and launched it over the wet grass of the field.

The Cloquet goalie crowded the near post as the ball ascended. Hawk forwards sped towards the net, jostling with defenders for position as the ball began its decline. There was a suggestion of a hook as the soccer ball sailed above the penalty square. As the player's fought for space in front of the goal, the ball turned sharply in the air, propelled by a defiant spin. The goalie set up to receive the kick. Offensive players shoved and pushed but could not break through to the net.

There are moments in life when reality slows as if preserved on film. Matt's corner kick is one of those moments. As the tender's gloved hands sought to control the spinning leather, as he stretched to the limits of his height, the unexpected happened. The ball skipped off the goalie's hands and landed smartly in the net.

My son's right fist rose triumphantly in the night air as he ran onto the field and met his teammates in front of the despondent Cloquet defenders. He looked up at the stands and found his parents. His mouth broke into a wide grin as the sweaty arms of his teammates embraced him.

After the game, I walked across soggy field towards Mack, intent on giving him my thanks. The Assistant Coach's grin was broader than my son's.

"That was one hell of a kick," my son's mentor observed. "Those shoes are really something."

I stopped my friend and corrected his perception:

"It wasn't the shoes, Mack. It was the heart."

A COUNTRY POND

When we bought the old Drew place, we didn't even know the pond was there.

At first glance, it doesn't look like much. If you're lucky and you lace up your skates in early November, you'll find our pond marginally skateable. But once the snow starts, our pond's surface becomes a challenge for even the most skilled athlete. To the casual observer, our pond, like a lot of things in life, seems flawed.

It's obvious that our pond is the creation of man. Its banks display the scars of a backhoe's handiwork. The creek that winds its way under the Taft Road and through the cedar swamp bordering our land is too lazy, too slow, to carve earth and form a pond on its own. One of the farm's prior owners, maybe Frank Kaneski, maybe Gerald Drew, or maybe someone we don't have any record of, gave the creek a hand. And so, a pond was born.

In some mysterious way, the quiet solitude one experiences when skating the creek bottom nurtures visions of a lost age, the age of the Ojibwa and the fur trade. Time spent on the pond during the deep cold of winter draws out a yearning for something that's past, of dreams left unfulfilled.

When my oldest son Matt was born, the thrill of America's Olympic hockey victory over the USSR and Finland took Minnesota by storm. As I watched the team's victory parade wind through downtown Minneapolis a world of possibilities seemed to loom in the future for my first-born son. Those were Minnesota boys who won that gold medal. Someday, he could be one of them.

As soon as Matt could walk, he was on skates. In our first years on the farm, we trudged across the pasture, shovels in hand, to clear the pond of snow. We fought the bitter wind and the unrelenting cold as well as the unpredictable onset of December thaws. Regardless of our efforts, nature inevitably tortured the early ice of November into layers of delicate, fragile crust. Despite imperfect conditions, Matt and I both learned how to skate. He was five. I was 29. In time, Dylan and Chris also learned to skate on the difficult ice of our farm pond.

Not so long ago, beaver moved in and built a dam across the creek. Their flawless engineering amplified the natural structure of the pond. The ice became smoother but it still wasn't perfect. It couldn't match what town had to offer.

When Matt became involved in organized hockey, he played and practiced outdoors. Then an arena was built. There was little reason for teams to play outside. Inside the new arena, there was no snow to shovel, no insufferable cold to contend with. The ice was perpetually smooth.

In time, our pond saw fewer and fewer kids using its ice. The pool's limited size and flawed surface couldn't compare with the manmade ice left by a Zamboni. There were no boards. We only had one net. Pucks sailed off the bumpy ice into the snow, never to be found again. Pressure ridges and beaver holes interrupted the continuity of the pond's surface. You had to be careful where you skated. The creek bottom ceased to echo with laughing voices. The pond sat vacant, waiting patiently for the boys to return. But the kids were in town, at the arena where everything was perfect.

A few weeks ago, hockey ended for our family. Eleven years of playing, running, fighting, arguing, driving, spending, cheering, crying, agonizing, worrying, counseling, and laughing came to a halt. A combination of things caused our involvement in the sport to cease. There was no one cause and no one is to blame.

The other day, reflecting on a winter without hockey, I walked down to our pond and stared out across the flawed ice. I'd come to the place where hockey began in our family. I'd come to question whether I'd done right by my sons. I asked myself whether I had fallen prey to a subtle desire to see my boys achieve something in their youth that I'd never achieved in mine. Had I tried to reshape my own childhood by living through them? I had no answer for my own questions.

A flock of Whistlers flew in. The duck's arrival was announced by the considerable speed of their wings. In unison, the ducks landed. The birds settled in open water near where the outlet of the creek joins the River. In the distance, the sun dropped behind the horizon, allowing shadows to form across the layered snow. Watching the sunset, I realized that I'd done the best I could as a father. I realized that, despite my fears, my boys know that as well. They'll be back, with or without hockey, to skate with their dad on the pond.

A VERY LONG FALL

You may or may not know that Rene' and I are once again proud parents. In the aftermath of my wife's 40th birthday and nearly ten 10 years after the birth of our third son Christian, Jack Bridger Munger was born. Jack is the caboose on our train of four sons.

Matt, our oldest son, was entering his senior year at Hermantown High School when Jack came into our lives. Dylan, the next boy in the Munger pecking order, was 13. Christian, as I said, was nearly 10. Rene' and I had been in the "discussion" stages of planning to have another child when God decided to make the plans operational.

Even with our past track record of three pregnancies and three healthy births, Jack's arrival proved to be less than optimal. Each of the other boys had arrived through technology. Labor was induced because the stubborn little buggers didn't want to exit the womb.

"When do you want to have the baby?" the doctor would ask.

"As soon as possible," my very large wife would say.

"How about next Tuesday?"

"Sounds good," I'd interject.

With Christian there were a few false alarms. One late-night trip to St. Mary's interrupted a quiet evening at the movies.

"Mark, I'm starting to get labor pains," my wife whispered to me in the inky blackness of the theater.

"Can't you wait until the movie is over?" I asked, intent on catching the conclusion of the film, which just happened to be *Baby Boom* starring Diane Keaton.

"This can't wait," Rene' replied, her voice becoming stern. "We have to leave now."

"Are you sure it's not a false alarm?" I questioned, just a hint of pleading in my voice. "The movie's almost over."

"Now," she said, struggling to rise from the hard plastic of the theater seat. "We have to leave now."

Of course I was right. We sat at the hospital, monitors hooked up to my wife, waiting for the miracle of spontaneous birth. It never happened. We made an appointment for Christian to be born by inducement two weeks later.

"Mark..." a nervous voice called out early one morning. "Mark..." The voice pleaded. "It's time."

My eyes were heavy with sleep. I thought I was dreaming. I looked at the clock. It was 6:00 AM. Rene' wasn't in bed. Something was amiss.

"Mark.... We've gotta go."

Sure enough, it happened. During my wife's fourth pregnancy, she finally followed the script. Rene's water broke. I won't share with you my entire bad behavior that morning as I careened around the house, a man out of control. All the logical thinking, all of my maturity was lost as I yelled, screamed, chased our older boys, and generally made a fool of myself. Thankfully my mom came over to take care of getting them off to school.

From the way Jack's story began, I knew I was in trouble. I mean, having lost all common sense the morning of his birth, I figured the rest of the ride was going to be bumpy. But you know what? It hasn't been. Because Rene' and I are older, we have infinitely more patience in dealing with Jack. At least that was true until last Sunday, up until the Very Long Fall.

I was somewhere in another galaxy when he started to scream. It is incomprehensible how a 17-month-old child weighing little more than 20 pounds can emit such a loud, piercing, wail. But he can. And he did.

"I'm gonna go get him and bring him to bed with us," Rene' remarked in her most maternal tone.

"Sure," I mumbled, turning my back to her spot in our bed. I listened as her bare feet trod down the hallway. Jack held his breath for what seemed to be a minute or more. I could feel the anticipation of his next scream beating against my temple as the silence extended.

"Lay down, Jack...", my wife admonished, placing the toddler between us.

"Awwwldone," Jack whispered. I felt his tiny hands exploring the hair at the base of my neck. His body tossed and turned. His feet pushed hard against my flank, nudging me out of near sleep.

"I'm gonna go downstairs," I declared, my words edged with annoyance.

Before Rene' could say anything, I threw off the quilt and stumbled out of the bedroom. The hallway was dark. I fumbled for the light switch but couldn't find it. I began to descend the stairs. I encountered the landing mid-way down the decline. My bare feet sank briefly into the carpet of the last set of stairs. Sleep on the couch beckoned.

And then, I was soaring. Not with the grace of a finely winged eagle caught in a draft. More like a loon flapping and struggling to make altitude before the end of the water. My foot pulsed in pain as it caught something near the bottom of the stairs and propelled me through the night. My arms flailed to either side, reaching for something solid to latch onto.

My left hand raced along the banister, probing, searching as my body fell. The fingers of my hand circled the large balustrade at the bottom of the railing. With all of my strength, I grasped the

166

smooth wooden ball and dug in. The balustrade pulled loose, just like in the movie *It's a Wonderful Life*, and I plunged towards the carpet.

As I cleared the top of the child-gate, my right foot struck a fence. Instead of landing safely on the carpet, my body twisted in mid-air. I came down hard on the last stair. Then the balustrade landed, striking me at the base of my right eye where the fine bones of the socket form a ledge. My face went numb as the wooden ball bounced off my cheekbone, grazed the top of my head, and came to rest on the carpet.

"Who in God's name left this _ _ _ _ gate on the stairs?" I roared.

"What's wrong, Mark?" Rene' responded from the warmth of our bed.

"I just tripped over the gate," I reiterated, sitting in the dark, rubbing my face. I noticed my toes were scrapped and bleeding. I couldn't see the blood: I felt it dripping onto our off-white carpeting.

"Are you all right?" my wife asked, her words quiet.

"No, I'm not all right," I responded. "I'm gonna sleep on the couch."

Then it hit me. I was the last person up the stairs. I'd stepped over the gate on my way to bed and had left the offending object in place.

"I wish you people would remember to put things away," I mumbled as I removed a blanket from the downstairs linen closet. But Jack and Rene' were already asleep and ignorant of my recriminations.

As I reclined on the couch and pulled the quilt over my burning cheek, I pondered the question of the moment:

Is a lie still a lie when no one is awake to hear it?

ANOTHER WINTER

The thermometer on the big spruce tree outside our kitchen window reads nineteen below zero. It's only November and the house is already filled with cold. An early winter snow has drifted over the driveway. Though we can negotiate the residue of the storm in our vehicles, the ruts will freeze if I don't get out and plow soon.

The kids and Rene' are off doing other things. I sit at a pine table staring out an arched window. The table, which was Rene's Grandmother's, has been with us for the duration of our marriage. We spent more money having the table refinished than it will ever be worth, but you can't always measure the worth of things, or people for that matter, by what others think.

I should be out shoveling. Instead, because it's Sunday, I listen to my new son Jack's exhalations. He's asleep on a blanket by my feet. While I listen to the delicate pattern of Jack's breathing, I try to work on my novel. It's a book that I started seven years ago. I had a publisher for it. The publisher went bankrupt. Now I'm on my own, fine-tuning the prose, hoping that someone else will be as excited about the book as I am.

The day draws to a close. The light fades and Jack stirs. I pick him up and talk to him. Not silly stuff like Rene' does. My theory is that you should use large words and a deep voice with infants so they'll recognize authority. "Goo goos" and "gee gees" don't cut it. I slip up. I find myself talking gibberish to the baby as Rene' and the boys come in.

"How's it going?", my wife asks, her voice hoarse due to a severe case of laryngitis.

"Fine. I just fed and changed him."

"I can see that. The label on the onesy goes in the back."

My wife pulls out the cotton tab under Jack's chin.

"I don't think he minds," I reply defensively.

"No, but it reflects badly on me if someone sees it."

After dinner, my parenting skills no longer in question, I find a pair of wool socks and pull them over my bare feet. Walking through the house in my long underwear, I pass Christian. He's sitting at the kitchen table complaining he's too full to eat any more. Resisting an urge to remind him about starving kids in Africa, I retreat to the basement.

By the light of a single bulb in our utility room, I step into my blue and white bib overalls. The waist seems a little more snug, the buttons a little more stressed, the denim, a little thinner than last year. I force my arms into the sleeves of my fatigue jacket. Though it's been sixteen years since boot camp, the jacket looks brand new. I cover my head with a rabbit-skin cap and pull the flaps of the hat snugly over my ears. I slide a pair of choppers over my hands to complete my stylish outfit.

Our 1962 International 606 is stubborn and refuses to turn over in the frigid air of the barn. Though I hooked a battery charger up to the vehicle before it snowed, my efforts to start the tractor drain the battery. I re-connect the charger and climb back on the machine. The vinyl seat emits a "crack" as I sit down. All three of our horses clamber into the barn and stare at me from behind a gate. Their large eyes plead with me for grain. I ignore them and concentrate on the International.

Brmmmmmmmmm..pop..Brmmmmmmmmm...pop....Brmmmm mmm.

The engine repeatedly starts and dies. It finally catches but runs at too high an idle. I push the accelerator lever forward, finding a comfortable pitch, shove the choke half way in, and climb down. I know that the tractor, like myself, is mature. Both of us need a little time to warm up.

Pushing snow with the bucket, the chains of the big rear tires slap in unison against the packed snow. I watch my ten-year-old son dodge behind the banks I'm creating. I know what will come next. A chunk of frozen water flies through the night air but falls short of the tractor. The ice ball bursts into blue shards.

"Ya missed, me, Chris," I tease.

Another chunk leaves a small gloved hand.

Splat.

The missile hits my neck. Pieces of snow and ice infiltrate my clothing and sting bare skin.

"Not this time, Dad."

"You must wanna die young, kid," I threaten, turning the tractor away from his barrage.

I leave the artificial light of the house and plow in darkness. Somewhere ahead of me, the open water of the Cloquet River threads its way through whitened ground. The moon is absent. Only the distant cool glimmer of silver stars punctures the evening. The old tractor churns forward, pushing a pile of snow in its bucket.

At the intersection of our driveway and the Taft Road, I draw a metallic lever towards me. The bucket tilts. With patience learned from past mistakes, I pull another lever to raise the scoop. The hydraulics groan in the cold.

Engaging in a process that will be repeated over and over until the driveway is free of snow, I manipulate the levers and extend the arms of the loader. The cylinders stretch to maximum reach and dump the load of snow, creating an ever-higher bank for kids to play on.

The 606 bounces towards the barn. I sense that my task, my chore, is a link to the real farmers, the real ranchers who inhabit snow country. I envision that somewhere out in Western Minnesota a dairy farmer is counting on an old International or an old John Deere to make it through another winter and I wonder if that farmer has to dodge errant snowballs when he plows his driveway.

FISHING THE BETSY

Brown water catches the embrace of an overhanging cedar bough. The branch bobs. I'm standing chest deep in the river's grip protected from the water's cold by thin synthetic material. Above and below my position, along both sides of the sandy banks of the stream, dozens of fishermen stand in virtual silence. We're all waiting for steelhead, migratory rainbow trout. The fish are supposed to be here by the thousands, seeking gravel beds in the swift water to procreate. Instead, there are only redhorse suckers, an undesirable rough fish, invading the river.

For years I've heard my father speak in reverent tones about the Betsy. I've seen photographs taken over his twenty or more seasons of fishing the river. Every year that he's made the twelve-hour drive to Beulah, Michigan, he's caught fish. Except this year, the year I decided to come with. This year, Grandpa Harry got skunked.

It's a long drive to Southern Michigan from Northern Minnesota. My father, his pal Bruce, and I packed our gear into my dad's Tahoe and headed out early Saturday morning with hours of road ahead of us. Because it is March, winter in Northwestern Wisconsin and the Upper Peninsula of Michigan is clearly on the decline. The snow banks lining the two-lane highway out of Bruce Crossing, a little hamlet located in Northern Michigan that offers visitors the choice of driving towards Marquette or Houghton, were half their former size, full of roadside debris and sand.

Our travels took us through the hardwoods of Northern Michigan, past the rough eastern coastline of Lake Superior, until we climbed the massive span of the Mackinaw Bridge, the only physical link between the part of Michigan that cheers for the Green Bay Packers and the rest of the State. Hundreds of feet below, water lapped against the concrete supports of the roadway, reminding me that my wife, a person not given to seeking out heights, would not enjoy driving over Mackinaw Straights.

To pass the time in the car, we listened to Walter Cronkite's memoirs on audiotape. It was necessary to supply something to listen to since every radio station along the way seemed to be dedicated to Patsy Cline and Waylon Jennings.

"I don't think I'm going to be able to ice fish this trip," Bruce observed, noting the lack of snow and ice on the Lower Peninsula side of the bridge.

"How's that?" I asked, somewhat puzzled since I wasn't aware we'd be doing anything but steelhead fishing.

"Bruce likes to go perch fishing on the little lakes near the Betsy," my father said. "I'm not quite sure why."

My dad is a rainbow trout fanatic. He'd stand in a river twenty-four hours a day if his seventy-three-year-old legs would let him. There was a hint of sarcasm to his words as he chided his buddy for seeking perch, fish that most Minnesotans toss back when fishing for walleyes, instead of trout.

"Harry, they're great eating. Jumbo perch like the ones I catch here aren't easy to come by."

Our destination was a small Ma and Pa motel standing within a stone's throw of the Betsy River: pretty meager digs when you consider that, as we passed through Traverse City, we marveled at row upon row of million-dollar-plus vacation and retirement homes lining the shoreline of Grand Traverse Bay.

When the alarm went off this morning, I left our cottage just after 6:00am. My dad was already on the river. Bruce continued to sleep.

Negotiating the river, I try to find spots that look like they harbor trout. My task is made difficult because the water is low and there are more folks fishing than there are good spots to wet a line. When I do find a place to try my luck, I catch sucker after sucker, never hooking a game fish. Each of the ugly rough fish provides a transitory thrill at the instant of attack: a thrill that quickly abates once the steady telltale pull of the sucker's effort is established. But it's a great week to be outside. The sun climbs high. A ceiling of sea-foam blue soars above the valley. Though white clouds sometimes race across the horizon, they never gather to form a front.

Upstream, a middle-aged woman stands in a pool tossing wet flies and streamers into the current. I marvel at her graceful approach to the sport. I'm unschooled in fly-fishing and generally end up wrapping my flies around tree limbs whenever I take a stab at using them.

The woman's hair, mousy brown turning gray at the temples, is tucked under a baseball cap. She stands knee deep in smooth water, water distinctly different in hue from that of the trout streams of the North Shore of Lake Superior.

Behind us, the forest clearly demarcates our geography. There are stands of oak and maple, hardwoods that aren't found in abundance in my part of the Midwest. Here and there, a cedar offers contrast to the grays and browns of the landscape. The leaves on the deciduous trees are still several weeks from breaking out.

"Fish on," the woman cries out.

Her rod bends and her reel whines as the fish, obviously not a sucker, seeks freedom. The angler cautiously follows the fish downstream. The woman's course brings her to an overturned stump in the middle of boiling water. It's clear to me that the steelhead is intent upon seeking refuge in the twisted roots of the cedar.

"I'll get him," I offer, resting my rod against the hollow trunk of a dead oak.

The woman raises her rod and controls the fish. I wade into the water. The stream's grip is forceful. I feel cold through the neoprene of my waders as I reach behind me for my landing net.

"Wait a sec while I ease him out from under that branch."

The angler doesn't divert her eyes from her rod as she speaks. Her voice is authoritative. I hang back until she persuades the fish to turn up river.

"Now."

A flash of chrome darts across my boots. I dip the net into the river and capture the fish. The woman slides over to where I'm standing and retrieves the steelhead from my net.

"Thanks."

She gently lifts the fish, a small rainbow trout that has lost its brilliant colors while living in Lake Michigan between spawning runs, from the mesh. With expert tenderness, the woman removes the streamer from her prey's mouth and releases the juvenile fish into the Betsy.

Later, as the sun fades over the hills and silent oaks standing to the west, I lean against the railing of a small concrete dam blocking the river. Behind the man-made barrier, the stream forms a pond, a momentary delay in the water's rush to Lake Michigan.

"Not many fish in the river," my dad remarks as he joins me. "They're spawning in small numbers. Got real warm in January, way too early. They've been running ever since."

"How'd you do?" I ask.

"Hooked a couple, didn't land any. How 'bout you?'

"Suckers. Dozens of suckers. I only saw one steelhead caught all day. I helped a lady land it."

"Any size?"

"Small. She threw it back."

"There's one."

My father points to a pewter missile struggling against the water spilling over the precipice of the artificial falls. A steelhead, compelled by ancient desires, tries to attain the calm relief of the pond just beyond the lip of the dam.

"Let's go see what Bruce wants to do for supper," my dad suggests.

"I'll be along in a minute."

My old man walks towards the cabin in opposition to the night's approach. Though we will fish for the better part of a week, none of us puts any trout in the cooler. Somehow, it really doesn't seem to matter.

SPRING WALK

My wife Rene' and I walk side by side over the pavement of the Taft Road. Jack, our six-month-old son, looks out at the newness of spring from deep within the three-wheeled cart that I'm pushing.

I didn't enjoy the false promise of this past winter. A warm January and February, a lack of snow, the unpredictability of it all was unnerving. Winter in Northeastern Minnesota is defined by storms, by below zero temperatures, and by mornings that beg for an extra layer of clothing. Not this year.

The spring sun warms our faces as we walk. Having escaped the brutal touch of ordinary winter, I want to deny the sun's impact on my soul. I want to proclaim the falseness of the day. I cannot.

Car after car passes us as we stroll together along the gravel shoulder of the road. Rene' and I speculate as to what the "Townies" are up to.

"Must be checking their cabins," Rene' postulates.

"Probably taking a look at the ice, trying to figure out when it will go out," I reply.

We walk by the house of a neighbor who recently died. Despite the fact that we've lived on adjoining land for over 14 years, I didn't know the man. In the country, geographic closeness does not always translate into friendship.

"I wonder who's at his house?" I ask absently, noting there is a vehicle parked next to his tidy doublewide. "Maybe a son or daughter," I suggest.

"Maybe," Rene' replies mutely.

Jack leans to one side. His body is suspended between nylon straps. My wife leans forward and looks into the cart.

"He's asleep," she reports.

"Seems like the smart thing to do," I offer.

Silently, I contemplate how nice a nap in the sun on our couch would be.

"He's snoring," Rene' remarks, slowing her pace.

"Just like mom," I tease.

"Keep the critique to yourself, Mr. Munger," my wife says.

Crows fly low, propelled by wind. The breeze is warm. A yellow caution flag attached to Jack's cart flaps annoyingly in my face.

"Poor design," I observe aloud, pushing the fabric away from my eyes.

"Maybe it's designed for taller men," Rene' says, striking a retaliatory blow.

We turn onto the Fish Lake Dam Road. We leave the blacktop and traverse rough gravel. An abandoned tavern, its windows covered by plastic, stands near the edge of the road. The vinyl rustles as captive air strains against staples anchoring the plastic to the building.

Walking past the bar calls to mind an evening from the past I spent with Matt, my oldest son, when he was still in elementary school. One winter night we walked to the tavern to watch a hockey game on the Inn's satellite dish. We shared a frozen pizza. Matt had a Coke and I sipped tap beer. At the end of the game, we pulled on our winter coats and walked home through an evening punctuated by beautiful stars.

The dish has long since been removed. The bar stands empty. I draw no symbolism from the vacancy of the building. It's simply closed.

A heavy residue of road sand lines the ditches. Yellow marsh grass and cattails poke through the debris. Despite the dirt in the channels, clear water, released by the melt of the sparse snowfall, courses downhill. The temporary stream bubbles and boils as it seeks union with Fish Lake.

Rene' was pregnant last summer. We haven't walked this road for over a year. Unexpectedly, the landscape opens before us. Where the path once abutted white pines and cedars rising on either side, the forest has retreated from the road. Here and there, sentinel pines remain, standing tall and alone along a freshly excavated right-of-way.

Jack wakes. He stretches his tiny arms and legs as we approach the still-frozen lake. Signs of activity clutter the parking lot of the resort that is our destination. Docks, vehicles, boats, and outboard motors await attention. The sun's reflection off the ice makes it hard to see. I shade my eyes with my hand. Jack squirms. The strength of the sun forces him to turn his head. I reposition the cart so that the sun doesn't strike his face. The child's eyes open and stare absently at the unfamiliar place.

"I should've put his cap on," Rene' laments.

Before I can respond, a high-pitched cry pierces the quiet.

"Peep...Peep..."

We strain to locate the source of the call. The sky is vacant. Only the spring sun hangs over the bare maples of the far shore.

"Osprey," I whisper.

My wife nods in agreement.

"It won't be long before the ice is out," I offer.

A ribbon of black water shifts uneasily between landfall and receding ice. Small waves gnaw at the hardened lake.

"Not long at all," my wife responds.

We turn and walk away from the resort. The wheels of the cart bounce over the uneven surface of the gravel. Within minutes, Jack is once again asleep.

THE HOCKEY STICK
(In Memory of Jeremy Byrnes)

My Oldest son Matt hasn't worn goalie pads in years. During his amateur hockey career, there were so many games, so many road trips and tournaments, that I don't remember the details of the contests. But I do remember the faces of the little boys he played with. There are objects that I've held onto from Matt's days on ice: team photographs, videotapes of games, snapshots from tournament trips with other parents and their families, and the like. And then there is the hockey stick.

It's about 18" long and made of maple. "Cooper"- the name of a Canadian hockey equipment manufacturer- is stenciled in black across on the stick's handle. Someone, a coach, the team mom, or the team manager colored in a blue ring around the stick's handle where the blade meets the shaft and added "Squirt C 1988-1989" in the same India ink.

I keep the stick in my office to remind me of simpler days, of more innocent times. The stick represents Matt's last year as a true Squirt, the last year of total enjoyment of the fastest game on ice without parental politics. The next year, and each year thereafter until his career ended, Matt faced tryouts and the prospect of "cuts": designations made by a panel of hockey coaches as to which level he'd play at. It's too bad I didn't understand what the future held in store that last year of Squirt hockey. I think I would have relished the season even more.

Youth athletics isn't just an opportunity for kids to make friends, learn a sport, and begin realizing that life, like games, involves competition: wins and losses, ups and downs. It's also an opportunity for the parents to learn a few things as well.

That year, our little team was coached by a guy I had, and still have, a great deal of respect for. Tim had a hockey background but that wasn't what made him a good coach. He had unflappable patience, a keen interest in the welfare of his little charges, and a steady hand for discipline. His son played on the team, a big, smiling kid with a wonderful sense of humor, and a love of good-natured competition. Tim's son and eleven other players signed the handle of that replica stick. I happen to have their autographs because I was an assistant coach that year.

It was an intense game, at least in my mind. In truth, I was so wound up watching my kid play I really shouldn't have been on the bench.

"Come on guys," I yelled at the top of my lungs. "Move your feet."

176

Jeff, the other assistant coach and I worked the doors to our team bench and shouted encouragement to our kids. Tim stood quietly on the bench surveying the play.

"Brian, get the lead out," Jeff shouted as his son lagged behind the rest of the Hawk forwards down the ice. Jeff's kid was little, fast, and had a good eye for the net.

"Yeah, Matt. Get up there and help out your team."

Matt turned and gave me look of disdain as he coasted by the bench. He was a forward. We called him the "Junkyard Dog" because he liked to park himself in front of the opposing net and slam the puck home. It was less work that way. Why waste all your energy trying to carry the puck up ice when someone else could do it for you?

I don't recall the score of the game. I know we were at home in the Hermantown Arena playing a regular season game. I also seem to recall that it was a close contest requiring extensive vocal intervention from Jeff and I to spur on our kids.

"What the heck is wrong with you, Ref?" I yelled in a belligerent tone when an official missed an easy offsides call against our opponent. My face was likely red, my testosterone rushing, as I got more and more heated. That's when Coach Tim took me aside.

"Mark. What do you think you're doing?" Tim asked. His head was bent forward so he could talk quietly, so that no one else could hear our conversation.

"The guy blew an off-sides call. They got a goal off that piece of garbage," I whispered.

"Number one, it wasn't that bad of a call. I've made worse," Tim interjected. "And number two, you're a coach. You're wearing a blue jacket with the words 'Hermantown Hockey' on it. What kind of example do you think you're setting for these young men?"

A lump formed in my throat. Tim was right. I was acting like one of the hockey parents that I'd always vowed I'd never emulate. I sheepishly looked away from the coach and pondered a response. Jeff stayed a considerable distance from us, unwilling to become the target of a similar lecture.

I am studying the names on the wooden stick sitting on my desk in the courthouse. Four of the names on the replica went on to play for state tournament teams at Hermantown High School. One kid played in two state tournaments as a goalie. Another never played high school hockey but went to state in track. Justin, one of two kids on the team to battle cancer, became a 1,000 yard rusher his senior year in football.

Five of the boys, including my son, went to college on the strength of their minds, not their bodies. In fact, David, a member of the group, graduated at the top of his high school class. And two of the players from that unit, maybe more, have given something back to the sport by becoming youth hockey coaches, by putting themselves on the line as role models for younger kids.

Some of the names on the little stick bring to mind distant events: some joyous, some tragic. Less than perfect memories reinforce the notion that not every kid who excels in a sport lives up to his or her potential. But there is one signature which stands out whenever I consider the names inscribed on that piece of maple. And when I scrutinize the gently crafted letters left behind by that little boy, the Coach's admonition rings as true today as it did twelve years ago:

"Mark, try and remember this isn't real life. These are just little kids playing a game."

THE BEAVER POND

Black alders cling to the surface of the stream. To walk downstream in search of brook trout, I must press my chest to the water and make myself small so that I can pass beneath the overhanging limbs. Behind me, my graphite fly rod quivers with each unsure step. Mosquitoes buzz me, ignoring chemicals I've applied to the bare skin of my face. Sweat forms on my T-shirt inside the impervious membrane of my neoprene waders. It's only 6:30 am and already the day's heat seeks to assert its authority.

My eleven-year-old son Christian and I came to the North Shore of Lake Superior seeking trout. We brought sparse provisions, a tent, our sleeping bags, and plenty of dry flies, wet flies, and dew worms. This is the first time Chris has been stream trout fishing. The weather is against us. It's nearly 90 degrees, the skies are cloudless, the days, brutally bright. But I didn't come to water with a need to catch fish. I came with a need to seek solace after a recent death in my family.

We fished a clean, open river not too far from Duluth the first day of our trip. Or I should say, I did. Chris's spin-casting rod was retrieved from the car with a broken tip. Despite my efforts at repairing it with a Band-Aid and a piece of used duct tape, the rod remained useless.

"I casted and the tip just fell off," my son lamented as he approached me across the cobbled surface of a gravel bar protruding into the river.

"Can't you get it to stay on?" I implored him as I fished a quiet hole under an overhanging red cedar.

"It won't work. I tried it a couple of times. The rod just falls apart."

"We'll stop in town and get you a new rod before we head up the Shore."

"Thanks. What should I do while you're fishing?" the boy asked, careful to keep his voice low, like mine.

"There seem to be fish here, " I suggested. "I'll hook 'em and we'll take turns bringing 'em in. How'd that be?"

"OK.'

We hooked and landed a few small brook trout, keeping one about six inches in length.

"Take a look at this fish, Chris," I remarked, holding the specimen in my hand.

"See the colors? Brook trout and lake trout are the only two trout native to Minnesota," I explained as he studied the beautiful markings of the fish.

Our path took us further upstream. The way was easy, the rocks open and obvious. There were no branches hanging in the

179

way, no tight places to negotiate. It had been years since I caught a rainbow trout in a stream. When I felt the tug, I assumed the fish was a brookie and handed the rod to Chris.

"Reel slowly and keep him in the current, away form the bank," I urged.

The tip of the rod, nearly nine feet in length, danced as the trout sought release. Chris cranked the reel slowly and brought the fish to me. I cupped the silver trout with my bare hands and raised him free of the river's embrace.

"Nice fish, Chris," I exclaimed. "I think it's a brown," I offered. "No, it's a rainbow, " I said, correcting myself upon seeing the slight glow of pink across the silver-green sides of the fish.

That was yesterday, when the river was easy to walk and we were within a few miles of civilization. Today we are in the deepest, most secret part of the forest, near the headwaters of another stream. Here, the fishing is not so easy.

Chris stays close to our campsite and fishes within a few yards of our tent. We've given up on flies. The warm weather left the trout with poor appetites. They will not rise for dry flies nor nibble at wet flies offered to them. We're using worms. I stumble downstream. Despite the heat, the water remains cold to the touch. Brook trout need cold water, water oxygenated by constant rapids and kept frigid by overhanging forest. I pause to dip my oilskin fedora in the river. As I place the hat back on my head, water pours out from under the brim and runs down my face and neck cooling my skin.

I find trout lurking in deep pools near the banks. Most of the fish are 6-7 inches long. A few are smaller. I let those go. I play and land one nice fish about eight inches long.

Ahead, a thick branch blocks the stream. Because of recent catastrophic storms a confusion of sticks left by dissipating water blocks the creek, forming a pool of mysterious quiet. I toss a worm into the middle of the hole and climb over a tree limb. My fly rod bends. A fierce, panicked exchange takes place. I feel the native power of a large brook trout pulling desperately as I try to keep the fish out of the flotsam. Placing one leg on either side of an alder branch, I keep the fish out of the debris and play the trout until it tires. The reds, blues, and yellows of the creature's flank shine as I lift the fish out of the dark water and into the afternoon light. I grasp the trout firmly and remove the hook. It's a beautiful, fat fish, a legendary trout, the sort of trout brook trout fishermen dream of. The fish surges in my hand, a primitive undulating pallet of color 14 inches in length. I reach behind me to secure the speckled trout in my game pouch. Before I know it, the fish flips out of my hand and returns to the welcoming depths of the stream.

"Crap," I mutter to myself as I watch the white tips of the trout's fins fade from sight. "I'll never catch another one like that."

I plunge on. The sun re-asserts its power. The weight of my waders begins to tire me. I catch and release another half dozen small trout. The course of the creek slows. Beaver have dammed the stream. With each step the water rises and threatens to breech the top of my waders. I climb a bank and gingerly negotiate hillocks of sedge grass. Encountering a beaver lodge, I stop to fish.

Slap.

A solitary beaver warns others of its kind of my approach before vanishing beneath the water. I toss a worm into the beaver pond. My line tightens. I feel the discrete inhalation of a trout. I begin to retrieve the line and encounter opposition. I tug, setting the hook. The fish is on.

"How'd you do, dad?" Chris asks as I stumble my way back into camp, my skin covered with bug bites and scratches from the underbrush, my clothes drenched with perspiration.

"I got a few. I missed a really nice one," I explain through a weak smile, trying to downplay how truly magnificent the lost brook trout was.

With ceremony and pride, I pull out five trout and add them to the four that Christian caught while fishing only ten feet from our tent. I note that my son is not sweating, that his skin displays few bug bites, and that he appears energetic and well rested.

"That's a nice one," my son remarks, looking at a fat 10 inch brook trout that gave up its life in the calm waters of the beaver pond.

"Yep," I say, carefully refraining from revealing the level of sacrifice I made to catch such a fine fish.

HARRY'S LAST RIDE

The sun sits diffusely in a June sky broken by innocent clouds. Rene' is looking for me but I'm engaged in the act of rigging Harry's saddle and reins. I hear her voice calling me to do chores. I ignore her. June days like this one, sunny, bright, with a slight bit of wind and no insects, are rare in Northeastern Minnesota. I know we're nearing the end of our time in our old farmhouse. I know I'm nearing the end of my relationship with my gelding Harry. I want one last, quiet ride on him before he goes away.

"Mark, what do you think you're doing?"

I pretend I can't hear my wife as I mount my horse. I know that she has something on her mind.

"Mark, are you listening?" she asks as she cruises across the lawn in my direction.

"I'm taking Harry out for one last ride," I respond.

"We need to get things packed. I need you to watch Jack," she asserts.

"The things will still be here when I get back," I tell her.

With words of protest stinging my ears, we move out slowly. Muscles ripple under the horse's roan skin. The gelding breaks into an easy trot. There's a familiarity to his stride. I leave my wife and don't speculate how she'll deal with me when I return. For now, I'm lost to her and to the rest of humanity.

The animal hesitates, as he always does, at the Taft Road Bridge. His reluctance to trust the bridge with our weight, with our lives, hasn't lessened with repetition.

"Come on boy," I urge, gently digging my tennis shoes into his ribs.

He balks for a second and then begins to canter sideways across the bridge deck. His nostrils flare as he examines the water of the River flowing below us. Like everything else on this ride, this is a last: the last time he will likely cross this bridge.

A low, grassy bank defines the north side of the River. Aspen and birch grow thick amongst the saw grass and cattails. Our neighbors have cut a riding trail along the bank's plateau. A slight breeze tickles the aspen leaves around us. Harry responds to my lead and ducks into the woods. As I ride along the River, I observe our home and outbuildings, our finely manicured lawn, our years of work and dedication to a place, from a distance. Sweat begins to bead up on Harry's neck and slide down his skin.

We negotiate our way around several deadfalls. The gelding hesitates at a small stream crossing the trail. The rivulet's banks are soft and muddy. I've learned that not all horses will cross suspect ground. Harry will do it for me. Not out of courage but out of trust: trust that I will not ask him to do something that will harm him. He dances a bit as I urge him forward and then, with one mighty leap, he clears the damp spot and moves on.

I loosen my grip on the reins to allow the animal to gallop up a steep slope. His mane, tinged with gold and highlighted by the intermittent rays of the sun, trails his effort and touches my face. At the top of the hill, the horse settles into a walk. His breathing is strong and defiant as if he is proud of his strength. The path meanders along the top of the river bluff through balsam, spruce, aspen, and birch. At intervals through the trees I can see our big pasture, the site where our new home will be built, across the River. Today, there is nothing on the pasture but grass and the promise of a new beginning.

The trail narrows and then plummets towards another creek. Someone has placed a crude log bridge, perhaps ten feet long and four feet wide, over a culvert at the bottom of the gully. Harry walks across the logs without fear. I feel his muscles tighten as his hooves dig into the dirt of the incline on the far side of the stream. I ease up on the reins, allowing him to bolt up the hill at his own pace. At the top of the slope, I urge him to stop by applying steady, gentle pressure to the bit.

"Good boy," I whisper to him as I stroke his mane and pat his flank.

I lift my bush hat off of my head to untangle the chinstrap. Sitting in the quiet of the forest, I wipe the sweat away from my hairline. The wind picks up, cooling my skin. Songbirds flit and glide on the breeze, serenading us in cautious jubilation. We ride on. We cross the remains of an old farm field. Harry and I wade through timothy that hasn't been cut in generations. There's no road to this dormant pasture. As we cross the grass, the heads of each plant swaying in the nervous wind, I wonder who first cultivated this plot of land. The trail narrows, becoming a single lane. I know, from prior trail rides that this path ends next to an abandoned hunting cabin sitting a stone's throw from the River.

There have been rumors of a new owner of the hunting cabin: gossip about a developer who wants to build apartments on the site, or, more recently, stories that a rich couple wants to build their dream castle along this stretch of the Cloquet River. The talk disappoints me because at one time I tried to buy the parcel to keep it wild.

As we approach the cabin, I find the trail blocked by aspen trees felled by an ax. We leave the trail. The horse selects a route through the forest. We rejoin the path next to the once-abandoned structure. Newly peeled aspen logs, obviously cut to serve as roof supports, lean against the walls of the cabin. Though the building appears decayed and suspect, the evidence of recent activity foreshadows an intent to claim and occupy this space. I coax the animal past the shack and down a riverbank stripped of vegetation. The big red horse raises and lowers his legs against the weight of the current. As Harry's hooves burst free of the River's hold, water trails from the thick hair of his fetlocks, creating tiny rainbows in the sun. I feel our combined weight press into the sandy bottom as we begin to move upriver.

I neck-rein the animal into the River's main channel. We negotiate large stones and boulders. Every so often Harry catches a hoof on an unseen rock and stumbles but never falls. His ears begin to twitch in anticipation of home. Our barn, its yellow metal skin brightened by the afternoon sun, comes into focus. The channel deepens. Only the horse's neck and head remain dry. Water, stained a deep bronze by its place of origin, laps at my thighs. I realize that Harry's hooves are still in contact with the river bottom. I wonder what it would be like to swim with him. I've never done that with a horse and I do not get the chance to do so on this ride. The water level recedes as we approach our place. The gelding begins to prance impatiently in preparation for a run to the barn. I hold him back.

Horse and rider clamber up the bank. Water slides off of the leather saddle and stirrups. My tennis shoes are momentarily stained brown by the River's embrace. My horse of eight years, my friend, pulls against the bit, seeking permission to gallop. Knowing that Harry has given me all that I ever wanted from a mount I release the reins and let the gelding break into a run one last time.

REQUIM

My college roommate was a hippie. I moved back home when I caught him partying with girls that were years too young for me, much less Rich, a guy in his twenties. There weren't many things that I learned from Rich during the three months we lived together in the old Ashtabula Apartments across from St. Mary's Hospital that would prove useful in later life. One important lesson Rich taught me was an appreciation for nurses. The other was an appreciation for folk music.

You see, up until I met Rich, I was pretty much a rock and roll kind of guy. When I moved in, I lugged (or more honestly, my friends lugged) hundreds of rock albums up the three flights of stairs. Ashtabula was a gothic palace: a warren of large apartments carved out of even larger spaces originally occupied by the near wealthy at the turn of the Twentieth Century. There was no elevator. My buddies helped me carry the heavy furniture of my childhood, my weight set, and my stereo up three steep flights of narrow stairs.

Rich told me he graduated from the University of Chicago with a degree in chemistry. For some unknown reason, he ended up in Duluth. We met when we both worked as janitors for a large custodial company cleaning downtown office buildings. My roommate had a couple of albums (yes, real vinyl stereo LP's) that caught my attention as soon as I moved in. One was a compilation of The Band's greatest hits. The other was an anthology of songs by a Chicago folksinger, Steve Goodman.

I'm sure you've never heard of him. But you've heard his music sung by others. Goodman's most recognized effort was made famous by Arlo Guthrie. You remember Arlo-the guy who took the song *Alice's Restaurant* and expanded it into an empire? Arlo sang one of Steve Goodman's compositions, often called the "best song about trains ever written", *The City of New Orleans*. Once I heard Goodman's deep, resonate baritone and his quick, accurate finger picking on the twelve-string guitar: once I listened to his satirical lyrics, I was hooked. Even after I moved back home, leaving Rich to his earthly pursuits, I continued to follow Goodman's career. I bought my own copy of his anthology. Then I found Rene'.

My future wife and I were going to school at the University of Minnesota-Duluth. After we became engaged in 1977, Steve Goodman came to town. So far as I know, it was his one and only appearance in Duluth. I might be wrong about that but it's the only one I'm aware of. Walking down the hallway in front of the UMD bookstore, you know, the one where the jocks sat coolly on the window ledge ogling passing girls, a poster caught my eye. It announced that Goodman was appearing in the Kirby Ballroom at

UMD. I don't remember the price of the tickets. I do remember I bought two that day.

"Who's Steve Goodman?" Rene' asked when I showed her the tickets.

"He's what they call an 'urban folksinger' from Chicago," I related. "He's coming here in a couple of weeks. I thought it'd be fun to go."

"Sounds great."

When we arrived for the concert, a few hundred students, a couple of dozen aging (they're fully aged by now) Flower Children, several rows of chairs, and an empty gray metal stool greeted us. We found seats a few footsteps away from the performer's perch. Someone dimmed the overhead lighting. The sparse fixtures cast an industrial pall over the place.

Goodman walked out, looking small and tired, a battered acoustic guitar dangling recklessly in one hand. I remember that he was short, balding, and dressed in a well-traveled T-shirt and faded blue jeans. The crowd settled in on folding chairs, forming a protective circle of the curious around the singer. He adjusted a weathered guitar strap across his shoulder. The guitar hung behind Goodman as he stood to sing:

> My name is Penny Evans and I've just gone twenty one
> I am a young widow in the war that's being fought in Viet Nam
> I have two infant daughters and I do the best I can
> Now they say the war is over, but I think it's just begun...

He enunciated the lyrics in a sweet a cappella voice. Even though I'd heard the song on vinyl dozens of times there was no comparison between the record and the real thing. The somber tones of *Penny Evans* gave way to the raucous humor of *Lincoln Park Pirates,* a tale about a dishonest car towing company, and the potent satire of *You Never Even Called Me by My Name* (a Goodman tune made famous by country artist David Alan Cole). The folk singer's energy was infectious. His smile, his powerful guitar style and boundless enthusiasm brought us to the edge of exhaustion as we clapped, cheered, and boogied.

I never saw Steve Goodman in concert again. Over the years, I caught him once or twice on public television. By then, my buddy Rich had disappeared. I tried to find his parent's telephone number in the Chicago phone book once when we were there on vacation but even his family had apparently disappeared.

Watching *Austin City Limits* one Saturday evening sometime in the 1980's, I heard the news: Steve Goodman had passed away. I stared mutely as old video roll across my television screen in tribute to an artist that few people had ever heard of.

"You're not going to believe what I heard on the radio today," Rene' told me as we were packing up to move not so long ago.

"What's that?" I asked.

"A Steve Goodman song about the end of the twentieth century," she advised.

"Really."

"It was written back in 1977 or so. I really liked it," Rene' added. "Apparently Steve Goodman and John Prine wrote it together."

Anyone who knows me knows that I'm compulsive about certain things, acquiring good music being one of those things. I had to find the song Rene' described. I made it my mission. A few days later, over the noon hour, I left the courthouse for a walk in the crisp December air. The currents over Lake Superior stung my face as I negotiated an icy sidewalk in downtown Duluth. The Electric Fetus on Superior Street was my destination. Bells chimed as I opened the heavy door and entered the warm interior of the music store. The smell of incense, a fragrance from another time, another age, greeted me. My black loafers beat an out-of-place cadence as I moved towards the folk music section.

I found what I was looking for. On the cover of a re-mastered CD, there was Steve; sprawled half naked across a piece of overstuffed furniture, looking back at the camera. I dug deep into the pocket of my trench coat and pulled out a piece of plastic. 25 years ago, there were no CD's, I had no plastic and no fancy overcoat. I was a "cash only" consumer acquiring my music on vinyl LP's and the only overcoat I owned was one I found at Goodwill.

Soon after my visit to the Electric Fetus my family moved into our new house. Enjoying a rare moment alone I delicately placed *Say it in Private*, the title of the Goodman CD I'd just purchased into the tray of our CD changer. Over the music's distant refrain, I heard Rene' climbing the front stairs.

"Listen to this," I said as she opened the door.

"Not another album," she moaned, knowing full well that there were boxes of albums, cassette tapes, and CD's yet to be unpacked.

"You'll like this one," I promised. "Listen":

Back in 1899 when everybody sang Auld Lang Syne
a hundred years took a long, long time
for every boy and girl
now there's only one thing I'd like to know
where did the 20th Century go
I'd swear it was here just a minute ago

187

all over the world.

Recognition stole across my wife's face. The tune continued:

Old Father Time has got his toes a' tappin
Standin' in the window grumblin' and a rappin'
Everybody's waiting for something to happen,
Tell me if it happens to you
The judgment day is getting nearer
There it is in the rearview mirror
If you duck down I could see a little clearer
All over this world.

The 20th Century is almost over
Almost over, almost over
The 20th Century is almost over
All over this world...

"That's the song I was telling you about," she observed.
"I know," I replied with a smile.

AN OLD MANTLE FOR A NEW HOUSE

Alvin Douglas wasn't a rich man. Successful, not wealthy, was how he saw himself. How others in St. Paul, Minnesota saw him was problematic. After all, it was the Great Depression and he was a banker. Whether he was a fair-minded man or a tyrant mattered very little in the whirlwind of financial disaster surrounding the farm economy of the Midwest. It was Alvin's job to foreclose on agricultural loans for the Farmer and Merchant's Bank of West St. Paul. Douglas' job was a thankless, dehabilitating task even during the best of times.

Oliver Krupp had been a good farmer. Before the drought, before the dry winds from the western plains seared his corn and dried up the watering holes used by his cattle on the 140-acre farm he owned in Rock County in the southeastern corner of Minnesota, Oliver and his family made a living off the land. But the winds, the sun, the lack of rainfall, and a corresponding lack of available money at the local bank forced Oliver out of his ponderous, careful ways. The events of 1932 forced him to take risks with his cattle, with his crops, with his land. Those risks involved going to St. Paul to ask for a loan, a loan that allowed Farmer and Merchant's Bank to acquire a mortgage against the Krupp place.

"I'm sorry, Oliver," Alvin Douglas related as he stood in front of the stark white façade of the Krupp homestead.

"There's nothing else I can do. You're sixteen months past due on your loan. I've given you all the rope I can. The board is forcing me to call the note, to foreclose on the mortgage," the banker said in a weary voice.

Krupp stared hard at the banker from beneath the brim of his brown Stetson. The farmer was deliberate and methodical by nature. Those traits served him well when the economy of the 20's was booming but spelled doom in the uncertainty of the Depression when quick action was often the difference between success and failure.

"Here's the thing," Oliver said, his voice parched and dry from the autumn wind. "Next spring my cattle will be fat and ready to butcher on account of the grain my cousin Albert give me. Albert's place went belly up. But before the bank came out, he sold me his grain crop at a bargain. That's what'll carry me through this tough spell."

The banker gazed out across the flatness of the place, seemingly looking for a distant mesa to concentrate his eyes upon. But there were no mesas. He was in southwestern Minnesota, not New Mexico. He wished he were in New Mexico. Alvin Douglas did not want to be here, telling Krupp that the farmer's life, his farm, was going to be taken away by economic forces beyond their control.

"I'd like to accommodate you, Oliver," Douglas offered, "but my hands are tied. I came out to see you as a courtesy before the Sheriff serves you with papers. There's nothing I can do to stop the process."

Krupp's huge hands balled into tight fists. The farmer raised his eyes against a forlorn sky. The banker sensed his adversary was near the point of crossing some deeply drawn Christian line. Douglas readied himself for the blows, which he sincerely believed were justified as an attack upon the financiers, the bosses, for whom he was a representative. But the farmer made no move towards the banker.

"How long do we have?" Krupp asked in a defeated tone as he returned his hands to the pockets of his overalls.

"I'm not sure. That's something I leave to the lawyers," the banker responded, knowing his reply was less than satisfactory to a man on the verge of losing his livelihood.

The farmer's eyes drew inward. The deep brown of Krupp's irises became lost behind his fatigue. Knowing there was little more to say, little more to comprehend, the farmer turned and climbed the stairs leading to the covered front porch of the farmhouse. Alvin Douglas watched the man's retreat with a sense of pity and shame, knowing full well that Krupp would accept neither from any man.

A fierce fire burned in the Krupp home's brick fireplace. Three children played on the floor within the embrace of the heat. Jonathan, the youngest Krupp child, pushed a tin tractor across a freshly varnished floor. The five-year-old made mechanized noises as the wheels of the toy creaked across smooth wood. Hilda and Oliver Jr., the Krupp's twelve-year-old twins, sat cross-legged around a board game throwing dice. Mrs. Krupp was upstairs, pale and weak from the effects of fighting the flu, moisture dripping noxiously from her limp blond hair as her body fought illness. She was asleep, caught in the shallow slumber of recovery, unaware of the pending demise of the farm.

Oliver poured himself a cup of sour coffee and walked quietly into the living room.

"Hello father," the twins said simultaneously before returning their attention to the board game.

"Hello children," Krupp answered dryly, sitting uncomfortably in a store-bought chair, an oak rocking chair crafted in the Mission style.

"Daddy!" the little one exclaimed, leaping onto his father's lap with exuberance.

The farmer studied the golden tones of the oak mantle surrounding the hazel colored brick of the fireplace. Quarter-sawn columns adorned the piece, revealing the wood's complex and intriguing grain. The mantle was new. It replaced a simple pine timber above the firebox and was the piece of craftsmanship on the place that Krupp was most proud of. It had taken him two months of careful work to design and build the artifact; two months of painstaking effort that relieved, for a time, the feeling of impending disaster brought about by the decline of the farm.

Oliver Krupp cradled the boy in his thick arms and studied the fire. He wondered how his family would respond when he told them that they were moving to Minneapolis. His sister Adeline had a house near Lake Harriet on the trolley line. That's where they would live. They'd leave the land, the sacred presence of the country for the uncertain chaos of the city.

I apply thin stain. I rub liquid deep into the freshly sanded oak with an old rag. There's no heat in our new home, a structure built only a few hundred yards downstream from our old farmhouse. Our animals are gone save for our two Labradors. The horses were sold so that we could move to the city while our new home was being built. Wiring, plumbing, and fir studs stand exposed as I work on the antique mantle that will define the atmosphere of the Great Room of our new home. The stain I'm applying accentuates the burl of the quarter-sawn oak. I marvel at the serious beauty revealed by the depth of the wood.

Outside, slick sheets of autumnal rain spatter the ground. The storm's barrage beats a consistent rhythm upon the building. The weather's cadence is at odds with a folk song playing over my transistor radio. I pause from my labor to think about the carpenter who built our mantle. I begin to spin fictional yarns in my head about a man named Oliver Krupp. My sense of history ties the Mission style of the piece I'm working on to the early 1930's. I imagine a farmer, on a distant plot of land, cutting down an old oak, planing the wood, and creating the object that sits before me. Myth? Perhaps. But it's my job as a writer to uncover the truth, or the possibility of a truth, layer by detailed layer so that the reader will understand. And when, as here, the people who know the truth are dead, it's my obligation to create a plausible substitute for the truth.

Oliver Krupp is such a creation. I'll think of his children, the children of the Great Depression, whenever I build a fire in our new house.

JACK'S BIG RIDE

It was one of the few days during the winter when riding a snowmobile was possible. There had been little snow. We needed wood for the fireplace. Our second oldest son needed to accomplish some chores to get back in the good graces of his parents.

"Dylan," I yelled downstairs, hoping to stir my son into action. "We need firewood."

There was a lot of mumbling. The words sounded non-compliant. I reminded my son that he was still in the doghouse and that he needed to redeem himself.

"If you want to go to Crosby next weekend for your hockey tournament," I yelled, holding the upcoming weekend over his head, "you better get outside and bring in some wood."

"All right," he replied with discord.

A few minutes later, I heard the single cylinder of our 1989 Ski Doo Citation snowmobile cough. The sound of the machine filled the quiet stillness of the late afternoon. I walked to the front window. My eyes followed the progress of the old conveyance as it carved a path through newly fallen snow. Dylan sat comfortably on the worn vinyl seat of the machine with Jack, his two-year-old brother, between his legs. Behind the snowmobile, an empty red plastic slider, attached to the Citation by a thick white towrope, bounced from side to side as Dylan roared down the driveway towards our woodpile.

A couple of minutes later I heard the sound of aspen and birch being stacked in the wood rack on the covered front porch of our new house. I opened the door. Jack sat contentedly on the seat of the Citation, hands firmly gripping the handlebars as he pretended to drive. The engine was turned off. A helmet covered most of Jack's face. Ski goggles protected his eyes.

"How's it going?" I asked Dylan as he staggered up the front stairs under the weight of an armload of firewood.

"Fine. How much wood do you want?"

"Fill 'er up. You can leave the rest of the pile out there until we need more."

Dylan, never one to waste words, nodded towards his younger brother:

"Jack likes the snowmobile."

"I can see that."

Satisfied that the work was getting done, I closed the door and settled into my recliner in front of our entertainment center. The latest Crosby, Stills, Nash, and Young album spun in the CD player filling the room with tight harmonies. Outside, the sun sank beneath the rim of the woods leaving only a few minutes of twilight for Dylan to finish his task.

"What's Dylan doing in the trees?" my wife asked a few minutes later as she looked out a window in our Great Room.

Curious, I rose from the comfortable leather of my chair and joined Rene'. Down the steep bank of our field's only hill, past a small stand of aspen, a single red light, the taillight of the Citation, glowed weakly from deep inside a tangle of black alders.

"That idiot," I moaned aloud. "How could he get stuck in the only trees on the pasture?"

"You better go help him. It'll be dark soon."

"No way. If he's stupid enough to drive into the woods he can get out himself."

"He can't do it alone."

"I'm going," I muttered, pulling on my well-worn leather boots and a quilted Hermantown Hockey jacket before walking out the door.

There was scant light as I shuffled through fresh snow towards the stricken Ski Doo. I heard the patterned rumble of the engine's idle above the dormant pasture. As I approached the snowmobile it became painfully obvious that the Citation was embedded deep in the brush.

"How in the world did you manage to find the only trees for miles around?" I asked, my inquiry edged with parental scorn.

Dylan rose deliberately from behind the buried vehicle, extended his gloved index finger, and pointed convincingly at his baby brother, a tiny bit of a thing no more than waist high, standing quietly off to one side.

"No way," I protested. "You're full of bunk."

A suggestion of an infantile smile broke across Jack's lips. The toddler spoke with the clear and obvious directness of a two-year-old:

"Jack goes fast."

Dylan gestured east, towards the pile of firewood remaining to be hauled:

"I bent down to put a piece in the slider. He was right next to me. The next thing I know, the Ski Doo is flying across the field with Jack holding the throttle wide open. "

The older boy smiled with pride as he recounted his brother's brush with the infinite:

"I ran after him but he piled into the trees before I could stop him."

"Did he fall off?"

"Nope. He was still sitting on the machine with the engine racing when I got here."

I positioned myself in front of the snowmobile and used all of my leg strength to free the sled. Dylan helped pull the machine into the open pasture. A slight moon rose behind us. The teen gathered

Jack in his arms and lowered the infant onto the Ski Doo's seat. I swear I saw my youngest son's eyes twinkle as he whispered:

"Jack goes fast in the trees."

I watched the Citation plow towards the pale lights of our new house at a deliberately cautious pace, leaving me to ponder how to explain Jack's new found interest in motor sports to his mother.

DRIVING TOO SLOW

I'm putting the finishing touches on a paint job in my wife's art studio attached to our new house. The phone rings.

"Dad," my son Christian shouts from the kitchen, "the phone's for you."

"Tell them I'm busy," I yell back, annoyed that my progress is being impeded by interruption after interruption. I took a week off of work to get projects done in our new home. I've accomplished little during the first two days of my vacation.

"It's Aunt Susanne," Chris says in an imploring tone. "She needs to talk to you."

Chris appears with the remote phone and hands it to me before I can object.

Outside, it's a dismal day. There's virtually no snow and little prospect of winter returning. I receive the phone and take note of my downhill skis leaning in one corner of the room. I haven't used them all year. There has been no time, no snow. It's the first winter since I was in law school that I haven't skied at least once.

"Mark," Susanne relates, "Auntie Ann isn't expected to make it. Wayne and I stopped up there yesterday. If you want to say goodbye, you'll have to do it today."

Auntie Ann is actually my Great Aunt, the last of my maternal grandfather's siblings. She's lived her entire life between the Iron Range towns of Biwabik and Aurora-Hoyt Lakes. She raised two boys to adulthood, took in my Great Uncle Stutz (Steven) when she was widowed back in the 1950"s, and has been a loving aunt, mother, and grandmother. Stutz's passing a year or so ago took a horrible toll on her. She's not been the same since. I try not to sound perturbed as I mutter a response:

"Okay. Maybe I can get up there," I say with strained credulity.

I hang up and return to my task. I begin to consider what the old woman dying in the nursing home in Hoyt Lakes has meant to me. Wasn't it Aunt Ann who, when I needed a recipe for roast turkey and stuffing for a stag party almost 25 years ago, patiently explained over the telephone what needed to be done with the bird? And when I couldn't get the stuffing right, wasn't she the one who told me to bring the ingredients over to her and she'd stuff the bird for me?

Wasn't it Auntie Ann who always had a sandwich and a beer ready for me when I stopped in unannounced? Wasn't it Auntie Ann who never forgot an important event in my life (confirmation, graduations, marriage, baby showers); who always had time for me even though our blood relationship is fairly distant?

"I owe her more," I tell myself, "than feeling irritated by a phone call."

"I'm going to drive up and see Auntie Ann," I tell Dylan and Chris as I wash my hands in the kitchen sink. "She's not going to make it through the day." I look at the clock. It's 12:15 in the afternoon. "I should be back by five."

I leave the older boys in charge of their infant brother and climb into my van for the trip up Highway No. 4. Clouds hang heavy over the field surrounding our house. The water of the Cloquet River swirls lazily as I pull away from our place. No. 4 is one of my favorite drives. My buddy Jeff has a farm up towards Whiteface that was the location of our high school and college efforts to build a log cabin. We succeeded in a fashion, though the building has long since fallen in upon itself. Driving the narrow two-lane highway north from Island Lake allows me to recall a past where the memories are always artificially pleasant.

At County 16, I take a right, then a left onto 99 and head towards Aurora-Hoyt Lakes. I think about my Great Aunt and the life she has led. Her father, mother, and my grandfather immigrated to this country through Ellis Island before the beginning of the 20th Century. There was work for immigrants from Slovenia in the forests and mines of Northeastern Minnesota. There was freedom from the prejudices of the Austrian Empire. Auntie Ann was born in Northeastern Minnesota. She fell in love, married, and buried her husband and all her siblings here.

A few miles outside of town, the sun begins to break through the overcast sky. The Lumina's engine purrs effortlessly as I pass old farmsteads, the remains of the toils of the Finns who tried to farm rocky, stubborn soil. Here and there, a brave soul still raises a steer or two. I see no milk cows. I see few tilled fields. Nature has reclaimed most of what the Finns tried to tame.

I swing into the White Community Hospital parking lot, turn off the engine, and pocket the keys. The building is familiar. Uncle Stutz spent his last days in this place, as did his other sister, my Great Aunt Mary. I visited both of them here. Even in the depths of dementia, during the middle of my campaign to become a judge, Stutz remembered his nephew "Markie", a person he saw but once or twice a year. That was true until my last visit when his mind would not allow him to recognize me.

I stop at the information desk just inside the door and ask for Ann's room. The attendant directs me down the hallway. I walk the final steps to my Great Aunt realizing that she likely won't recognize me, knowing that she's probably unconscious. It doesn't matter. The visit is as much for me as it is for her.

Arriving at the nurses' station, I note that the place smells fresh and clean, not at all like other nursing homes I've visited.

196

"I'm here to see Ann Sale," I tell a LPN manning the desk.

I sense something is amiss when the LPN looks over my shoulder and calls out to a RN down the hall:

"This gentleman is here to see Ann."

A woman about my age, dressed in a dark blue slacks and blouse, straightens the stethoscope around her neck and advances briskly down the hall towards me.

"And you are...?" she asks politely.

"I'm Ann's nephew from Duluth," I mumble.

"I'm sorry. Your Aunt passed away around 12:15. Is there anything I can do?"

"Were her sons here?" I ask weakly.

"Yes. They left about a half hour ago."

"Thanks. I'll stop by and visit them."

I don't ask to see Ann. She isn't here. There's no point in my looking at something that isn't her. I make my way into Hoyt Lakes and stop to visit my cousin Johnny. Over coffee, we tell stories about his mom, marveling at the patience and kindness she shared with us during the ninety years of her life. Silently, I ask her to forgive my selfishness and my slow driving.

A WALK IN THE WOODS

I looked at a wall in our new home and realized that I missed quite a few spots when I was touching up the paint. This realization shouldn't be stressful. After all, it's only one small wall. At most, it will take half an hour to fully repaint the surface.

But it's more than just one wall. There's oak trim that needs to be stained and varnished. I thought I had it all done before the carpenters tacked it into place. I was wrong. We were short on the original order. To move in on time, the workers had to put up unstained trim, leaving another job for me to complete. Small and seemingly inconsequential, the staining looms larger and larger as I aggregate all of the little tasks left to be completed. Like the windows. The trim around them is stained and finished but the windows themselves, constructed of clean white fir, are not. Neither are the French doors. Another small, insignificant task to add to my mental "to do" list. Maybe not so insignificant when you start to add it all up.

Then there are the interior pine doors. I was only able to get one coat of polyurethane on each of them. I need to buff down the first layer of varnish and apply another coat. On 24 doors. Add the need to apply a second layer of varnish to the kitchen floor because I thought a little elbow grease and steel wool would harmlessly remove splotches of white paint spattered on the oak flooring, and the list becomes unmanageable.

"I need to go for a walk," I said to my wife as I stared up at my less than perfect paint job. "This place is overwhelming me."

"Why don't you do that?" she responded as she chopped carrots at the kitchen counter.

For the first time since we moved into the new place, I pulled on my well-worn Sorels and bundled up against a less than fierce January afternoon.

"Here Maggie, here Sam," I yelled as I walked down our long gravel driveway. I called loudly, my voice solitary and harsh against the quiet of the valley. Since June, our dogs have lived with our new neighbors, the Kaas's, in our old farmhouse. It's apparent to me that the dogs would rather live with our neighbors in familiar surroundings than join us at our new home. Every time I let the dogs out, they bolt towards the old place, returning only when I offer them a meal.

Sam responded first. I watched his yellow torso bound across the thin white blanket of winter defining the distance between past and present. Maggie, fat and lazy from too much food and attention, waddled slowly across the pasture. The yellow dog met me where a whitened hayfield meets a row of transplanted Norway pines. Maggie appeared a few seconds later with her tongue hanging loose from effort.

"Good girl," I praised, scratching Maggie's ample belly as she wiggled on her back in the snow. "Good boy," I said to Sam, patting his thick corn-colored neck.

It was nearly evening when we crossed an abandoned field and entered my ski trail. The dogs walked in front of me on the narrow path. In the distance, the mournful wail of a Duluth Winnipeg and Pacific locomotive sounded as the train crossed a bridge over the Cloquet River nine miles away. If the dogs heard the train's call, they ignored it. I noted that someone had spent considerable time removing deadfall from my trail. Recently trimmed balsam bore evidence of a chainsaw at work. To the south, the distinctive rumble of snowmobiles on Fish Lake also disturbed the forest's silence. I stopped and listened to the constant whine of the machines three or four miles distant, recognizing that the lake was the only place they could safely run due to the winter's disappointing snowfall.

I stopped to watch the black water of the River. I sat in a folding chair that someone had abandoned next to a declining cabin. The chair's webbing was fragile and decayed. My dogs pranced and snuffled, looking for mice and moles under the snow. Night covered the valley with its carefully orchestrated arrival. It was time to head back.

I shuffled through minimal snow, keeping my eyes focused on the artificial light emanating from the building. Though I didn't see anyone inside the house, I imagined each member of my family occupied in some pedestrian task. The dogs dashed across the white expanse of the pasture, their paws kicking up tufts of snow as they broke for home.

"How was your walk?" my wife asked as she opened the front door and stepped outside to greet me.

"Just what the doctor ordered," I responded.

"Wish I could've come with."

"Me too."

The smell of pot roast baking in the oven welcomed me as I climbed the stairs towards my wife.

THE TOILET BOWL

It's pitch black as I drive north on Highway 53 towards Hibbing, Minnesota. Somewhere to the east, below the ridgeline of Lake Superior's hills, the sun is reaching for open sky. *West Coast Live* echoes from the radio of my old Pontiac Transport as the tires slapped against the road. Dylan, my second son, the reason I'm up before dawn on a quiet Sunday morning, leans against the passenger door, sound asleep.

Two days earlier. Rene' was invited to the dedication of an alcohol treatment facility in Virginia, another town on Minnesota's Iron Range. She's an employee of Range Mental Health and the building, named in honor of United States District Court Judge Donovan Frank, is run by her employer. A week or so before, she asked if I wanted to attend with her.

"You know Judge Frank," Rene' said, recalling that we both went to his investiture ceremony at Hamline University a year earlier.

"Sure," I replied. "We worked together on *Lawyers on the Line* on channel 8. He's a great guy. I'd love to go."

Because of our work schedules and a plethora of weekend athletic tournaments involving our sons, we determined that the only way we both could attend was for each of us to drive separate vehicles to Virginia and meet there. Christian, our twelve-year-old, had a basketball tournament in Two Harbors the next day. Dylan had a 9:00pm hockey game in Hibbing that Friday evening. Someone needed to be recruited to watch Jack, our two-year-old. We're much too astute as parents to try to bring a toddler to a formal dinner. Been there, done that.

"Mom," I said on the telephone a couple of days before the dinner, "can you watch Jack this Friday evening? Rene' and I have a chance to go to a shindig on the Range. We need someone to watch him."

"Sure," she responded. "He can even stay the night."

I assured Grandma Barb he didn't need to spend the evening, that Rene' would pick him up after the dinner. That Friday, I came home from work, picked up Dylan, his gear, and a small bag of my own clothes and essentials. My plan was to drive to Hibbing, drop Dylan off at the Memorial Building and then make it to the Coates Hotel in downtown Virginia in time for the dinner. Rene' was home, getting dressed. Jack was sleeping. Dylan had his hockey bag, his uniform bag, and his homework packed.

The lights of Hibbing welcomed us as we drove in on 169 from Virginia. It had been a few years since I watched a hockey game in the Memorial Building. Playing against type, I actually stopped to ask for directions to the arena at a corner gas station.

Driving down the residential streets of Hibbing, the arched superstructure of the Memorial Building loomed large against the streetlights. We arrived in front of the place at 5:30pm, right on schedule. I handed my son a ten-dollar bill and told him I'd be back to see most of his game.

"We'll check into the motel when I get back," I promised.

"OK," he responded, shuffling his way towards the ice rink under a heavy load.

I met my wife at the appointed place and time. We ate with some of my judicial colleagues and their wives from the Range. During after-dinner conversation, I noted that it was 8:45 p.m. Dylan's game was set to begin in 15 minutes. I said my good-byes and kissed Rene' on the cheek.

"I'll call you in the morning."

"I'll be in Two Harbors," she observed.

"Oh, that's right," I replied. "I'll call you on your cell phone after his game tomorrow," I offered.

"Don't forget."

"I won't."

Traveling at sixty-five-miles-per-hour wouldn't get me to the game on time but I reasoned that I'd make most of the second and all of the third period if I drove the speed limit and if our 1991 Transport with nearly 200,000 miles on the odometer continued to defy the odds. Thankfully, the vehicle raced along without hesitation.

The parking lot at the Memorial Building was, to my surprise, packed with cars as I wheeled in from the street. Something was wrong. It was doubtful that a Bantam B hockey tournament, even on the Iron Range, could generate such interest. Walking into the arena, my suspicions were confirmed.

The stands were packed. Two very fast and very talented high school teams raced up and down the slick ice. The distant ceiling of the place resounded with the cheers of the crowd. I looked optimistically into the stands for any sign that Dylan's team was seated together, waiting to get on the ice. I saw no one I recognized.

"Excuse me officer," I asked a uniformed policeman working the crowd. "Is there another ice rink in town?"

"Sure. About six or seven blocks east, over by the old fairgrounds," he answered professionally.

"I'm looking for my son. He's a Bantam and he's in a tournament," I confided.

"That's where he is," the cop continued. "The tournament is over there tonight and tomorrow, then over here on Sunday."

"Thanks."

I glanced at the clock on the wall as I raced out of the lobby. It was nearly 10:00pm. There would be a little bit of the game left.

But was Dylan there? Maybe he hitched a ride to our hotel with someone. I wasn't nervous: he's a big boy, capable of taking care of himself. It was obvious I'd left him at the wrong place. At least he was in the right town.

Walking into the fairgrounds ice shelter, I saw familiar parents standing in the tight confines of the arena.   My eyes scanned the ice. When I found a place to stand I spied Number 18 lining up a Shattuck player. Dylan leveled the kid with a check. I turned to one of the other dads from our team:

"Do you have any idea how Dylan got here?"

The man gave me a puzzled expression.

"Didn't he come with you?"

"To Hibbing," I answered. "I left him at the Memorial Building five hours ago. I'm trying to find out how he made it here."

"Beats me, " the dad said, a knowing grin on his face. "Maybe he hitch-hiked."

The Hawks lost. Dylan and his pal Ryan shared a room with me at the Motel 6. On the way to the motel, Dylan explained that he'd asked a coach from Hibbing where the bantam teams were playing. The gentleman gave Dylan a lift.

Now it's Sunday morning. My resourceful ninth grader is snoring loudly in the front seat of the van. We're on our way back to Hibbing, this time to play a game in the Memorial Building. Normally, I'd be excited about watching my son. Not today. Because Dylan's team lost twice during the tournament, he's scheduled to play at 8:00am Sunday morning in the "Toilet Bowl", the last place game against International Falls.

I-Falls is easily the worst team we've played all year. It doesn't matter. Our kids play without emotion. There's no incentive for them to do well. It's a shame to play such poor hockey in such a storied arena but that's what happens.

My son and I catch breakfast at McDonald's on the outskirts of Hibbing. During the drive home, I listen to a Vikings game on AM radio, hoping that the Minnesota team gives St. Louis a battle. For one half of football, my hopes are met. During the second half of the contest, the Rams demolish the Vikings. I turn the game off and concentrate my attention upon the barren January marsh and forest we pass along Highway No. 7 on the way home.

OUR DAD ISN'T SAM COOK
(Part One)

(Note: Sam Cook is a nationally known outdoors writer from Duluth, Minnesota. Nearly every time Sam sets foot in the north woods, his adventures turn to gold. This set of stories paints a very different picture of a wilderness trip into the Boundary Waters Canoe Area in Northern Minnesota.)

I planned our Memorial Day fishing expedition to Perent Lake over the past winter. I used the BWCA's website (everyone, even the wilderness, has a website these days) to make reservations for a trip down Hog Creek into Perent Lake. Matt, my oldest son would be back from college sometime before Memorial Day. The trip would reunite all of the Munger boys with their parents. Right off, my concept of "family togetherness" ran into significant resistance.

"You can't be serious. I'm not taking a baby in diapers into the woods."

My wife's opposition to my plan surprised me. When Christian, our twelve-year-old, was an infant, we made a similar trip into Perent Lake without appreciable difficulty. Of course, we were younger then.

"You can take the older boys. Jack and I will stay home and fish," Rene' said, ending any further debate on the matter.

I intended to inventory my fishing equipment, camping equipment, and the like well before the month of May rolled around. Other things got in the way. Like Opening Fishing. Like teaching Confirmation Class. Like laying sod. A week before our scheduled trip, I was asking significant questions:

"I wonder if the tent leaks?"

"Do I have enough fishing rods?"

"Do the lantern and the cook stove still work?"

During 1999, we moved to town while our new home was being built. Our camping and fishing equipment had not been touched for a year. I was uncertain as to its condition. But I knew one thing. We had no sleeping bags of merit. I quickly computed the minimum I'd have to spend to purchase four serviceable bags. Not the fancy mummy bags that Sam Cook and other professionals swear by for their winter excursions into the Canadian taiga. Just four simple bags that would afford modest protection against spring's chill. I figured at least $25.00 a piece.

Sunday, May 21st. I'm rummaging through the garage for camping and fishing equipment. I find I'm down to two decent fishing rods, not counting the one I bought Rene' last Mother's Day. I know she'll want to toss a line in the Cloquet River over Memorial weekend. I don't dare requisition her rod and reel.

"That's another sixty bucks," I moan. Expensive stuff, equipment like the stuff famed fisherman Babe Winkleman uses would cost me hundreds of dollars. I cringe at what my wife's reaction would be if I spent that kind of money on fishing gear destined to be stepped on, thrown into the water, or left behind on some portage.

I find a Duluth Pack in the pile. I locate a couple of duffel bags with shoulder straps from my days in the Army. I retrieve my father-in-law's duffel bag dating from WWII. The mice have chewed big holes through the canvas, leaving a container of dubious utility. I'm certain that we'll need another pack because we don't have enough bags to carry the equipment and food four people will need for four days and nights in the woods.

A tent proves to be my biggest challenge. We have two of them. My wife doesn't understand why we have two of them. She would never understand why we need a third one. I try to envision my sons and me crammed into a two-person tent. Our five-person tent is only suitable for backyard tenting, not real camping. The last time we used our big family tent, my sister-in-law Colleen slept with the three older boys on Sawbill Lake in the BWCA. It poured for two days. Their stuff, including their sleeping bags, floated inside the porous confines of the shelter. Rene' and I remained dry in our two-person dome tent.

"A $100.00 minimum for a decent four-person dome tent," I muse. "This is really starting to add up."

Tuesday afternoon. I purchase two rods and reels at Gander Mountain. I buy myself the cheapest sleeping pad the store sells. I'd like one of the self-inflating models. My budget doesn't allow it. We had four pads but during my inventory, I found we were down to three:

"Dylan, do you know where the fourth sleeping pad went?"

"It was in my fort the last time I saw it. I think the mice chewed it up."

Sure enough, a trip to Dylan's shack confirms my son's memory. Little bits of blue foam litter the interior of the structure. I'm forced to buy a low budget replacement for the destroyed pad.

The local Gander Mountain store has decent sleeping bags on sale. I buy four, keeping my cost below the magic $100.00 ceiling. I also purchase two disposable propane tanks, mantles, and a glass globe for our Coleman lantern, and batteries for three flashlights.

"How much is all of this costing?" my wife asks when I return.

"Not that much."

"I hope you're watching the check book."

"I am."

"It sure looks like you're spending a lot."

"At least I'm not buying a tent."

Wednesday evening, waiting for Dylan to finish Driver's Education, Chris and I stop at Super One to grocery shop. I scan my prepared menu as we race through the isles, filling a grocery cart with boxes of Rice A Roni, Shore Lunch, Kraft Macaroni and Cheese, and other essentials. The bill at the cash register gives me a headache. I remember going to the Boundary Waters with my high school buddies. The whole trip, gas, bait and food included, used to run less than twenty bucks a person. My stomach begins to turn over.

At home, I carefully pack all of the items according to the meal plan. Jack scurries around, stealing packages and hiding them amongst his toys. I catch him with the disposable camera I just bought before he hides it in a desk drawer.

"Jack, Daddy needs that."

"Jack take picture."

"Not now. Daddy needs to pack the camera."

With the supplies neatly tucked into the Duluth Pack, I begin to organize our fishing gear. In the midst of trying to place line on one of my new reels, the entire reel disintegrates in my hands. I mutter some not so nice words under my breath.

"What's wrong, dad?"

"Nothing, Chris. I'll have to bring this reel back."

Thursday. Departure day. Both Dylan and Chris are in school. I can't find the maps used on prior trips to Perent Lake. Matt watches Jack while I run errands. On my way back to town, I make a decision:

We need a new tent.

I stop at Wal-Mart and buy the cheapest four-person dome tent in the store. I return the broken reel to Gander, pick out a replacement, and get a five-dollar credit. I feel lucky. I head downtown to buy maps.

"We're phasing out our maps. What we've got is in the cabinet over there."

I'm in the place where I always buy my BWCA maps. The two maps I need are missing.

"You could try Gander Mountain."

Hmmm. Why didn't I think of that?

I walk to Minnesota Surplus, a few doors down, muttering the whole way. I'm in search of a cheap alternative to a Duluth Pack. The surplus store has used duffel bags for $14.95. At that price, I can buy ten of the rugged sacks for the cost of one Duluth Pack. I buy five. I look up and see a display:

We have McKenzie Maps.

"So you have McKenzie maps?"

"Sure."

"I wonder why the place next door wanted to send me to Gander Mountain."

"They should know better. I send them enough business."

Refreshed by a warm sun, I approach my vehicle only to find a parking ticket waiting for me. I rip the citation from beneath the wiper blade and shove it viciously into my jacket pocket. Then, on the way up the hill, the van's voltage indicator goes berserk. Soon, all of the needles of the vehicle's dashboard dials are thrash wildly inside their housings. I sense that my alternator is about to die. I detour to Downtown Service, a couple of blocks away.

My mechanic Woody is a fisherman. He understands my predicament. It's nearly noon. I have to run up to Tofte, more than an hour away on the North Shore of Lake Superior, to pick up our BWCA entry permit and be back to load the kids by 5:00 PM.

"If you leave the van here, I can put in a new alternator."

I look around the place. There are ten cars with appointments waiting to be repaired.

"I need to get Matt and drive to Tofte. I can have it back here by 1:30. Is that enough time?"

"That'll work. Just don't turn the car off. You're down to 11 volts on the meter. It won't start again."

Back at home I load two canoes on a snowmobile trailer. Without thinking, I turn the van off. It takes 20 minutes to jumpstart the vehicle using Matt's little four-cylinder Mazda. We drop the van at Woody's by 1:30pm and race up the North Shore in the Mazda. Jack contentedly munches on McDonald's food as he watches our frenzied pace from the vantage point of his safety seat.

At the Tofte Ranger Station, I get another surprise:

"You can't go into the BWCA until tomorrow. Enter before midnight, and you're in violation," a Ranger explains.

I'm sure my reservation was supposed to begin today. Too tired to complain, I accept the permit and leave.

OUR DAD ISN'T SAM COOK
(Or Taking Pictures Without a Camera, Part II)

Our family's Pontiac Transport van sits in the Isabella Lake parking lot, the ultimate destination of our four-day canoe trip down Hog Creek. It's dark and nearly 9:00pm as my Chevrolet Lumina van bounces along Forest Service Road No. 354 towards the Creek with my three oldest sons, myself, our gear, and a snowmobile trailer loaded with two canoes in tow.

"What the heck is that?" Matt yells as an enormous shape bursts onto the roadway in front of us.

"It's a moose," I reply.

"A bull moose" Dylan observes. "He's got a small rack."

The animal lopes in front of the vehicle, running straight down the middle of the forest service road just within the light cast by the van's headlights. For a couple hundred yards, the animal's hooves slash and pound the road in fury, seeking to outrun the artificial light until the moose finally turns and vanishes into the forest.

"Cool," Christian murmurs as he watches the moose disappear.

"That was cool," Matt agrees.

We negotiate twenty-seven miles of dirt road before we come to Hog Creek. Over that distance, the only other critter we cross paths with is a terrified cottontail that refuses to yield the roadway for a considerable distance. In the Hog Creek Parking Lot, we set up the new tent. It goes up with ease. Three of us roll out our sleeping bags and take shelter for the night.

"I'm sleeping in the car," Dylan advises.

"OK, Dyl. But you're going to be cramped."

I watch my fifteen-year-old son stretch out on the back seat of the van and cover himself with a new sleeping bag. He doesn't respond to my admonition.

"What's for breakfast?" Dylan asks the next morning. A brilliant sun peaks over the balsam forest and warms my bones.

"I've got some oranges in the food pack," I say.

"I'm hungry. Don't we have something else?" Dylan moans.

"It's all we've got. We'll have lunch when we get to the Lake."

The oranges burst with juice and taste good. We launch the canoes, fill them with our gear, and head down the creek, a slow trough of muskeg affected water that empties into Perent Lake. Chris and I take the lead. Matt and Dylan follow. Soon, the rhythm of paddling the narrow craft and negotiating myriad turns in the stream's course takes over. We're quiet as we work.

Once we're out on the big water, we're disappointed to discover that our favorite island campsite is taken. A mild breeze greets us as we paddle through a narrow channel. We find a campsite on the mainland. It's not our first choice but a quick survey reveals that the place will do.

"I'm going to take a picture of our first camp."

The older boys pitch the tent while I dig into the Duluth Pack for the disposable camera. The camera is nowhere to be found. I remove all of the food and supplies on the off chance that the camera has shifted inside the bag.

"Nuts."

"What's wrong, dad?" Chris asks.

"I think Jack stole the camera."

"No way," Matt interjects.

"He was really interested in it. I took it away from him once. He must have taken it out again when I was doing something else."

"That kid's going to be a juvenile delinquent when he hits puberty," Chris opines.

"Oh, oh."

"Now what?" Dylan inquires.

"I forgot to pack the rain tarp. It was in another duffel. I forgot to put it in here," I admit.

Over the span of a few minutes, I determine that we have no camera, that we will have no photos of our trip, and that we are missing our rain tarp. Trying to ignore my mistakes, I inventory the food to locate any perishables that need to be kept cool. I make another disappointing discovery. Four packages of lunchmeat, along with a brick of cheese, are missing. Then I remember. I pulled several items out of the freezer and packed them but I never bothered to double-check the refrigerator. Rene' and Jack will have plenty of ham and cheese to eat while we're gone.

Things get worse. I discover that one of the new collapsible fishing rods I bought is missing its last guide. The rod must have been damaged on the trip in. I find an old rod tip in the campfire pit and jerry-rig the new rod so that it's useable.

"You should bring that back to Gander, Dad," Matt observes.

"For a quarter I can put a new tip on it."

"Yeah, but it's brand new. Why not just get a another one?"

I ponder my oldest son's suggestion. Chris and I decide to go fishing. Matt and Dylan join us. The older boys insist on still fishing in the lee of a gigantic boulder. They catch nothing. Chris and I drift spinners and dew worms across rocky reefs under a clear blue sky. A breeze sets up a perfect "walleye chop" and propels our canoe across the water at just the right speed. Chris and I catch several fish apiece. We keep two walleye for the frying pan. The other canoe is skunked.

The night air is cool. I burrow deep inside my new sleeping bags and dream of wilderness. There is no sound but the whistling of the wind, the lapping of the waves, and the solitary call of a loon gliding gently off the rocks in front of our camp.

"Crap," my oldest son remarks late the next afternoon.

"What's wrong?"

"I lost your fishing rod."

"You what?"

"I just lost your rod."

"It's brand new. You're gonna have to pay me back. Forty bucks, mister."

This exchange takes place as Chris and I work the shores of an inconsequential island. On each pass through the narrow channel we pick up fish. Sometimes we have two walleye on at a time. Up until Matt lost his rod and reel, he and Dylan were catching fish as well. But Matt made the mistake of trolling the shoreline without securing the rod.

"I lost my spinner," Dylan says in a tone mimicking the lament of his older sibling.

My patience wears thin.

"Matt, you know better. You should've tucked the rod under the seat so it couldn't be pulled out if you got a snag."

I'm not sure why I'm giving my oldest son a retroactive lecture.

"You two might as well head in and get supper ready."

"Matt, you're a bonehead."

"Shut up, Chris," Dylan retorts in defense of his older brother.

I watch the other canoe fight waves as it heads back to camp.

Chris and I catch and release another ten walleye before the day is done. When we're ready to turn for home, we stop in the vicinity of the great rod disappearance. I toss a monster Daredevil from shore towards the spot where Matt lost the equipment. After a half-hour of trying to snag the submerged rod and reel, I give up.

"Let's try one more pass for fish."

"Sure Dad."

We lower our spinners into the dark water. The sky becomes overcast but there's no threat of moisture. The woods are tinder dry. There's a great need for the sky to open up and douse the forest. I study the trees and the clouds as Chris reels his line in.

"I think you caught Matt's line," I observe.

"I thought it was yours."

"Nope. Hold on while I try to pull the rod in."

I fumble with the line trying to determine which end the lost rod is attached to. The bail on the reel is obviously open. I pull handfuls of twisted monofilament line into the bottom of the canoe until there is no more line to retrieve. I gently pull on the line, trying to coax the rod free of the rocks below.

Snap.

The line breaks. The adventure is over.

"I prayed that we'd find the rod. I guess God answered my prayer," Chris explains quietly.

"That he did, son, that he did."

Back on shore, I fillet eight fine looking Perent Lake walleye on a rocky slab of the Canadian Shield. Matt takes the fish and batters them Cajun-style as I paddle across the straits to chop up and deposit the leavings for seagulls. White birds circle above me, drawn by the smell of freshly cleaned fish. As I pull myself away from the rocks, the gulls land with boldness and claim the carrion.

"This stuff is spicy," Dylan says between mouthfuls of fish.

"You're a wuss," Matt replies.

"He's right Matt. I need more Kool-Aid. This fish is spicy."

"You too, dad? Jeez, what a bunch of pansies."

We sit on jack pine logs in front of a reluctant campfire and watch the evening pass. Pale pink light glows from somewhere beyond the western horizon. For a moment, the lost rod is forgotten. For a moment, the only sound to be heard is the contented munching of four hungry fishermen.

OUR DAD ISN'T SAM COOK
(Or "I'm Never Going Canoeing Again", Part III)

We hope that the sun breaks through the high gray clouds so that we can see the lost rod and reel in murky water. Matt lost my new fishing rod close to shore. Without direct sunlight, our chance of seeing anything on the bottom of Perent Lake, even in the shallows, is non-existent.

Our canoes drift lazily over the uneven lakebed. I'm positive the rod is wedged between boulders.

"I'll go in and see if I can feel it."

Dylan, a high school freshman, volunteers to strip to his boxers and wade into the icy water in search of the lost implement.

"You're nuts," is our universal response.

Matt eases the green plastic Old Town canoe into shore. Dylan carefully removes his clothes and stacks them in a neat pile on top of the Duluth Pack. Both canoes are loaded for the trip down the Perent River. We're leaving the great fishing and easy life of Perent Lake for adventure. At least that's how I've been selling our departure to the boys.

I know that there are 12 portages ahead of us. None of them are long. But the respite between them is short, making it necessary to pace yourself. Dylan's skin bristles with immediate goose bumps as he embraces the frigid water. He has no luck finding the lost rod. I study a map and determine the direction to the first portage. I steer us up a small creek several miles off course. I realize my mistake only after I note the water is flowing against us: we should be headed downstream, not upstream.

"Can't you read a map?" Dylan scolds.

"Give me that thing," Matt demands.

"Chris, just paddle. Let's get away from those Yahoos," I urge.

My partner pulls hard. Our Coleman canoe, fully loaded with duffel bags, plows through the tannin clouded waters of the lake as I try to escape my critics.

"Wait up. I wanna see the map."

I ignore Matt's request and push on.

"Oh great, he's looking at the map again," Dylan chides.

I pull out another map. My error is obvious. I was relying on a map of the Isabella Lake area. We're too far east for that map to be of any help. It's useless to stop and explain my discovery to those behind us. They'll simply reply with more catcalls, heaping further denigration on their old man.

We arrive at the first portage, the longest we will encounter, and empty the canoes. In short order, the packs are safely across the isthmus.

211

"I think we can make it."

"Whatever you say, dad. I'm game."

Matt and I study the rapids. The water is low. There is not much force behind the river. We decide to run the turbulence in empty canoes. We do so without incident.

At the far end of the first portage, I dig into the food pack and pull out makings for peanut butter and jelly pita sandwiches. Using pita bread is a stroke of rare genius. Pita bread maintains its shape and stands up to the rigors of the trail. A bright sun covers us in light as we eat. I pull several pesky wood ticks off of my shins and feel the warmth of spring enter my body.

At the second portage, Matt struggles to carry the Discovery by himself.

"It's not about strength," I tell him. "It's about balance. Both you and Dylan are stronger than me."

"It feels like crap."

"Put a life jacket under the portage bar."

"That doesn't help."

I double-portage the canoes on the first few portages to help out. The boys carry my packs. We run another set of rapids. This time, both canoes get stuck on rocks. I stand waist deep in devious water holding our canoe while Chris sits patiently in the front seat.

"Let Chris go down by himself," Matt urges.

I look at the vicious tongue of water downstream of us. I hold the canoe against the current. Out in the open water of the next pond, Dylan is swimming with the Discovery. The big green canoe is full of water, making it difficult for my son to tow the craft to shore.

"No way, dad," Chris moans.

I detect fear in my twelve-year-olds' voice.

"Don't worry, Chris. Get out on a rock. I'll guide the canoe down."

Chris complies and stands timidly on solid ground. I send the canoe crashing through the gorge. Matt tries to guide the vessel away from the rocks with a rope but slips and bangs his knees. Big bruises appear instantly above the kneecaps. He curses out loud.

Later on, we run another set of rapids. No one is injured. The gear and canoes make it through without incident. By the seventh portage, Matt and Dylan have discovered that, with the two of them working together, they can portage a canoe.

We pass through a succession of placid ponds. A small flock of Goldeneyes takes wing. A pair of mergansers hangs with the other ducks for protection. Muskrats dive from warm perches into the cool water at our approach. Chris and I try unsuccessfully to sneak up on three mud turtles basking on a bleached log. The air is clean and filled with nature.

At the eighth portage, the trail climbs an onerous ridge before it plummets back to the river. I follow Matt and Dylan on the trail as they struggle with their canoe.

"Look at the size of these white pines," I whisper in admiration.

"Ya, right. That's just what I was thinking too, Dad."

"Come on Dylan, you've got to appreciate these trees."

The portage trail splits two magnificent white pines. Both trees tower in excess of a hundred feet above the forest floor. I watch my older sons plod onward without so much as a glance upward.

Towards the end of the day, we stop and discuss whether we should try to make Isabella Lake.

"I'm not going any further."

Dylan is dragging his feet. He wants to camp at the first available site.

"We might as well make it to the lake, Dyl."

"Matt, shut up. I'm not going any further. This is the stupidest trip I've ever been on. Why couldn't we just stay on Perent Lake and fish?"

I admit to myself that the boy has a point. By portaging twelve times in one day, we've covered distance but have not really accomplished anything, unless you count the subtle lessons the boys have learned regarding teamwork. I don't tell them that one last portage awaits us before we achieve our destination, Isabella Lake.

"We'll stop at the first campsite," I agree.

Our camp at the end of the Perent River is perfect. We situate our tent high above the water on a stone outcropping. A cool breeze keeps the black flies and mosquitoes away. Chris and I take separate canoes to do some perch fishing. In less than an hour, we catch and release a dozen small perch and northern.

Monday. Our last day. The howl of a stiff west wind greets us as we rise. Concerned about the weather, I urge the boys to move fast. The sky looks like rain. When the clouds clear, the boys are left even more skeptical of my outdoor skills. We make the short portage into Isabella Lake without complaint. By now my sons are old hands at packing their gear and the canoes over the trail. It' a long paddle against the wind across the lake to the trailhead.

"What'd ya think of the trip?" I ask the boys as we land on the south shore of the lake.

"I'm never going canoeing again," Dylan responds.

"Really? That hurts my feelings."

"No offense Dad, but your trip didn't make any sense. We should've stayed on Perent and caught fish rather than portaging thirteen times."

I mull over Dylan's observation as I walk to the car. The trail leading to the parking lot passes through an arid, desert-like grove of pines. I'm astounded that the place hasn't burst into flames before now. This is not an area of blow down. There is no fire ban on here. Yet, the woods are tinder dry, ready for disaster.

In the parking lot, I study the left rear tire of our Transport van. The tire is dangerously low. It's 30 miles one-way to Hog Creek and the other van. I scrutinize the wheel.

"Well, it's not flat yet," Matt advises.

I motion for Matt to get in the Pontiac. We leave the other boys sitting on top of our gear as we drive back to get the other van.

I'm bone tired and thirsty when I pull back into the Isabella lot driving the Lumina with the trailer in tow. Matt is just ahead of me driving the Transport. Just before reaching the Isabella lot, the suspect tire on the Transport gives up the ghost. I'm too far gone to complain. I pull out the tools and the jack, lower the spare from beneath the rear chassis, and change the tire. I'd taken a bath in the frigid waters of the river the night before. The grime of the road and the exertion of changing the flat leave me substantially less than clean.

We stop at a little tavern in the Village of Isabella. I have $26.00 to my name. Matt is broke. Thankfully, both vans have full gas tanks.

"We can only spend $4.00 apiece," I tell Matt and Dylan. Chris is outside and doesn't hear my instructions.

Once he's seated, Chris tries to order a $6.00 item. I quietly admonish him. He pouts. The boys order sodas. I order a cold tap beer. It tastes good. It tastes like another. I can't chance it. I don't want to end up doing dishes. My stomach is in knots in anticipation of the bill. The total comes in under budget. I have enough money left after the tip to give the boys a buck apiece to buy a cold soda for the road.

"Dylan, would you change your mind about going again if I made some concessions?" I ask as we stand on the dusty gravel of the tavern's parking lot getting ready for the return trip to Duluth.

My son's blue eyes stare back at me as he tries to fathom what I'm up to.

"Like what?"

"Like letting you boys help plan the next trip."

"That might work."

I hope it does.

BLACK WATER

When my oldest son Matt came back in June from a Boundary Waters trip with three of his buddies, I experienced trout envy. The brook trout Matt displayed on our kitchen counter were huge. They ran one to three pounds each. I stared at their fat, swollen bodies and wondered how they had fought, how Matt's eyes must have lit up when he pulled the first fish clear of the clean waters of the little border lake he was fishing.

In desperation, I took a package of my stream trout out of our freezer in an attempt to mollify my jealousy. When I placed the brilliantly colored trout next to Matt's gargantuan's, the result was predictable. My heart, rather than being uplifted, sank into a fisherman's depression.

I thought about Matt's brookies all summer. An opportunity arose for me to try out brook trout fishing on Minnesota's Iron Range when my wife Rene' drove up to Biwabik, Minnesota for work. With Rene' safely entrenched behind a desk, I pulled our Lumina van out onto the blacktop and drove north. I'd read about an Iron Range stream that was labeled, at least in the book I consulted, as the premier brook trout stream north of Virginia. There were also rumors of huge brown trout, reported to be reproducing naturally in the cold waters of the river.

The thing about trout envy is that, once it hits you, you can't shake it short of going fishing. No amount of golf, walking, weight lifting, or biking can substitute for taking your shot at native trout in wild water. Lake fishing is a poor second cousin. When you're in a stream, wading through the coursing rapids with unsteady balance in search of that next great pool, it's you against God and the fish. No locators, no gasoline engines, no trickery.

The sky was heavy. There was no question the North Country needed a deluge. Dust kicked up as my Lumina made each tenuous corner on the logging road. It was cool and dimly pleasant as I stopped just beyond a plank bridge crossing the stream. A pickup passed by as I pulled my jeans and golf shirt off in favor of shorts and a T-shirt. I brought extra clothing in anticipation of stopping at Howard Street Books, a local bookstore in Hibbing, when I was done. I had a new novel to promote, one invoking memories and scenes from the Iron Range. I didn't want to show up at the store, asking for a book signing date, smelling like fish. The driver in the truck waved as a cloud of fine dust settled over my van. I pulled my waders on, wrenching my neck in the process, and picked up my fly rod.

The bottom of the stream was partially sand, partially loon crap. Gaining consistent footing was problematic. Black alders hung over the banks. Norway and Jack pines loomed above the marsh grass on either side of the water. There were few birds. It was as if the avians anticipated a storm that would not break.

I felt the tug of something. It was obviously not a trout. I pulled a 4" shiner from the cold river. The minnow dropped off the shiny hook, taking my nightcrawler with it. Minnow-1, fisherman-0.

My path wading the stream became more difficult. It was obvious that beaver had been at work along the river and that humans had used extraordinary efforts to destroy the rodents' handiwork. Here and there the remains of lodges and dams interrupted the natural flow of water. Silt had settled deep in these artificial pools, making walking nearly impossible. At intervals, I caught more minnows. There were no trout interested in my offerings.

I came upon a gorgeous pond. Switching to dry flies, I awkwardly presented several types. My efforts yielded more minnows. The wind picked up. I sensed that it was about to storm but the weather remained noncommittal.

It was the middle of the day, a poor time to try to pick up native brook trout, or to raise always-skittish German Browns. I'd hoped my diligence and effort would result in a few strikes, a few fish. It seemed my faith in books about trout was misplaced.

Wandering further downstream, I encountered a large Jack Pine log blocking the river. On the left, a high bank soared. On the right, the landscape boasted lowland marsh filled with thistle. There seemed to be no path open to me but straight down the channel.

The bottom of the stream lost its stony solidity as the bank sloped towards the pine. My boots sank into mush. I struggled to grab hold the pine. I was a few inches short of connecting with the log when I felt the streambed give way. Lunging forward, I snagged the palm of my left hand on a sharp branch. I held on to the limb, allowing the water to float my boots free of the bottom. Exhausted, I pulled myself onto the log.

Blood oozed out of my hand in bright red whispers. There was no pain, only a constant flow of red. Pulling my shirt out of my waders I wrapped the tail of the T-shirt around the wound. I rested momentarily on the rough surface of the dead pine. My rod and reel balanced precariously on another log. I felt a sharp pain in my left calf as I tried to shift my weight to gain stability. When I'd pulled my left leg out of the grip of the mucky bottom, I'd apparently strained my hamstring.

My T-shirt was soaked with blood. I dipped my hand into the river and let cold water disperse a rising ache. After a few minutes, I examined the wound. It wasn't deep. I'd merely peeled back a layer of skin, exposing white fat. The sore was clean and dry. The bleeding stopped.

It took some doing to negotiate the steep bank. I climbed heavily before making the crest of the ridge. My drive back to Hibbing was reflective. I convinced myself to give up the notion of catching fish, of satisfying my trout envy. Sometimes it's safer to admit that you've been bested.

MUSIC LESSONS

"Remember we're going to that CD release party at Fitger's tonight," I remind my wife over the telephone.

"That's right. I forgot. What time?" Rene' responds.

"It starts at eight. We'll get one of the boys to watch Jack and we can grab a bite to eat."

"Where?" Rene' asks.

"How about Chi Chi's?" I suggest, mentioning a well-known Mexican restaurant. "It's right there in the complex."

"Who are we seeing again?"

"Brenda Weiler. She's that young singer I heard at the Bayfront Folk Music Festival."

"I know who she is. You've been playing her CD's nonstop for the past two months."

As a middle-aged male with a wife and four sons, I feel a little weird enjoying Ms. Weiler's music so much. I guess my angst comes from the age difference thing. I'm old enough to be her father and yet, I find that her lyrics, her style of music touches, some chord deep within me.

I climb the stairs to the theater intent on buying tickets. A large-boned young man sits on a metal stool near the doorway. The exposed brick of the converted brewery frames the man's bulk.

"Where can I buy tickets for tonight's concert?"

"There aren't really any tickets-just a six dollar cover charge that you pay at the door."

"OK," I say, retreating from the encounter, uneasy that the show might sell out before Rene' and I finish dinner downstairs.

I notice a young lady sitting behind a table displaying Brenda Weiler T-shirts and CD's. I study her profile. My mind puts the pieces together. I head towards the woman.

"I'm Mark Munger. Nice to meet you," I say, extending my hand to Ms. Weiler.

The folksinger returns the gesture. She's a pretty young woman dressed like a thousand other pretty young women back in her home state of North Dakota on a Saturday night.

"You sent me your new CD. I'm planning on writing a review of tonight's concert for *The Hermantown Star*, my hometown paper," I offer.

"Thanks. I appreciate that," she says in a voice remarkably devoid of power. Her eyes betray shyness. I suspect she's trying to figure out what motivates someone my age to take an interest in her music.

"If the concert's anything like the album, I'll write only good things."

She nods her head. I sense that I've overstayed my welcome. Not because of anything she says or does. An instinctual feeling compels me to withdraw. It strikes me that it must take great courage for a shy person to sing songs of deep personal meaning in front of a theater full of strangers.

Rene' and I return to the upper level just in time for the show. I try to pay with a twenty-dollar bill. A rush of customers hesitates while the heavy-set guy searches for change. I'm antsy to get in and find a seat. I haven't been inside the Spirit of the North Theater in years.

Brenda takes the stage and begins her set with a song from her new album, *Fly Me Back*. She hits the mark on her own compositions *Bold* and *Breath*. Her covers of *Motherless Chile*, an old spiritual, and Tori Amos' *China* show her versatility and depth as an artist. Throughout the evening, I study the songwriter and try to understand what it is about her voice, her guitar work and her style that is so compelling. Her lyrics and music on *Tease* and *Trickle Down* carry a harsh, angry edge. When Ms. Weiler lashes into one of her more disturbing pieces there's no hint of deception apparent in her presentation.

She performs this night, washed by the subtle glow of candlelight, without a band, singing her new songs in solitude, the way she wrote them.

After two hours of contemplating the words and textures of Ms. Weiler's music, it finally dawns on me why I came to see this young woman perform.

I'm a middle-aged male locked into responsibility at home, at work, even at my place of worship. Because of my position in society, I try to influence young men and women by my actions, by my words, by my conduct. I spend so much time trying to tell my kids, and other young people, what I think (and what I think they should think) that I've forgotten youth's uncanny ability to impact the way older folks view the world.

The stage lights are turned up. Rene' and follow the departing crowd. I sing my favorite Brenda Weiler song under my breath as we exit the old brewery:

I'm going dancing in my pretty white dress
I'm ready to go dancing in my pretty white dress

But no one will go dancing
God no, not with me
No one will go dancing
At least not with me

I can dream of my dress and of all the others

And all I see is me by myself in the midst of
All the others

But no one will go dancing
God no, not with me
No one will go dancing
At least not with me.

For a brief moment, I'm an awkward fifteen-year-old boy afraid to ask the girl standing across the gymnasium for a dance.

SWIMMING WITH LOONS

Round Lake sits peacefully against a backdrop of hardwoods and pines. It's a simple day in Becker County. It was a complicated journey from Fargo, North Dakota. Our oldest son, Matt, is changing colleges. After two years at Michigan Tech located in Upper Peninsula Michigan, he's had enough snow. He's had enough five-to-one boy-to-girl ratio. He's had enough serenity and contemplation.

It was nearly impossible to convince our two oldest sons that the six of us should cram into our minivan and drive to Fargo to visit North Dakota State University and our old friends, the Flom's. I was amazed that I was able to prevail and insist on 100% family attendance. We did end up taking Spencer, our pro forma adopted son, along. Seven seats. Seven people. I didn't object to Spence coming with. It seemed like the environmentally sound thing to do.

We pull into Moorhead just after 11:00pm. I uncharacteristically stop at a service station, look in a phonebook, and find Jan and Joel's address. I verify our location on a map so that I won't be wandering aimlessly through cornfields in search of their house.

Traveling down the highway, I spot the side road I'm supposed take. I pull onto gravel under a barrage of criticism:

"They don't live on a dirt road" Rene' enjoins.

"You've gone too far. We're in the sticks," Matt laments.

"I'm thirsty," Christian whines.

"When we gonna be there?" Dylan intones.

I mumble under my breath, pull a U-turn and head back north.

"Jan, this is Rene'. We're on No. 75. How do we get to your place?"

There's a slight pause as my wife listens.

"Jan says you missed the road that would have taken us right to their place," my wife directs. "She can see our van from her living room window."

I mutter. The dirt road I'd been admonished to pass by was the correct road.

"She says to take the next right, follow it around the bend by the river."

I start to say something about my being correct. Objections from my kids and wife silence me in mid-sentence. Rene' continues to chat with Jan. Unexpectedly, I hear Mrs. Flom's voice call out over the tiny speaker of the cell phone:

"Turn here!"

A woman appears out of nowhere, standing defiantly in the light of the van's headlamps. The Lumina stops only inches from our friend. Mrs. Flom is standing in her pajamas in the middle of the road pointing at her house.

"Jan, you're nuts," is Rene's only response.

The Flom children are growing up. A.J., their oldest boy, is a senior at Moorhead High School. Sara, the middle child, is entering ninth grade. Both are active athletes. Peter, the youngest, is a musician. Joel and Jan were law school classmates of mine at William Mitchell College of Law in St. Paul. They wed shortly after we all graduated, a year or so after Rene' and I were married. Then they moved to Moorhead where Joel became a partner in his own firm. Jan hung up her briefcase and became a mom, watercolor artist, and sculptor.

Matt, Rene', Jack, and I tour NDSU the next day. We weather moments of minor conflict but handle our differences well despite the ninety-eight-degree heat. We've made a visit the Flom's nearly every year since our friends bought their place on Round Lake. Their cabin is an hour drive from Fargo-Moorhead, and is located in the rolling hills and black earth of Becker County between Detroit Lakes and Park Rapids. Joel and A.J. journey ahead of the group to open the place up. I'm responsible for getting all my boys and Spencer to the lake in the Lumina. Rene' and Jan will be following in Jan's Blazer with groceries.

I glance at the van's fuel gauge as we leave Moorhead. Over a quarter of a tank, plenty of gas to make it to Detroit Lakes. Fully loaded, with Jack slumbering behind me in his car seat, I turn onto US No. 10. About fifteen miles from Detroit Lakes, the van starts to act up. It chugs and wheezes. I glance at the fuel gauge. It still reads above a quarter of a tank. I pull over to the side of the road. Vacation traffic flies by us as I contemplate my next move.

"Must be vapor lock. I'll just let it sit for a minute or two," I say.

"Try it without the AC," Matt offers. "Maybe that'll help."

We open the windows, allowing hot, dry air to engulf us. The vehicle travels a few miles before it begins to labor again.

"I'm gonna turn off here and let it sit," I explain.

We exit and park next to a gasoline pump at a convenience store. I examine the fuel level again. Nothing has changed. I turn the key. The car starts fine. We move a few hundred yards down the highway before the engine quits. Matt calls Rene' on the cell phone. Jan's Blazer pulls in behind us. After a brief consultation, I transfer the four younger kids to the other car. Matt and I decide to wait for a wrecker.

Sitting in the rising heat, I study the gas gauge. It hasn't moved. I look at the trip odometer. 378 miles. I can do the math in my head. The van gets a little over 20 miles to the gallon. It has an 18-gallon tank.

"Matt," I say slowly, as if defeated, "we're out of gas."

"No way."

"Look at the odometer."

"Didn't you pay attention to the gas gauge?"

"See for yourself. It's still above a quarter. It's busted."

When the women come back, I send them for a gas can. Twenty minutes later the Lumina's tank is full. We're back on the road.

A soft, hot wind greets Rene' and I as we stroll past the Flom's log cabin to look at the lake. The cottage is stained a dark brown. An eclectic stone fireplace chase interrupts the horizontal harmony of the old logs. Clear water laps expectantly against rock riprap along the shore. I lower my hand to take the lake's temperature. I look back at the cabin with renewed focus. Somehow the nostalgia of the place acts as a subtle barrier against the assorted complexities and demands of the Twenty First Century.

Early the next morning I'm in need of a shower. I pull on my swimming trunks and wade into Round Lake. The sun is absent, though tendrils of light are beginning to climb the eastern sky. The water shimmers like a vast emerald. Rene' walks onto the dock with a mug of coffee in her hands. Steam rises from the cup in the morning air.

"Look, a loon," my wife observes.

Without my glasses, I have difficulty seeing. Squinting, I confirm Rene's discovery. I submerge and move silently towards the bird. When I surface, the loon is further away.

"Swimming with the loon?" Rene' asks with a hint of humor.

"Loons, plural," I reply. "After yesterday, I feel like one."

TRAVELING BLUES

I was, as always, in a hurry to make it to an event. I figured if I got out of court by 3:30pm, I'd have an outside chance of making it to the cross-country meet in Maple, Wisconsin. My twelve-year-old son Christian was running in the race as a seventh grader. I made sure of the time and location of the event by cross-examining Chris earlier in the morning:

"What time is the meet?"

"4:00."

"Where?"

"Northwestern. The golf course."

"You mean Norwood?"

"That's the one."

"You're sure?"

"If that's the one in Maple."

My afternoon calendar allowed me to leave the courthouse by 3:30. I raced across town and picked up Jack well before 3:45. I had 15 minutes to make Maple. The odds of doing that without a speeding ticket were against me.

The colors had not yet peaked as my van roared along US Highway No. 2 east of Superior. Hints of autumn touched the highest reaches of the maples. The aspen and birch were as yet undisturbed. Jack watched the panorama of rolling farm fields, wild trout streams, and adolescent forest pass by from his safety seat.

As I approached Poplar, Wisconsin, I noted a golf course sign on my left. I veered from the highway onto a county road. It was 4:05. I figured I'd get to the course just in time to pretend that I'd seen the race and congratulate Chris on a fine run. What the kid didn't know wouldn't hurt him.

There was only one car in the golf course parking lot. The lack of big yellow school buses parked alongside the verdant green of the course convinced me that my kid was running somewhere else. An old man ambled gingerly across one of the fairways pulling his golf cart and clubs behind him. He was the only soul around. I didn't stay to watch his game.

The Chevrolet accelerated towards Maple, where Northwestern High School is located. I was certain that the only golf courses around were in Poplar, where I'd already been disappointed, and to the south, on the road to Solon Springs. I wanted to make sure the teams weren't assembled and running somewhere close by.

The Northwestern Tigers football team was practicing when I drove past the school. I saw no cross-country runners in the area. Jack continued to view his surroundings. We headed south.

Norwood Golf Course was deserted. It was 4:30. I'd missed Chris' run, wherever his meet was being held. We stopped at a filling station along Highway 53. Jack came into the store and picked out a candy bar and a sucker.

Back on the road, I figured I'd been misled as to the meet's location. I headed back to the Hermantown Middle School to await the arrival of the cross-country team. Given it would be nearly 6:00 by the time I got to Hermantown, I calculated that we'd only have to wait an hour or so for the team bus.

"I play on the swings."

"OK, Jack."

I lifted my youngest son out of the van. He ran towards a playground next to the Middle School. There was a boy's varsity soccer game going on. While the game held my interest, I kept one eye out for the cross-country bus and another on Jack. The soccer contest ended. It was nearly 7:00 pm. Still, there was no bus. I called home to find out whether anyone had heard from Christian. I used the free phone in the school's lobby.

"Chris called about a half hour ago. He won't be in until nine," Dylan advised.

"Nine? Why would it take until nine to drive back from Maple?"

"Maple? Dad, I hate to tell you this but Chris is in Grand Rapids."

"What?"

My voice took on an explosive edge.

"His meet is in Grand Rapids. At the golf course."

I hung up the phone. Muttering under my breath, I grasped Jack's hand and walked quickly through the deserted hallway of the Middle School. It was difficult maintaining my composure when I picked up Chris later that evening.

"How was the meet?" I asked in a patronizing tone.

"Fine."

"When did you realize that you'd sent your father to the wrong state, 140 miles away from where you were running?"

The boy remained silent.

"Was it when you got on the bus to leave Hermantown?"

No answer.

"Was it when the bus drove northwest across the State of Minnesota instead of southeast across the State of Wisconsin?"

Christian remained mute.

"Was it when you arrived in the wrong city, in the wrong state?"

More silence.

Then, in a timid voice, Christian finally advanced this admission:

"It was when I crossed the finish line and realized that you weren't there."

OCCURRENCE AT HUNTER LAKE

This past winter I got the bright idea (no pun intended) to go cross-country skiing during the eclipse of the full moon. Now at first blush, that concept seems fairly noble and straightforward. But think about it. Yes, the moon would be full. Up until the eclipse. But once an eclipse comes to fruition...Do you see the problem?

I skied hard and fast as the sun slowly disguised the yellow globe of the full moon. Darkness enveloped the trail. The night took on an eerie, dangerous aspect. I started to wonder why I hadn't brought my two Labradors, Maggie and Sam, with me. I started to think about the timber wolves and cougars in the forest surrounding our home, both of which are active at night and not at all bothered by winter. My heart raced. I picked up the pace. I made my way back to the house safely despite the eclipse.

I tell you this so you can understand that not all of my ideas for adventure along the banks of the Cloquet River are well thought out.

"Do you and Ron want to go canoeing tonight?"

I'm eves-dropping as my wife Rene' calls our friend Nancy to find out if she and her husband want to come over and canoe from our house down to Hunter Lake, an ox-bow in the River, a one and a half hour canoe trip from our place.

"They're going to try and make it. Randy and his girlfriend want to come with," Rene' explains as she hangs up the phone. Randy is the McVean's middle son. He's a resident medical student living in LaCrosse, Wisconsin.

"Randy's got a new canoe. Ronda's coming down tonight so she'll want to go too," my wife adds, noting that her good friend and blueberry picking partner from Ely will be staying the night with us.

I scurry around, locate four canoe paddles, stock a cooler with beer, pop and ice, and ready two of our canoes for the journey. Nancy stops over with her mom around dinnertime. She wants to firm up our plans and show her mom our new house.

"I'd like to pull the canoes out at Wahlsten's," I suggest, knowing that Nancy is a good friend of the Wahlsten's. For some reason, I leave my reference to our take-out site oblique. Though there are no words of understanding exchanged, I believe that Nancy understands that its her job to call the Wahlsten's and warn them that we'll be landing on their shoreline sometime after midnight.

A haze descends over the woodlands. The moon rises in the east as a mere dim bulb cloaked by interference. There's enough light to see but not enough light to make the evening memorable. At approximately 9:30 PM, the McVean's arrive.

"We need lifejackets," Nancy laments. "We forgot ours at the lake."

I wander out to our garage and locate four adult life preservers.

"Nance, you really don't need these. The water's only thigh deep and the current isn't moving much."

"I'll feel better if we take them."

"Suit yourself."

The moon's limited illumination isn't much help as we descend the steep bank to the River. I've made it a priority sometime during the summer to put in stairs. I haven't hit that part of my chore list yet. I help Randy carry his canoe, a fine Kevlar beauty, down the boulder-strewn slope to the water. His girlfriend Jen slips 1 and audibly bangs her knee.

"She's already got a concussion from water skiing," the doctor-in-training observes. "Are you alright?"

A slight nod from Jen. The first canoe enters the water. Randy and his companion sit in the Kevlar craft suspended in the current, waiting for other boats to launch. I help Ron and Nancy into my Old Town Discovery. They promptly paddle backwards into overhanging brush. A few critical comments later and their canoe is drifting free. Ronda and Rene' hand me the cooler and paddles. The women step gingerly into our 15' Coleman canoe, its red plastic skin worn thin by encounters with various boulders and rock ledges. Rene' claims the front seat. Ronda sits on a cushion on the floor in the middle of the watercraft. I push the canoe away from shore and sit down on the rear seat. We begin our trip.

There are only two places along this stretch of the Cloquet where canoes are in danger of hanging up on rocks. Both our vessel and the one carrying Ron and Nancy manage to find those places. The delays caused by the rocks are brief and thankfully dry. Noting our plight, Randy tosses a derogatory comment or two our way. My response is honest and forthright:

"Hey, take a look at the weight in this canoe. I've got beer, two middle-aged women, and an out of shape dad in the stern. You've got two twenty-something's in a light weight Kevlar. Is it any wonder we're hitting bottom and you're not?"

I ignore the angry looks that Rene' and Ronda flash my way.

"How can the moon be on our left and then straight ahead of us?" Nancy asks sometime later.

"Simple, Nancy, the River is changing directions and we're following it," I explain.

"It doesn't make any sense."

"Rene', I notice that you're very conservative with your strokes," Ron needles.

My wife and her pal from Ely engage in extended conversations as the shoreline slips by. The depth of their discussion momentarily engages my wife:

"I paddle only when I need to," she responds sometime later.

The pale light of the moon never increases in intensity. There's scant current to assist our efforts. Just before Hunter Lake strains of a John Mellancamp tune echo over the water. Bright porch lights appear from around a sharp bend in the River. The music is loud and out of place. We drift by a rustic cottage fully expecting to see throngs of partying people. There's no obvious movement in or around the building.

Randy and Jen break out into Hunter Lake. Their canoe is a slash of yellow against an otherwise black and white world. We pass our take-out point and continue into Hunter Lake. There are no bugs. Here and there, the faint glow of artificial light denotes an occupied home or cottage along the shoreline. The far side of the lake remains shrouded in darkness. We turn and head towards Wahlsten's. Approaching the landing, I turn on my flashlight. Inadvertently, the halogen beam reflects off of a window in the Wahlsten home.

"Watch your light," Ron cautions. "You'll wake them up."

A flashlight beam appears from behind the trees. Someone is approaching us. The lamp illuminates Ron and Nancy as the bow of their canoe strikes shore.

"Hi Bruce. It's Nancy," the woman says in greeting to Mr. Wahlsten.

"You scared the heck out of me, Nancy. I was in bed."

It doesn't take long to figure out what happened. Nancy thought I called the Wahlsten's. I thought she'd take care of that chore. No one had bothered to tell our neighbors that seven adults would be stumbling around their yard at half-past midnight.

Mr. Wahlsten helps us land the canoes.

"Good thing you recognized us," Ron says with a smile as he shakes Bruce's hand.

"Good for you, you mean," the landowner says warily, patting what appears to be a holster underneath his pajama top. "Mom's up in the house with the back-up gun, just in case."

As we load the canoes onto the snowmobile trailer, I ponder whether Mr. Wahlsten is serious about the gun. I can't ask him. He's already on his way back to bed.

A BIG SNOW

"You're crazy. No one's going to show up for a book club on a day like today. You're going to end up eating breakfast at the Buena Vista by yourself."

My wife had a point. Snow continued to fall at a steady pace. Our quarter-mile long driveway looked to be socked in. I was supposed to meet with a book club at the Buena Vista restaurant, read selections from my debut novel, *The Legacy*, to the group, and discuss the book and the writing process with the ten or so female members of the book club. Looking at the considerable snow that had already fallen, it seemed unlikely that there'd be much of a turnout.

I'm a male. Big snow means a chance to explore the world. My wife just happened to buy a Toyota Rav4 Mini-SUV a few weeks back. I hadn't driven the car in snow. The book club excursion was the perfect excuse to try out the vehicle's all-wheel drive capabilities.

"I'm sure at least some of the members will show up."

"No way. Women are not going to go out into this weather for a book club. Why don't you call the woman in charge and re-schedule it?"

I was already out the door when my wife's suggestion floated across the warm air of our kitchen.

Of course, she was right. I made it to the restaurant in plenty of time. I ate wild rice pancakes, sausages, and fried eggs by myself and drank piping hot coffee in the silence of the near-empty establishment. Wind driven snow pelted the thick windows of the place. There were only three or four other brave souls eating, holding private conversations in distant corners of the room.

"They canceled the meeting," I said to my wife in a perfunctory tone when I returned home several hours later.

"What'd I tell you? I made a nice breakfast and you missed it."

"The wild rice pancakes I had while I was waiting were really good. We'll have to go there for breakfast sometime."

"I knew it. You ended up reading your paper and having breakfast by yourself, didn't you?"

"Yep."

I contemplated editorializing further about the quality of the food. For self-preservation, I declined further comment.

"Did you find Jack's money?" I asked later in the afternoon as we were getting dressed to cross country ski.

My question was spurred on by the events of the past week. On Wednesday evening, in the back seat of the Toyota, Jack, our three-and-a-half-year-old son, decided to ingest currency for the first time. The only admission he would make to Rene', as he simulated choking, was that he had "swallowed a penny".

A trip to an urgent care center confirmed Jack was a serious saver: there on the black and white x-ray was the proof. A large, bright circle denoted a coin's progress through our son's digestive tract. The kid had swallowed a quarter. The coin had already cleared Jack's stomach and was on its way through. Rene', being the mom, was assigned the job, by me as the dad, of making sure the money was retrieved upon exit.

"No. I haven't seen it. He keeps getting on the toilet without telling me. I'm not sure if it's been passed yet."

Knowing better than to criticize my wife's efforts with respect to fecal inspection, I zipped up my nylon pullover and headed out the door.

White cloaked the field in front of our house as I waxed our skis. Fragments of frozen water, more sleet than true snow, drifted down from the clouds, adding to the twelve inches of new precipitation already on the ground. There was no wind. The air was full of moisture.

Our skis cut slow, steady paths through shin-high drifts blanketing the trail. At one point we stopped and rested, listening to the distinctive rumble of a Duluth, Winnipeg, and Pacific locomotive. Further down the trail, Rene' and I stood quietly beneath an arbor formed by stately Norway pines crowning the highest point on our land. We didn't talk as we stood beneath the canopy. We simply breathed deeply of the fresh air and the quiet.

The shadows of the landscape lengthened. A northwestern zephyr formed a subtle row of snow across our driveway. My wife headed up to the house to warm up. I made for the garage to put on my Sorels and my insulated bib overalls Once properly dressed against the gale, I fired up my International tractor and began the slow process of removing snow drifts from places that I didn't want them to be.

SAILING

My son Christian and his buddy Spencer stand in refreshing water. They're waiting for me to rig the jib and mainsail of a Hobie Cat sailboat. With thick fingers and the limited dexterity of age, it takes me a spell.

We came to Round Lake in rural Becker County to spend a couple of days with old friends from law school. It's a ritual that we've kept up as a family for the better part of a decade. The Flom's come over from their home in Moorhead, we drive west from Duluth. We meet at their 1930's vintage log cabin by Detroit Lakes. There's never a lack of food, kidding around, or friendship at their place.

The boys sit on the catamaran's pontoons. The sails begin to gather wind. It takes several false starts before we're able to tack consistently and work our way out of the protected bay in front of the log cabin.

Round Lake is part of the Ottertail River. Being part of a flowage, the water is clear and clean. Osprey and bald eagles soar above us seeking the benefit of the same wind we rely upon to move. The boat begins to gather speed. I learn how to use the jib and weave a path out into the main lake. The catamaran glides along the surface of the water.

"Mission Impossible," Chris shouts as he hangs below me, moving hand over hand along ropes suspended beneath the flexible tarpaulin that forms the boat's deck.

"Indiana Jones," Spencer responds.

A gust of wind bends fragile reeds in the lake's shallows, alerting me that the boat's pace will accelerate.

"Hold on, boys," I shout.

The pontoon carrying Chris dives beneath the waves. The float carrying Spencer rises out of the water. I arch my back and lean heavily away from the submerged float. Rope sings in the wind and burns my bare hands. I hold the rudder in place by using my legs to pin the handle against the canvas deck.

We dance across the lake, colorful sails full of brisk country air. Though it's Saturday, there are virtually no other boats on the water.

Several hours later, we beach the boat and the boys pull the Hobie Cat onto land for the night. I notice Jack looking out the cabin's big picture window. He's waving at us. Later that evening, my older sons, Matt and Dylan, join the Flom's, Jan and Joel, playing contract rummy with my wife Rene' and I. The action is lively: the banter, unforgiving. The other children, Peter-the youngest Flom, Christian, and Spencer play video games. A.J., the Flom's oldest offspring, naps on a leather sofa. It's amazing that he's able to sleep with the racket we make playing cards.

The next morning, Joel and I drive to Moorhead to pick up Sara, Joel and Jan's daughter, and one of Sara's friends. When we arrive back at the cabin, Jack is waiting for me.

"Go in the boat, Dad?" my three-year-old son asks.

"Sure, Jack, but you need a lifejacket."

"Go fast in the boat, Dad?"

I study the lake. Sparse ripples barely disturb the water's calm. What little breeze there is seems unpredictable. I look at my son's face. There's little I can do but agree to try. I enlist Chris and Spencer to assist me with the sails. Once the boat is in the water, it becomes apparent that the older boys have got to go. In the light air, their weight precludes the vessel from making progress.

"Ouch," Chris cries as I smack his bare fingers with my elbow.

My son's hand grips a rope hanging just below me. My gesture forces him to release his hold. He drops into the lake as the sailboat gathers speed.

"Hey, watch it," Spencer exclaims as I gently shove him off the canvas deck into the water.

The boat surges forward.

"All I had to do was lose the dead weight," I tease in a voice loud enough for the dispossessed boys to hear.

"I'll get you for this," Chris threatens. His words are an idle challenge. The catamaran has moved into deep water.

"Lay down, Jack."

My youngest son, his bare arms and legs brown from the summer sun, reclines on the tarp. His orange life vest is larger than his diminutive body. Pools of dark brown stare at me from within his eyes.

"That's it. You don't want to get hit by the boom," I instruct, pointing at the horizontal piping connected to the bottom of the mainsail.

Jack seems to understand. I follow a familiar course and clear the bay. Though I'm newly skilled at using the jib to make the boat come about, the wind remains limited. Jack doesn't seem to mind. Once or twice, we catch temporary gusts of strong air. In these fleeting moments, water moves rapidly beneath the catamaran and Jack smiles:

"Dad go faster."

"I'll try son."

Soon it's dinnertime. I turn the boat around. Approaching the shoreline, I see Rene', Jan, and Joel lounging in lawn chairs, sipping gin and tonics in the shade of tall spruce trees. The smell of grilled sausages permeates the still air. I lower the mainsail and bring the boat to shore. As the pontoons of the Hobie Cat touch sand, I study the earnest smile of my youngest child and realize there's no better way to spend a weekend.

ABOUT THE AUTHOR

Mark Munger is a life long resident of Northeastern Minnesota. He and his wife Rene' and their four sons live on the banks of the wild and scenic Cloquet River north of Duluth. When not writing fiction, Mark writes a regular column for *The Hermantown Star* newspaper and is a Minnesota District Court Judge.

OTHER WORKS BY THE AUTHOR

The Legacy (Distributed by Cloquet River Press, ISBN 1886028486)

Set against the backdrop of World War II Yugoslavia and present-day Northeastern Minnesota, this debut novel combines elements of military history, romance, thriller and mystery. Rated 3 and 1/2 daggers out of 4 by *The Mystery Review Quarterly*.
Trade Paperback $19.95

Ordinary Lives (Cloquet River Press, ISBN 09720050053)

A collection of short stories, and a novella, depicting the human condition and the geography of the heart. These tales contain a fictional survey of life in modern America as seen through the eyes of a new writer from the Midwest.
Trade Paperback $17.95

Available at All Fine Bookstores or Directly from Cloquet River Press at:
5353 Knudsen Road Duluth, Minnesota 55803
or via the internet at
Mlitlgator@msn.com.